Building a
Canadian–American
Free Trade Area

Brookings Dialogues on Public Policy

The presentations and discussions at Brookings conferences and seminars often deserve wide circulation as contributions to public understanding of issues of national importance. The Brookings Dialogues on Public Policy series is intended to make such statements and commentary available to a broad and general audience, usually in summary form. The series supplements the Institution's research publications by reflecting the contrasting, often lively, and sometimes conflicting views of elected and appointed government officials, other leaders in public and private life, and scholars. In keeping with their origin and purpose, the Dialogues are not subjected to the formal review procedures established for the Institution's research publications. Brookings publishes them in the belief that they are worthy of public consideration but does not assume responsibility for their accuracy or objectivity. And, as in all Brookings publications, the judgments, conclusions, and recommendations presented in the Dialogues should not be ascribed to the trustees, officers, or other staff members of the Brookings Institution.

Building a Canadian–American Free Trade Area

Papers by DONALD S. MACDONALD, MAX BAUCUS
RICHARD G. HARRIS, PETER MORICI
TOM BURNS, JOHN J. LAFALCE
ROBERT E. HUDEC, CARL E. BEIGIE
JOHN H. MCDERMID, HARRY L. FREEMAN
JACQUES PARIZEAU, WILLIAM NISKANEN
T. K. WARLEY, R. R. BARICHELLO
JOHN A. SCHNITTKER, CLAYTON YEUTTER
*presented at a conference at the Brookings Institution
chaired by Bruce K. MacLaury on February 3, 1987*

Edited by EDWARD R. FRIED, FRANK STONE
PHILIP H. TREZISE

THE BROOKINGS INSTITUTION
Washington, D.C.

Copyright © 1987 by
THE BROOKINGS INSTITUTION
1775 Massachusetts Avenue, N.W.
Washington, D.C. 20036

Library of Congress Catalog Card Number 87-71507
ISBN 0-8157-2973-1

9 8 7 6 5 4 3 2 1

About Brookings

THE BROOKINGS INSTITUTION is a private nonprofit organization devoted to research, education, and publication in economics, government, foreign policy, and the social sciences generally. Its principal purpose is to bring knowledge to bear on the current and emerging public policy problems facing the American people. In its research, Brookings functions as an independent analyst and critic, committed to publishing its findings for the information of the public. In its conferences and other activities, it serves as a bridge between scholarship and public policy, bringing new knowledge to the attention of decisionmakers and affording scholars a better insight into policy issues. Its activities are carried out through three research programs (Economic Studies, Governmental Studies, Foreign Policy Studies), a Center for Public Policy Education, a Publications Program, and a Social Science Computation Center.

The Institution was incorporated in 1927 to merge the Institute for Government Research, founded in 1916 as the first private organization devoted to public policy issues at the national level; the Institute of Economics, established in 1922 to study economic problems; and the Robert Brookings Graduate School of Economics and Government, organized in 1924 as a pioneering experiment in training for public service. The consolidated institution was named in honor of Robert Somers Brookings (1850–1932), a St. Louis businessman whose leadership shaped the earlier organizations.

Brookings is financed largely by endowment and by the support of philanthropic foundations, corporations, and private individuals. Its funds are devoted to carrying out its own research and educational activities. It also undertakes some unclassified government contract studies, reserving the right to publish its findings.

A Board of Trustees is responsible for general supervision of the Institution, approval of fields of investigation, and safeguarding the independence of the Institution's work. The President is the chief administrative officer, responsible for formulating and coordinating policies, recommending projects, approving publications, and selecting the staff.

About the Institute for Research on Public Policy

FOUNDED IN 1972, the Institute for Research on Public Policy is a national organization with offices in Victoria, London, Ottawa, Quebec, and Halifax.

The raison d'être of the Institute is threefold:
—to act as a catalyst within the national community by helping to facilitate informed public debate on issues of major public interest;
—to stimulate participation by all segments of the national community in the process that leads to public policy making; and
—to find practical solutions to important public policy problems, thus aiding in the development of sound public policies.

The Institute is governed by a Board of Directors, which is the decisionmaking body, and a Council of Trustees, which advises the Board on matters related to the research direction of the Institute. Administration of the Institute's policies, programs, and staff is the responsibility of the president.

The Institute operates in a decentralized way, employing researchers located across Canada. This ensures that research undertaken by the Institute will involve contributions from all regions of the country.

The Institute's independence and autonomy are assured by the revenues of an endowment fund, built through contributions from the federal and provincial governments and by the private sector. In addition, the Institute receives grants and contracts from governments, corporations, and foundations to carry out specific research projects.

The Institute promotes public understanding and discussion of issues of national importance, whether they be controversial or not. It attempts to publish its research findings with clarity and impartiality. It is not the function of the Institute to control or influence the conduct of particular research or the conclusions reached thereby. Conclusions or recommendations in a publication of the Institute are solely those of the author and not the Institute, its Board, Council, or contributors.

The Institute is now concentrating its core research program around three themes: international economic issues, governability, and social policy. In addition, the Institute has research programs on the small and medium-sized business and on environmental policy. It publishes comments on issues of public policy through its *Newsletter,* through *Choices* (an occasional newsletter supplement), and through its magazine, *Policy Options.*

Preface

THE NEGOTIATION of a free trade agreement between two major trading nations is a large venture in international affairs. Not surprisingly, the current Canadian-U.S. effort to build a free trade area has drawn mixed responses on both sides of the border. There are hopes for significant benefits to be gained from the removal of obstacles to the efficient use of resources. But there are also serious reservations about the economic and political implications of free trade between economic units of disparate size and, in important respects, different traditions.

Most economists reason that free trade will raise productivity and the potential for growth in each country. At the same time, the proposed agreement, like other international accords, will put new limits on the exercise of national sovereignty. Canada, still in transition from an economy dependent on natural resources, could find its future economic policy options constrained. The United States, which must work its way out of a massive external trade deficit, could similarly come to consider commitments to bilateral free trade unduly binding.

For Canadians, of course, concern for economic sovereignty is mingled with long-standing fears about maintaining an independent national identity in North America. The strongly expressed need for protecting Canadian cultural sectors from American dominance is an important reflection of those fears. In the United States, attitudes are more clearly linked to regional or sectoral economic anxieties. Moreover, despite the potential benefits, in neither country will the proposed agreement have an easy passage through political waters roiled by allegations of unfair practices on the part of trading partners.

Widespread support exists in both countries for devising better rules to govern the huge flows of goods, services, and capital across the border. The basic argument for adopting such rules remains: there are large economic gains in sight that both sides would share. Whether this argument will prevail over the many misgivings and reservations will be determined, not at the end of the negotiating day, but after the political process has run its course in Ottawa and Washington.

The Brookings Institution and the Institute for Research on Public Policy are pleased to publish this volume in the Dialogues on Public Policy series. We are grateful to the American Embassy in Ottawa, the Canadian Embassy in Washington, Cargill Inc., Pfizer Inc., and the H. Smith Richardson Charitable Trust for help in financing the conference and the publication.

The editors are indebted to Carol Delaney of the Brookings Center for Public Policy Education and to Lynda Lennon of the Institute for Research on Public Policy, who managed the organizational arrangements for the conference; to Alice Carroll and Jeanette Morrison, who prepared the manuscript for publication; and to Janet Smith, who typed successive versions of the text.

The views expressed here are those of the authors and should not be ascribed to the organizations whose assistance is acknowledged above or to the trustees, officers, or other staff members of the Institute for Research on Public Policy or the Brookings Institution.

ROD DOBELL
President
Institute for Research
on Public Policy

BRUCE K. MACLAURY
President
Brookings Institution

Contents

Summary

EDWARD R. FRIED *and* PHILIP H. TREZISE

THAT SOMETIME STAPLE of political oratory about Canadian-American relations—"The longest undefended border in the world"—is rather out of fashion today. Still, the reality remains. Few people in either country would think it odd that destroyers do not patrol the Great Lakes or that forts and defense installations are nowhere to be found along the border. The fact that their governments have chosen not to use resources for those purposes is taken by Americans and Canadians alike as a part of the natural order.

The commercial border is another matter. There, barriers defend a variety of perceived American and Canadian interests. These protective works are costly, just as navies on the lakes and frontier garrisons in Ontario and New York would be costly. But they have been in place over the entire history of the Canadian Confederation's relations with the United States. They have thus acquired a status in the public mind not altogether different from that held by the geographic border.

An argument can be made that the commercial border is an historic accident. If Generals Montgomery and Arnold had been a bit luckier at the city of Quebec on a snowy night in the late fall of 1775, the Canadian provinces would very likely now be a part of the American customs union. Or suppose that William Pitt the Elder rather than Lord North had won the argument in London in the 1770s, or that General Washington had fallen into the Delaware on the way to Trenton on another snowy night a year after the Americans had failed at Quebec. Then Canada and the United States might well be joined in a North American customs union, but one having a different political character.

Pursuing these speculations, the current free trade negotiations can be seen as a latter day effort to undo some of the economic consequences of those eighteenth century accidents. For the directive given by President Ronald Reagan and Prime Minister Brian Mulroney to the American and Canadian negotiators was to work for an agreement to dismantle most—perhaps eventually

1

all—of the barriers erected by the two governments to control and hamper the flow of goods, services, and capital across the commercial border. To be sure, they did not propose a full customs union, which would have political implications too large for either government to contemplate. (Interestingly enough, however, Western Europe's customs union, in operation for a quarter of a century, has had much less political impact than had been anticipated.) Nevertheless, the comprehensive negotiations envisioned by the two leaders at the Quebec Summit could be expected to alter in far-reaching ways the accustomed economic relationship between the United States and Canada.

The papers and conference discussion recorded in this volume essentially focus on three questions: what is involved in going off on this bold negotiating venture; is it feasible; and is it going to be worthwhile?

Political views   Donald Macdonald's answer, reflecting the analysis and argument of the state paper of the Royal Commission on Economic Union and Development Prospects, is that Canada has an overriding economic interest in the removal of trade barriers between the two countries. Canadian standards of life have benefited during the years since World War II from a major and sustained expansion of natural resource production and exports. However, past rates of growth in the natural resource sectors cannot be expected to continue. And Canadian manufacturing industry will be unable to make up the difference needed to support economic growth unless it can escape from the constraint of a small domestic market. As a practical matter, making this escape depends on substantially free trade with the United States.

Economic logic, Macdonald warns, will not necessarily be determining. The adjustments required of Canadian industry under bilateral free trade will be sizable and in some cases painful. Beyond these concerns is the fear that closer economic relations with the giant neighbor to the south could fatally prejudice Canadian political independence. Well founded or not, this kind of reservation about a free trade agreement is a political fact. That is why matters like "cultural sovereignty" are important to the negotiations. Many Canadians want reassurance that their country's separate identity will not be overwhelmed in a free trade agreement with the United States.

The parliamentary secretary for international trade, John McDermid, observes that Canada, like the United States, has traditionally relied on the General Agreement on Tariffs and Trade

(GATT) for obtaining better and more secure access to foreign markets. Now, the slow pace of the GATT and the complexity of the issues before it call for another approach to U.S.-Canada trade relations. A comprehensive bilateral agreement, which offers predictability and stability to cross-border trade, will be much in the mutual interest. Predictability and stability, however, will depend on agreed rules governing subsidies and other practices which frequently attract countervailing responses. Canada is not seeking exemption from the so-called trade remedy laws of the United States, McDermid emphasizes, but it does make a claim for bilaterally agreed rules defining unfair trade practices and for strong joint institutions for settling disputes.

Senator Max Baucus and Representative John LaFalce have been prominent in the U.S. Congress's consideration of a possible free trade agreement with Canada. Both agree that bilateral free trade promises substantial economic opportunities for the United States and Canada alike. Baucus stresses the need for a congressional role during the negotiating period. Absent a satisfactory Congress-executive branch partnership in sorting out the issues in advance, an agreement could fail of approval in the legislature. Among the troubling issues for the Congress are agricultural trade, the potentially differential impact of free trade on regions in the United States, and the exchange rate. On the other hand, Baucus suggests, ways to meet Canadian worries about the application of the American laws against dumping and subsidies may not be out of the question.

Congressman LaFalce, whose New York district borders Ontario, presents a broad review of U.S.-Canadian economic relations and the proposed free trade agreement. He foresees, among other potential benefits from free trade, gains for U.S. firms from the phased elimination of high Canadian tariffs and from the reform of cumbersome and expensive customs procedures that, he observes, work to discourage companies from entering the export trade. Like other contributors, he considers that a joint commission is needed to mediate and reconcile differences over trade, with special reference to problems arising under trade remedy laws. He suggests that if nothing else can be achieved, the creation of such a dispute settlement mechanism will have justified the negotiations.

Economic views

Peter Morici's comprehensive essay examines the current negotiations against the background of the close and extensive economic ties that have developed between the two nations. He points out that the economies north and south of the border differ in the role assigned to public authorities, with Canadian governments, federal and provincial, typically being the more interventionist. Reconciliation of the policies and institutions that have grown up under relatively distinct governmental economic philosophies will be a basic task for the negotiators. Morici nevertheless expects that an agreement will be reached and will deal with most of the specifics at issue. That, he thinks, will give U.S. firms meaningful advantages—both greater access for goods, services, and investments, and greater certainty about the official rules governing these activities. On the other hand, he fears that a failed negotiation would be likely to impel Canada to more inward-looking policies, with a resulting serious deterioration of the bilateral economic relationship.

Econometricians have applied much ingenuity to measuring the probable welfare outcome of a move to free trade. Estimates for the U.S.-Canada case have varied widely—for Canada, from large gains in gross national product to small losses. Richard Harris, whose models have been among the most sophisticated, presents the strongly positive estimate that free trade would raise the long-term level of real income in Canada by 5 percent, and this without incurring unacceptably disruptive short- and medium-term adjustment costs. He finds that much of the gain will come in manufacturing industry, which will experience sharp reductions in average costs through rationalization. A sobering feature of Harris's paper is in his simulation of the possible impact of a swing to protectionism in the United States. For Canada as a whole, real growth would fall by nearly 2 percentage points for the first three years, net exports in affected sectors would drop 20 percent to 30 percent, and nominal wages in all industries would fall 4.3 percent within five years and 8.6 percent in ten years.

The distribution of gains from free trade for Canada and the United States is brought up at several points in this volume. The standard judgment is that Canada, as the smaller partner, will have larger proportionate gains. No participant challenges this conclusion. Ambassador Clayton Yeutter, however, questions the concept itself. If a free trade agreement makes sense, he argues, both parties will be winners. To concentrate on relative shares is to miss the central reason for seeking an agreement. And William Niskanen, in a slightly broader context, challenges the belief that more information will make it easier to reach agreement. The allocation of the benefits deriving from "good rules"—more efficient economic arrangements—is fundamentally unpredictable. Forecasts of probable outcomes are more likely to obstruct agreement than to hasten it.

Trade barriers Canadian and American officials have negotiated bilaterally within the GATT framework ever since 1947 but these negotiations have been confined mainly to bargaining over tariff reductions. The free trade negotiation between Canada and the United States is intended to cover broader ground. Frank Stone and Tom Burns provide a review of the agenda items, beginning with tariffs and proceeding to less standard fare like government purchasing practices, trade in services, rules relating to investment, and—a key issue as seen from Canada—so-called trade remedies, particularly the operation of U.S. antidumping and countervailing duty statutes. They suggest ways to resolve differences over these points, with emphasis on a new mechanism for settling the disputes that they expect are bound to arise under free trade.

Robert Hudec's paper centers on the antidumping, countervailing duty issue. He dismisses immediately any supposition that the relevant laws can be effectively set aside in a free trade agreement. This solution is both unrealistic and illogical. Legislatures will not repeal the laws. And if the imposition of dumping or countervailing duties is wrongheaded, the wrongheadedness is not limited to trade between Canada and the United States. The illogicality extends as well to proposals for narrowing the application of the laws—for example, by attempting to measure "net" subsidies. Hudec, nevertheless, does see room for a possible bilateral agreement. He suggests that dumping might be dealt with by promoting "reverse" dumping—that is, an agreement clause that would facilitate the return of underpriced exports to the country of origin, thus discouraging use of this practice in the first place. As for subsidies and countervailing duties, he would have the negotiation first define carefully the kinds of subsidies subject to countervailing duties and, that accomplished, give to a joint commission the responsibility for supervising the practices followed in each country. In the longer run, in his vision, the evolution should be toward the harmonization of those national laws that bear directly on the functioning of the free trade agreement.

Carl Beigie in his commentary worries about the difficult challenges to achieving a comprehensive bilateral accord between two such disparately sized economies, each of which clings to national myths about the other. He believes that a powerful impetus to an agreement in Canada is the concern that rising U.S. trade barriers will otherwise seriously impair Canadian exports. Even so, he has lingering doubts that the Canadian government, in the end, will be able to gain approval of a comprehensive package, whatever the economic arguments favoring its acceptance.

Services and investment

Among the priority objectives of the United States in the bilateral negotiation—as in the multilateral GATT negotiation—is to arrive at rules that will serve to liberalize both trade in services and international flows of investment. Harry Freeman of the American Express Company sets out the form that an agreement on services trade should take. It would provide an umbrella code or framework of principles—for example, national treatment and the right of establishment—applicable to service sectors generally. Subsequent agreements would be sector-specific and would include these principles but would also treat issues peculiar to individual sectors such as telecommunications, financial services, or tourism. Like others, Freeman remarks that a bilateral services agreement, highly desirable in itself, would have the further useful effect of spurring the GATT contracting parties toward a multilateral agreement.

Jacques Parizeau, writing from experience with Canadian provincial laws and administrative practices, has a closely argued essay on investment and services issues. He offers reasons why Canada's heritage from the 1970s of protective measures against nonresident ownership does not preclude formal commitments to nondiscriminatory treatment of foreign investors. As for the services field, where provincial regulatory structures are generally operative and often differ province to province, Parizeau despairs of creating a true common market in Canada by way of an agreement between two central governments. He believes that a workable answer for purposes of the bilateral agreement is to define national treatment of a foreign firm in, say, Ontario as the treatment Ontario is committed to give to firms in other Canadian provinces. In short, he sees the realistic objective as being "concrete . . . arrangements rather than broad statements . . . that may be satisfying to the soul but have little chance of becoming operational."

In his comment, William Niskanen suggests a like approach as the way to bilateral agreement. It is wishful, he says, to expect the free trade idea per se to attract the necessary political support, at least in the United States. What will be necessary will be practical trade-offs between what American interest groups would like and what Canadian interest groups desire. That might mean, for instance, American concessions on trade remedies balanced by Canadian concessions on investment rules and services trade. Following through along this traditional bargaining path will offer the best hope for an agreement that will gain political acceptance.

Agricultural trade

Agricultural trade appears to be the least tractable problem facing the Canadian and American negotiators. The agricultural industries on either side of the border are protected and subsidized by a variety of techniques, many of which differ as between the two countries. These arrangements have created compelling material interests in their perpetuation, interests that politicians have been extremely wary of challenging. T. K. Warley of the University of Guelph states as a given the "unequivocal opposition" of Canadian farm organizations and commodity groups to free trade between Canada and the United States. As he dissects the situation, each major farm group can readily grasp the potentially adverse impact of bilateral free trade on incomes, asset values, or numbers of farmers. The possible gains, by comparison, seem speculative. Warley nonetheless thinks that U.S. insistence on its inclusion will bring agricultural trade into an eventual agreement, though necessarily on a product-group-by-product-group basis.

John Schnittker, a long-time observer of U.S. agricultural policy, is less sanguine than Warley about the outcome. He views the United States as having the basis for only the "most limited" concessions on agricultural trade with Canada. The significant changes in laws and practices that might be made will be reserved for bargaining in the larger GATT tent. An accord on less important measures and programs that hamper trade with Canada would be welcome and ought to be pursued. Whether even that can be accomplished in the current climate remains to be seen.

Ambassador Yeutter, speaking from the vantage of a negotiator, is a relative optimist about trade in agricultural goods. He agrees that the big agricultural trade questions, centering on grains, clearly belong to the GATT round. There remain a host of lesser issues in U.S.-Canada agricultural trade—tariffs and differing sanitary and health standards are examples—many of which could be dealt with to the benefit of both countries.

As for the bilateral negotiation as a whole, Yeutter characterizes it as the most important ever for the United States. He recognizes that free trade would require adjustments in both economies, for individual firms and for entire industries. But adjustments will have to be made anyway; a free trade arrangement will merely speed up the process. The material benefits to Canada and the United States and the likely positive effect on the multilateral talks will make a successful negotiating outcome an eminently worthwhile achievement.

A sensible perspective

A final point, made by Clayton Yeutter in one of his responses to questions at the conference, is worth brief elaboration. To a question about the influence of the 1986 U.S. trade deficit of $170 billion on congressional willingness to approve a Canada–U.S. agreement, he replied that while the deficit of course was of immediate concern, the envisioned bilateral free trade regime would not come fully into effect until the end of the century. Hinging the negotiation on a 1986 event or problem, he implied, would be to suppose that change, far from being inevitable, would never occur.

In fact, the briefest reflection suggests that many matters thought to be of great moment today doubtless will seem quite trivial a few years hence. Other problems, many of them not at all foreseen, will appear. The goal of the negotiators must be to devise a set of rules and principles that will make the evolution from the present situation to free trade as steady and as certain as possible. But no agreement, and certainly not one written under the time duress that the negotiators face, can anticipate events or assure that they will be seen in the same light by the two parties. The various proposals for a joint disputes settlement mechanism are a recognition of this reality.

A long view will not guarantee an agreement in 1987 and its ratification in 1988. Still, among the perspectives offered by the contributors to this volume, the most telling is the advice that things should be put in sensible perspective.

The Politics and Economics
of Bilateral Free Trade

Canadian Perceptions

DONALD S. MACDONALD

THE PERCEPTION of the Royal Commission on the Economic Union and Development Prospects for Canada was of Canada as a country undergoing a fundamental change in economic circumstances. It was an opinion arrived at after a considerable program of academic study, but also based on extensive consultations with all sectors of Canadian society. It is a perception that I believe is shared by an important segment of Canadian business, although I think the full realization that we are undergoing and have undergone an economic change has not yet dawned on many Canadians.

Canadians have always seen themselves, quite rightly, as the residents of a major resource producing country. In recent years, however, they have been inclined to underestimate the extent to which economic activity in Canada has been stimulated by the manufacturing and service industries. Nonetheless, it is true that over the years Canada has run a substantial merchandise trade surplus by selling resource or resource-derived products to foreign customers, using that surplus to buy foreign manufactured goods or, in some cases, to buy foreign services such as shipping, insurance, and cultural products. In the postwar period, not only was there expansion in areas of strength such as grains, forest products, and minerals, but there was also an enormous development of resources we had not previously tapped: oil and natural gas, uranium, coking coal, and iron ore. The resource expansion enabled us to enjoy almost unbroken increases in the standard of living in this country, and it also enabled Canadian manufacturing, behind the wall of a protective tariff, to develop capacities that it had previously not deployed.

For a variety of reasons, it has now become apparent that the rate of growth of the resource sector in Canada will not continue. If we were to be dependent on the resource sector alone, the rate of improvement in the Canadian standard of living would drastically slow down. The reasons for the change are various. In some cases such as in copper or grains, it is because of the

11

emergence of competitive foreign suppliers. In others, because of technological change—for example, in the displacement of copper wire by fiber optics—there will be a drop in demand. Or there have been shifts in end-use production of certain kinds of merchandise—for example, automobiles—to parts of the world that do not use Canadian commodities.

Canada will continue to be a competitive and a versatile supplier of resource commodities. Those commodities will continue to be important to our economic base. But they will not grow at the past rate and therefore will not produce the same rate of general economic growth that we have known. That is the important reality to which Canadians must adjust.

I have said on many occasions that if the Royal Commission were entitled to give only one message to the country, it is that continuing on as we have is merely to assure a decline in the economic well-being of Canadians.

Although the world and Canadians themselves have perceived Canada as a natural resource producer, that perception has underestimated the capacity of the Canadian economy to produce manufactured goods and services. Manufactured products have had an important share of Canadian exports. Much of this share, it is true, has been from arrangements such as the Automotive Agreement, but a range of other products is included in these figures. Canadian industry has considerable competitive potential. From work done for the commission we concluded that if Canada entered into a free trade area agreement with the United States, while there would be substantial adjustments needed in virtually every manufacturing sector, each sector would be able to survive and become an effective competitor in the wider market.

The key for Canada's future economic development, as we saw it, and for the continuation of close economic relations between Canada and the United States is clear: economic logic argues for a removal of trade barriers between the two countries. The question is, are the political systems of the two capable of bringing about such an historic change?

While I watch carefully the turn of political events in the United States, other participants in these meetings are in a better position to comment on free trade as seen from the American viewpoint. Therefore, I would like to talk about the politics of the proposal from a Canadian standpoint.

Fear of free trade

Despite the economic arguments I have mentioned, which I think a broad spectrum of Canadian economic opinion accepts, there is a notable reluctance on the part of many Canadians to see the country become a participant in a free trade area agreement with the United States. Their concern is that too close an economic relationship with our large neighbor may put in jeopardy the fundamental political decision taken more than two centuries ago to maintain an independent political community in the northern half of North America.

The simultaneous attraction and repulsion of a closer trade relationship with the United States has been a source of Canadian ambivalence and of political difference within Canada for well over a century.

In the middle of the nineteenth century, the Canadian provinces achieved limited favorable access to the U.S. market through the Reciprocity Treaty of 1854. And for the twelve-year life of that treaty, it was an economic benefit to Canada. Termination of that treaty by the United States in 1866 was one of the factors that the Fathers of Confederation weighed in deciding in favor of the Canadian Union in 1867. Renewal of the favorable arrangement was the object of both Conservative and Liberal governments in the new Dominion in the first decade after Confederation. In 1878–79, however, A. T. Galt and John A. Macdonald turned their backs on the U.S. market in favor of a protected Canadian market behind a high tariff wall.

The National Policy of Macdonald met the expectations of some Canadians but it was not popular with others for whom closer trade relations with the United States continued to be a political objective. In the last decades of the nineteenth century, there was little American interest in such a mutual arrangement and it was only at the end of the first decade of the twentieth century that the objectives of the two governments came into parallel with the negotiation of the trade agreement of 1911.

While in 1866 it had been the Americans who were reluctant to maintain the relationship, in 1911 it was the Canadian electors who were negative. Responding to the appeals to nationhood and to the imperial connection, Canadians in that year voted out of office the Laurier government which had proposed the treaty.

Since that time, it has been a political axiom in Canada that to seek a comprehensive economic arrangement with the United States is to court Canadian political disaster. We have been told that Mackenzie King, who was the most successful of Canadian prime ministers, faced but backed away from a similar compact in the mid-1940s. While there has been a whole range of functional and sectoral arrangements between the two countries, Brian

Mulroney is the first Canadian prime minister in seventy-five years prepared to stake the life of his government on a comprehensive trade arrangement with the United States.

What are the political realities of the free trade cause in Canada in 1987? The response is necessarily subjective, although I believe and some evidence indicates that a majority of Canadians do favor the economic benefits that would come with the negotiation of a free trade area agreement. That majority, however, depends on the way in which a number of specific concerns are addressed by the agreement itself.

While there are many persons who will express support for the concept of a more comprehensive arrangement, many among them exhibit a visceral concern that closer economic relations may well remove some of the protective supports that sustain Canadian political independence. They cannot be reassured nor their concern dispelled by the marshalling of facts or the exercise of logic. Even those who are persuaded by the mind that it is the right course of action cannot overcome a gut anxiety about the political consequences.

Analogies to other free trade arrangements are not of much assistance in clarifying this issue. In three foreign examples— relations between Austria and Germany, Ireland and the United Kingdom (before their accession to the European Community), and New Zealand and Australia—one can say confidently that the independence of the smaller partner has not been prejudiced by closer trade relations. And in those cases the elements of disparity of size and common language, which are so often referred to in the Canadian-American context, were present. On the contrary, those who argue against the relationship by historical or other analogy have to go back to the nineteenth century to the Zollverein (which of course was designed specifically by Bismarck to bring about the union of the German states), or to the relationship between Hawaii and the United States to find support for their arguments. I do not find a great comparability between the position of Hawaii in the middle of the nineteenth century and Canada in 1987.

My response has been that Canadian independence ultimately will not depend on the nature of tariff arrangements between Canada and the United States. What really counts is the will and conviction of Canadians, a will and conviction that has been in existence now for over two centuries, to continue to maintain an independent country in the northern half of North America. In my opinion, the sense of national community, of national pride, is even stronger in Canada now than I remember it during my boyhood, and that despite much closer economic ties between the two countries. But the concern about independence is a sensitive nerve and it is capable of being activated by what are seemingly the most trivial incidents.

Need for cultural sovereignty

A more specific aspect of that concern about national sovereignty is the concern about what Canadians call cultural sovereignty. This is a matter that is very difficult to discuss with Americans because since the days of Nathaniel Hawthorne, Americans have not had any particular fear of being dominated culturally. To talk about this is to talk about an experience that Americans simply have not known and therefore do not understand.

Since the report of the Massey Commission in 1951, the goal of assuring a Canadian statement in the arts has been widely shared by Canadians. Through publicly owned institutions, through regulatory requirements, or through ownership restrictions, Canadian governments have sought to reserve a place for Canadian expression within the cultural life of our community. This has not meant, as some of the more extreme critics of these Canadian policies have alleged, that Canada has shut out foreign products. Over 70 percent of the magazines and periodicals in the Canadian market are of foreign origin, over 80 percent of the prime-time television presentations are from foreign sources, and equivalently large percentages of book publications or of recordings come from outside the country. Of all the members of the Organization for Economic Cooperation and Development, Canada is the largest per capita importer of cultural products. A Canadian-American agreement that fails to acknowledge the legitimacy of this concern of Canadians, just as it would acknowledge the concern of Americans that American broadcasting stations be owned by their own nationals, would simply be a nonstarter with a large number of Canadians, including apostles of free trade like myself.

It has not been helpful, therefore, to have the response to this legitimate Canadian concern take the form of a statement that all issues, including presumably this one, are still on the table. That kind of response has brought into the lists against the free trade negotiation an important and articulate Canadian group that need not have been provoked. We are told regularly that "you Canadians have got to take into account the legitimate political concerns of the U.S. Congress." Well, there are some political concerns in Canada that have to be taken into account. I believe that a little greater sensitivity would make our relationship easier and the task of our negotiators more manageable.

Other opposition to free trade

Who are some of the other groups within Canada who oppose the negotiations? Most articulate has been the trade union leadership. One should not be surprised at their opposition, since they too are in politics. Their electorate is made up of members of trade unions who, in some cases, will be adversely affected by the industrial change that a broader market will bring. The leaders are not elected to represent the broader interests of the Canadian work force, but only those members within their unions. Of course they are going to direct themselves to their unions' specific interests. I believe that the wider Canadian community recognizes and discounts this special interest, just as it recognized the special interest of the Canadian Labour Congress in campaigning against the anti-inflation program. Nevertheless, the trade union leaders represent an important and articulate minority in the Canadian community and they will be listened to.

While the farm community has been less articulate, it also may be expected to oppose an agreement. Both Canada and the United States have put in place a cat's cradle of subsidies and special support mechanisms to sustain the farm communities. It would be surprising if the farmers did not feel apprehension lest these supportive measures be phased out. And in the case of some of the Canadian measures such as the supply control marketing boards, there would be a serious prospect of them being brought to an end. The problems of the farming communities of Canada and the United States are the same, as they are the same in Western Europe; fundamentally they are too productive for their own good. These are problems that can only be resolved in meetings among the major agricultural exporters. They cannot be confined to a negotiation between Canada and the United States. It is for that reason that I have expressed the view that agriculture might well be left to one side for discussion in a broader forum.

I will make one further observation. That is about what may be the most serious political problem for the negotiations in Canada, namely the continued imposition of what Americans refer to as "fair trade measures" and what we in Canada call "contingent protectionism."

The right to impose antidumping duties, to levy countervailing duties against subsidized exports, even to take emergency action to safeguard against certain kinds of imports are all recognized in the General Agreement on Tariffs and Trade to which both Canada and the United States subscribe. Canada may well want in the future to be able to have resort to antidumping duties, in legitimate cases where its interests are adversely affected. But the imposition of trade penalties on Canada where formerly the American tribunal could find no unfair Canadian trading practices, as in the case of softwood lumber, or where no unfair trading was asserted at all, as in the case of shakes and shingles or the proposed quota on Canadian steel, poisons the wells of political goodwill in Canada that will have to be drawn on to get national support for a trade agreement.

The United States has organized its trade laws in such a way that the initiation and continuation of such measures rests with the most prejudiced group within the American community, namely those who are seeking the relief. American spokesmen have been fond of using the sporting analogy that all they seek is a level playing field. To Canadians, picking an analogy from our national game, it has looked more like wanting to appoint the referee to call back our goals when we look like we might win.

I have observed that unless Canadians can have some assurance of a fairer and more objective application of these GATT articles between Canada and the United States, then an agreement is not worth having. I think that the skills exist on both sides of the negotiating table to develop a set of principles under which the fair trade laws—both the use of subsidies and the employment of fair trade laws—will be fairly monitored, and to provide some objective process to resolve disputes where they occur. In the long run, I think the problems from these kinds of measures are soluble between our two countries and that they will be resolved. In the short run, just as a "standstill" agreement was arrived at between the GATT contracting parties at Punta del Este, so it would be desirable to achieve a standstill in Canada-U.S. relations of contingent protective measures, whether they be against American corn or Canadian products like softwood lumber.

A Congressional Perception

MAX BAUCUS

A GREAT DEAL has been said about the benefits of a free trade agreement between the United States and Canada. The liberalization of the world's largest bilateral trade relationship offers tremendous opportunities for both countries. It also presents a tremendous challenge. I will focus on what must be done to make it a reality.

If the negotiations between our countries are to succeed, the United States must be united in its desire for an agreement. The administration, the Congress, and the relevant groups in this country must all feel that the United States is getting a "good deal" out of the negotiations. That requires the administration to build a strong consensus in favor of the agreement.

I do not feel that is happening. In fact, the administration is repeating past mistakes. If it does not improve its performance, it is very unlikely that a free trade agreement will be ratified by Congress.

Fast-track authority

The history of the administration's actions surrounding the Senate Finance Committee's approval of "fast-track authority" for the negotiations is instructive. In December 1985, the president, as required by statute, asked the committee for fast-track authority—that is, for permission to reach an agreement that Congress would approve or disapprove within ninety days of its submission, with no opportunity to amend. Under the terms of the statute, the authority would be granted automatically if neither the Senate Finance Committee nor the House Ways and Means Committee disapproved the president's request within sixty calendar days, a period ending in April 1986.

The statute is clear. Once the president has notified Congress of his desire for fast-track authority, he has a statutory duty to consult with Congress. Yet until approximately two weeks before

Bob Kyle, legislative counsel, presented the paper on behalf of Senator Baucus and represented him in the discussion.

18

the consideration period ended, the administration had sent no one to Congress to discuss the free trade agreement with me or, as far as I know, other members of the Senate Finance Committee. In my judgment, that was a fundamental mistake; the administration assumed that lack of expressed opposition meant support. As a result, it failed to undertake the consultation necessary to lay the groundwork for congressional approval of fast-track authority.

The consequences became clear about a week and a half before the fast-track vote was required to take place. Absent consultation, opposition to granting fast-track authority had spread like wildfire. Some of my colleagues and I opposed granting the necessary authority because outstanding trade disputes, notably over lumber, indicated that the climate was not right for negotiating a free trade agreement with Canada. Other members were upset because they viewed the lack of consultation as a general failure by the administration to include Congress in trade policymaking. Ultimately, the fast-track authority was granted by only one vote.

I fear that the administration is making the same mistake today. In the week before the vote last April, administration officials involved with the negotiations met with me four times. In the ten months since then, administration officials have met with Finance Committee members only twice. The conclusion seems inescapable that the administration—having gotten the authority—has decided once again to treat Congress as an afterthought.

Before the vote last April, the administration interpreted congressional silence—stemming from preoccupation with tax reform and other important matters—as support for fast-track authority. Today, the administration apparently is again mistaking silence for support. Can the administration really believe that an agreement potentially affecting such critical industries as automobiles, steel, and agriculture will not arouse intense concern among members of Congress?

Some observers have suggested that the Finance Committee's opposition to the fast-track authority was an aberration. They suggest that the committee's opposition sprang solely from dissatisfaction over the relationship between the Congress and the president on trade policymaking generally and had nothing to do with Canada. They suggest that if the president works with Congress this year to fashion a trade bill, resistance to the free trade agreement will evaporate.

In my judgment, that is a misreading of the committee's actions. The committee saw the fast-track issue as symptomatic of a broader problem, but an instance that had significance in and of itself. Even if the administration chooses to work more closely with Congress this year on trade, the committee will be resistant to a free trade agreement unless the administration through systematic consultation is able to allay congressional concern about specific issues in trade with Canada.

The deadlines imposed by the current fast-track authority require the administration to address congressional concern as soon as possible. The authority expires on January 3, 1988. Under the terms of the relevant statute, the president would be required to notify Congress that the administration had reached an agreement by September 1987.

The administration cannot afford to wait until September to address the myriad of congressional interests involved, then expect Congress to approve an agreement. It must begin to work with members of Congress now. The administration should identify sources of congressional opposition and begin building a consensus that can provide broad-based congressional support for an agreement. Failure to do this will risk dangerous consequences that were barely averted last April.

I do not wish to suggest that our negotiators are not working hard on this agreement or that they are trying to put something over on Congress. In fact, they are extremely understaffed and overworked. However, I am saying that they are not paying sufficient attention to the congressional consultation process that is part of the fast-track procedure and that must be followed as a practical matter if they are to achieve congressional approval of an agreement.

It has been suggested that Congress might include an extension of the fast-track authority in the trade bill that it is now drafting. Putting aside the argument that the negotiations will proceed more expeditiously if the negotiating deadlines stay as they are, I think it is unlikely that Congress will want to extend the authority, so long as the administration continues to fail to consult adequately.

Article 1, section 3, clause 8 of the Constitution gives Congress, not the president, the power "to regulate Commerce with foreign nations." Over the years, Congress has delegated substantial authority to the president, because, as a practical matter, our country must have one strong voice at the bargaining table. But Congress is in fact an active partner in these negotiations and must be treated accordingly.

I stand ready to help the administration work with Congress. I would be anxious to help ratify an agreement, if it is balanced and in the best interests of the United States. But such an agreement is not likely to be negotiated unless the administration begins to build a consensus in Congress now.

Areas of concern

I will not go into the many areas that an agreement should address, but I would like to touch on four areas of concern that could play an important role in gaining congressional approval.

Regional Effects

Although a U.S.-Canada free trade agreement may benefit the United States as a nation, it may not affect the entire nation equally. Analyses of the issue have suggested the effects a free trade agreement would have on certain sectors of the economy, such as services, manufacturing, or agriculture. However, I have seen no analysis of its regional effects.

Such an analysis is important. Currently, many of our exports to Canada consist of manufactured products, while many of our imports consist of natural-resource-based products, such as timber and minerals. Would a free trade agreement promote exports from the manufacturing-based states of the East and encourage competition in the natural-resource-based economies of the West? Or are current trade flows the result of barriers that are already low, suggesting that free trade would not have much impact on a regional basis?

None of these questions has been discussed. But they are critical to legislators from different regions of the country. For that reason, the administration must be able to assess the regional effects of an agreement, so that it can build a national consensus in the Congress.

Agriculture

A second area of concern is agriculture. It is becoming increasingly apparent on both sides of the border that it will be difficult to include agriculture in this agreement. Our marketing systems are too different, and our respective third-country trade interests would be too affected by changes in those systems. I agree with many of these arguments.

However, this should not deter the negotiators from addressing strictly bilateral agricultural trade issues, such as animal quarantine and health restrictions that unduly burden trade between the United States and Canada. These restrictions can and should be a proper topic of negotiation.

Exchange Rates

In my judgment, the exchange rate issue should be addressed before any agreement is struck. The Canadian dollar currently is about 25 percent below parity, giving Canadian exporters a tremendous price advantage in the U.S. market. I do not want to go into the causes of the depressed Canadian dollar. I only want to note that an exchange rate that places U.S. producers at a disadvantage creates a bad climate for congressional approval of any free trade agreement.

Contingent Protection

One of the most important issues in this negotiation is contingent protection. In discussing contingent protection I refer to the question of the extent to which Canada, under any agreement, would be treated differently from other countries under U.S. countervailing duty and antidumping laws.

At the outset, it is important to recognize that our two countries have fundamentally different views of the U.S. countervailing duty and antidumping laws. It is my view—and the view of most of Congress—that those laws are the means by which we enforce our rights under the General Agreement on Tariffs and Trade and ensure free trade. They are the chief mechanisms for discouraging an escalation of subsidies and unfair pricing practices. If Canada truly trades freely under the agreement, these provisions will never be invoked.

Canada sees things differently. Canadians believe that these laws are mere protectionism, that the procedures under which they are applied are highly political and subjective. I can only assure them this is not the case. My entire experience with these laws indicates that they are imposed in a quasi-judicial manner, separate from political considerations.

I also want to assure you that the U.S. view is not likely to change. In the view of Congress, any agreement to exempt Canada from these laws would be tantamount to signing an agreement, then eliminating the means to enforce it.

Does this mean that there can be no agreement over contingent protection? No. In my judgment, Congress might be willing to go so far as to consider the establishment of a bilateral commission to examine disputes between the two countries. Such a commission might be modeled along the lines of the Boundary Waters Commission. However, it is extremely unlikely, in my judgment, that Congress would permit such a commission to make binding determinations, but it might endow a commission with recommendatory authority.

Conclusion

During the Finance Committee vote on the fast-track authority, many members of the Senate Finance Committee indicated that they favored free trade agreement negotiations in the abstract but had not been persuaded in practical terms that the negotiations should proceed. The same kind of thinking exists today; many members of Congress believe a free trade agreement holds great opportunities, but they must be persuaded that the specific agreement negotiated is in the best interest of the United States.

We can negotiate a good agreement, or we can negotiate a bad agreement. There is no immutable law that any agreement will be advantageous to the United States. Therefore, we cannot expect legislators to stand for a "free trade agreement" in advance. But the administration can increase the chances that Congress will accept an agreement, if it has been consulted along the way. If it is not consulted, the road to an agreement will be rocky indeed.

Economic Impact on Canada

RICHARD G. HARRIS

WHAT IS the potential economic impact of a free trade arrangement between Canada and the United States on the Canadian economy? I have used some fairly large scale models in the general equilibrium tradition to examine the effects of economywide microeconomic policies such as a free trade deal. The general conclusion from my work is that such an agreement would have produced large benefits for Canada in the mid-1970s, and that about half of these benefits are still potentially achievable. To be precise, looking at a free trade deal initiated in late 1987 covering all significant tariff and nontariff barriers, I would guess that in the long term the level of real income in Canada would rise by about 5 percent. Of course, such a precise number requires that I explain my key assumptions. In this paper I review the most controversial of my results, including possible terms-of-trade effects, the significance of scale economies, and the estimated values of the nontariff barriers.

I also discuss what the adjustment process is likely to involve in terms of job losses. Those estimates must be qualified because analysis of adjustment to a far-reaching policy change such as free trade is complicated by problems of the timing of investment and disinvestment both by workers and by firms. One further aspect of the economic effects that I assess is the impact of potential protection by the United States on Canadian industry, and the importance of market access for Canadian manufacturing. Here the evidence is clear, reasonably uncontroversial, and sobering to say the least.

Since the report of the Royal Commission chaired by Donald Macdonald was issued in 1985, no studies have been published that change the basic picture of Canada-U.S. trade developed in the 1970s and early 1980s.[1] As of 1987, however, the presence of significant competition from newly industrialized and developing

---

1. See *Report of the Royal Commission on the Economic Union and Development Prospects for Canada* (Ottawa: Ministry of Supply and Services, 1985).

countries has made the future of U.S. and Canadian manufacturing less clear. This is a problem that has not been addressed in a quantitative way.

Background   The model commonly used in analysis of international trade patterns and the impact of protection on income, prices, production, and employment is based on the Heckscher–Ohlin/Ricardian model developed in the first half of this century. It explains trade in terms of differences in production technologies or resource endowments between countries. It is a neoclassical model, in that it assumes fully flexible prices, which clear all commodity and factor markets, and perfect competition in all markets. Thus, no individual buyer or seller exerts any significant power on the price in his own market. This model usually incorporates the assumption of constant costs in all industries, so that as industry output expands or contracts, unit cost of output remains constant. The trade economist is thus able to ignore the individual firm as a unit of study and focus on how resources are allocated among industries. And the model is logically consistent with the perfect competition model in assuming away increasing returns to scale, or decreasing costs of production. Economists have recognized since the 1930s that scale economies are inconsistent with the perfect competition model.

There are problems, however, with an analysis of trade policy based on perfect competition. From the early days of economic theory, many economists realized that assumptions of perfect competition, while perhaps useful, are patently at odds with the facts for many industries and markets. During the 1960s, a number of practical-minded trade economists like Eastman and Stykolt and the Wonnacotts realized that the competitive model was not appropriate for a small economy such as Canada. They began writing about the impact of protection on industries that were oligopolistic and characterized by decreasing costs.[2] At the same time, Bela Balassa was writing on similar matters with respect to the effect of the formation of a European customs union.

For the most part, these scholars emphasized a set of factors ignored by most trade theorists. Within Canada, the new views became well known and were a basis for development of the free trade position. Their basic point was that protection, both foreign

2. H. Eastman and S. Stykolt, *The Tariff and Competition in Canada* (Toronto: Macmillan, 1967); R.J. Wonnacott and P. Wonnacott, *Free Trade Between the United States and Canada: The Potential Economic Effects* (Harvard University Press, 1967). See *Canadian Public Policy,* special supplement, vol. 7 (October 1982), for a summary of the literature.

and domestic, was anticompetitive in its effects, producing inefficient domestic firms. One major form of inefficiency was highly diversified manufacturing plants with production runs too short to realize the scale economies available in larger countries. These economists demonstrated that trade barriers contributed to high prices, low wages, low productivity, and poor export performance in the manufacturing sector.[3] The position they took was fairly controversial, one reason being that until 1982 no one had done a quantitative disaggregated general equilibrium analysis of these issues.

The GET policy simulation model

In an attempt to quantify the effects of trade barriers, I developed a general equilibrium trade (GET) model of the Canadian economy. The model is complex, emphasizing the role of relative price changes in the economic adjustment process.[4] A rise in demand in one sector raises the price in that sector and the model tracks subsequent adjustments throughout the industrial system. The model is logically consistent in that supply must equal demand in every market and all markets are linked together in the appropriate ways—hence the term *general* equilibrium. This model, regarded as medium sized, contains thirty commodities, two primary factors of production, and twenty-nine industries. Exports and imports are explicitly treated as responding to the various exogenous and endogenous variables, including relative price changes due to protection. An innovative assumption is that capital—both physical goods and financial capital—is mobile across the Canadian border. The implication is that any departure of the long-run rate of return on investment in Canada from that in the United States would be met by a capital flow that would completely remove this differential in the long run.

The main innovation within the model is the treatment of the manufacturing sector within Canada. Each of the twenty manufacturing industries is regarded as imperfectly competitive to some degree. The extent of imperfect competition is determined within the model. Firms rationally set prices in response to perceived demand for their goods and their competitors' reactions. Each firm has a cost structure with average cost declining over some

3. Richard Harris with David Cox, *Trade, Industrial Policy, and Canadian Manufacturing* (Toronto: Ontario Economic Council, 1984), reviews the debate and literature on free trade.
4. The structure is described in ibid.; Richard Harris, "Applied General Equilibrium Analysis of Small Open Economies with Scale Economies and Imperfect Competition," *American Economic Review*, vol. 74 (December 1984), pp. 1016–32.

range of output. Firms enter and exit from industries in response to profits and losses. The explicit recognition of firms, their cost curves, and entry and exit allows the model to identify what is commonly called the rationalization of industry. For example, a reduction in the number of firms in an industry, accompanied by increasing output per firm, would allow the industry as a whole to produce at lower cost. Tariffs play a crucial role in this rationalization. Domestic tariffs restrict entry and result in non-competitive pricing by the protected firms, which in turn induces low output per firm and high costs. Foreign tariffs are equally important, for different reasons. With reduced access to world markets, Canadian firms may not be able to attain sufficient size for the kind of specialization and rationalization effects that would be most desirable.

The GET model was explicitly designed to answer questions regarding rationalization and protection within a long-run framework. Because it is a general equilibrium model, it is not limited to single industries but can be used to examine the complex interaction between the various product and factor markets. It turns out, for example, that in determining the extent of rationalization, it is crucial to consider what happens to the equilibrium Canadian real wage, and in a general equilibrium model the wage is endogenously determined.

Aggregate results of trade liberalization policies

Table 1 shows some of the results obtained with the GET model of the removal of the 1976 barriers, both domestic and foreign, on trade between Canada and the United States as well as on unilateral and multilateral bases. The model incorporates some nontariff barriers, though many that were too difficult to quantify, such as government procurement policy, are not included. The model is based on econometric estimates from the early and mid-1970s, and the input-output table in the model is based on 1976 data. Some of the parameters are only imprecisely known and hence results refer to what are known as the best-guess or reference-parameter values.

The most surprising result in table 1 is the gain in real income from the unilateral removal of Canadian import barriers—about 3.5 percent of base gross national product for Canada. This is a very large number compared with other estimates, which are typically less than 1 percent of GNP. The real wage rises by about 10 percent, with an increase in labor productivity of about 20 percent and an increase in total factor productivity of about 8.5 percent. The major source of these productivity and real income

Table 1. *Change in Key Variables of the Canadian Economy under Bilateral, Unilateral, and Multilateral Free Trade Relative to 1976 Barriers*
Percent

Variable	Bilateral free trade	Unilateral free trade	Multilateral free trade
Wages	27.6	9.98	25.21
Real gross national product	6.5	3.49	7.02
Welfare gain[a]	8.9	4.13	8.59
Length of production runs[b]	90.0	41.40	66.84
Labor productivity[c]	29.9	19.57	32.62
Trade volume[d]	87.3	53.13	88.61
Labor reallocation index[e]	6.7	3.93	6.15
U.S. trade[f]	97.9	. . .	. . .
Diversion index[g]	76.3	. . .	. . .

Sources: David Cox and Richard G. Harris, "Trade Liberalization and Industrial Organization: Some Estimates for Canada," *Journal of Political Economy* (1984), table 1; David Cox and Richard Harris, "A Quantitative Assessment of the Economic Impact on Canada of Sectoral Free Trade with the United States," *Canadian Journal of Economics*, no. 3 (August 1986), pp. 377–94.

a. Hicks equivalent variation as a percent of initial gross national expenditure.

b. Weighted average of output per firm in each manufacturing industry, where the weights are the industries' shares of total manufacturing output.

c. Output per unit of labor, based on the weighted average of labor productivity in each industry, where the weights are the industries' shares of the total output of all industries.

d. Sum of the value of exports and imports across all industries, including noncompeting imports.

e. Percentage of all labor that must shift intersectorally.

f. Percentage increase in trade volume with the United States.

g. Percentage of total Canadian trade volume accounted for by trade with the United States.

gains is reductions in the average cost of production through industry rationalization. Rationalization in this case leads to an average increase in output per firm of around 40 percent. In some industries this means a fairly dramatic decline in the number of firms. The most prominent effect of unilateral free trade is the rationalization it induces at the level of the individual industry.

When both foreign and domestic trade barriers are reduced, the effects are even greater. The aggregate real income gain under multilateral free trade is 8.6 percent, and the real wage rises by 25 percent. These are clearly very substantial gains. Trade volume increases enormously, from $84 billion (in 1976 Canadian dollars) to $160 billion. This is accompanied by an increase in inward investment flows as a result of the more capital-intensive production techniques adopted in many industries in response to the higher relative price of labor. This is particularly true in the natural resource and service sectors of the economy.

On bilateral free trade the basic results are striking. First, bilateral free trade gives welfare gains of 8.9 percent—slightly larger than the 8.6 percent gains under multilateral free trade, which are based on somewhat lower tariff estimates. The larger number clearly arises from the preferential access to the U.S. market under a bilateral arrangement. As the small country in the arrangement, Canada benefits by the diversion of U.S. trade from other countries toward Canada. Given the existence of scale economies in Canadian industries, the larger market afforded by the diversion of U.S. imports toward Canada clearly benefits Canada. Diversion of trade within Canada—estimated as the proportion of total Canadian trade accounted for by the United States—increases from a base equilibrium of 71 percent to 76 percent under bilateral free trade. And under the assumption of bilateral free trade, total Canadian foreign trade increases by over 87 percent, and trade with the United States by over 97 percent.

The conventional wisdom is that the impact of protection on the Canadian economy is to shelter manufacturing industries and throw most of the burden on the resource sectors. Results of the 1976 simulations that are not included in table 1 suggest the opposite. Total employment within manufacturing rises by 12 percent and employment in the service and resource sectors declines. The major cost of Canadian protection is an inefficient manufacturing sector.

The overall pattern of reallocation of resources suggests that adjustments occur both within and among industries. In aggregate terms, the percentage of trade within industries changes little in response to either multilateral or bilateral free trade. This, however, masks an increasing specialization of production within the manufacturing sector. Bilateral free trade is likely to bring about substantial gains in the use of resources only as it induces significant shifts in the allocation of resources among industries.

Under bilateral free trade, fifteen of the twenty manufacturing industries experience an increase in real output of more than 10 percent (table 2). Ten of the twenty-two are winners on employment grounds; seven are significant losers, including miscellaneous manufacturing, furniture, electrical equipment, and agricultural equipment. Manufacturing as a whole moves from a significant trade deficit position to a trade surplus position. In total, exports rise in all but two manufacturing industries, and in construction, communications, electric power and gas, and services. Imports rise in all industries. The common characteristic of the losers is a fairly labor-intensive technology. Winners have one and often more of the following characteristics: unexploited economies of scale; low levels of initial protection against U.S. imports; a capital-intensive technology; high export elasticities; and moderate degrees of import competition.

Table 2. *Change in Key Variables in Twenty-two Canadian Industries under Bilateral Free Trade Relative to 1976 Barriers*
Percent

Industry	Output	Productivity	Employment
Textiles	126.7	31.5	72.5
Steel	27.9	23.3	3.7
Agricultural equipment	−10.1	23.2	−26.9
Urban transportation equipment	94.4	26.7	53.5
Chemicals	23.4	23.1	0.2
Food and beverages	24.6	26.9	−1.8
Tobacco	27.6	41.7	−9.9
Rubber	38.2	30.2	6.2
Leather	24.8	34.1	−6.9
Knitting	98.4	39.1	42.6
Clothing	478.9	60.1	261.6
Wool	15.0	30.9	−12.1
Furniture	−15.2	35.5	−37.4
Paper and allied products	59.9	21.4	31.7
Printing	35.9	19.8	13.5
Metal fabrication	14.7	22.9	−6.6
Nonagricultural equipment	−18.0	22.8	−33.2
Transport equipment	104.7	26.2	62.2
Electrical products	−0.5	26.9	−21.6
Nonmetal minerals	21.5	22.3	−0.6
Petroleum	23.5	33.4	−7.4
Miscellaneous manufacturing	−18.8	21.8	−33.3

Source: Cox and Harris, "A Quantitative Assessment," pp. 377–94.

Distribution of Gains and Adjustment Patterns

Any change in trade policy creates losers and gainers. Furthermore, the labor adjustment burden will be inequitably distributed. The results on bilateral free trade show that some of the conventional wisdom about losers in manufacturing and gainers in resource industries is misplaced. For example, the GET model suggests that the biggest loser from protection in the 1970s was labor in the manufacturing sectors. While consumers as a whole faced higher prices on imports that were protected, their loss is about one-quarter that of labor in the manufacturing industries as a whole. Within manufacturing the picture is more varied. The biggest employment losses are in labor-intensive industries, and this is where the major labor adjustment burden must be borne. Both winning and losing industries are concentrated in Ontario and Quebec, so that adjustment is largely confined to central Canada. Both the west and the east are (small) gainers from trade liberalization.

Another aspect of the pattern of labor adjustment is the distribution of shifts within and between industries. Some economists are of the view that intraindustry adjustment is less costly than interindustry adjustment. Such is often said to have been the European experience since the formation of the European Community.[5] If this view is correct, the results from the GET model are not comforting. Bilateral free trade is estimated (in table 1) to require about 6.7 percent of the Canadian labor force to shift intersectorally, mostly within manufacturing and partly out of services and resources into manufacturing. While 6.7 percent of the labor force is not a large number, it is substantial in terms of the retraining and relocation that would be required.

The model also indicates a significant amount of intraindustry adjustment in the form of a fall in the number of firms within certain industries, both those expanding and those contracting. In some heavily protected industries the number of plants is cut in half. Estimating the actual cost of adjustment associated with reductions in the number of firms is difficult. Some economists believe that this type of cost is relatively low, given that it does not involve human resources directly. Others believe that even when plant closures are beneficial in terms of rationalization, they create severe dislocation costs for employees within those plants. There is, no doubt, something to this latter view.

In summary, the long-run equilibrium results from the GET model suggest that the gains arising from trade liberalization are substantial and accrue largely to labor within central Canada's manufacturing industries.

Unilateral Sectoral Trade Liberalization

One of the policy simulations done with the GET model investigates the effects of unilateral free trade within a single sector. The results of this simulation, reported in table 3, provide a rough indication of the effect of import competition in each of the twenty industrial sectors.

In general, the picture is quite positive. In ten of the manufacturing industries, unilateral sectoral free trade is employment-creating. Furthermore, in each case, exports increased by more than imports in percentage terms. Finally, in all but three there is a positive aggregate gain in real income to the economy. The numbers are not small. For example, in the food and beverage industry, the real income gain is about $1 billion (in 1976 Canadian dollars). When the domestic side is viewed alone, the results suggest that unilateral free trade in individual sectors, while not

---

5. This view is commonly attributed to Bela Balassa.

Table 3. *Change in Key Variables in Twenty Canadian Industries under Unilateral Sectoral Free Trade Relative to 1976 Barriers*

Industry	Welfare gain (millions of Canadian dollars)	Percent change in				
		Price of goods produced	Employment rate	Value of exports	Value of imports	Labor productivity
Food and beverages	1,069.73	−7	−2	51	47	13
Tobacco	218.04	−14	0	113	139	26
Rubber and plastics	172.41	−5	6	73	21	6
Leather	−11.17	−8	−21	91	40	12
Textiles	130.25	−8	3	88	30	9
Knitting mills	−14.95	−12	−37	159	85	19
Clothing	−17.40	−13	−48	308	187	30
Wood	242.90	−3	8	20	12	3
Furniture and fixtures	23.72	−6	−20	94	87	10
Paper and allied products	373.91	−4	16	31	21	4
Printing and publishing	84.22	−3	0	32	15	3
Primary metals	499.86	−3	18	57	11	3
Metal fabricating	347.41	−4	4	69	21	6
Machinery	5.18	−3	2	44	10	3
Transportation equipment	2,673.45	−4	53	95	62	13
Electrical products	108.82	−5	−4	54	26	6
Nonmetallic mineral production	193.46	−4	10	56	11	4
Petroleum and coal	94.63	−1	−1	6	7	1
Chemical products	101.34	−3	4	42	14	3
Miscellaneous manufacturing	49.01	−4	−2	101	30	7

Source: Richard Harris with David Cox, *Trade, Industrial Policy, and Canadian Manufacturing* (Toronto: Ontario Economic Council, 1984), table 23.

as beneficial as complete free trade, is for the most part a good thing in terms of net economic efficiency.

For those industries with a positive welfare gain, the rationalization effects are responsible for most of the gains. In three industries—leather, knitting mills, and clothing—unilateral free trade turns out to be welfare-decreasing. The negative welfare effects point out the limitations of reductions in protection for specific sectors. Because these three industries are highly labor intensive and heavily protected, cutting domestic protection results in a substantial outflow of employment into other industries. Since protection is still in place in these other industries and they are not rationalized, the additional resources are employed inefficiently and actually lead to a deterioration in the terms of trade in the receiving industries. One virtue of complete free trade is that this cannot happen, because all sectors are rationalized simultaneously.

Sensitivity

As of 1987, the estimated static gains from bilateral free trade should probably be about half of those estimated for the 1976 figures. By the end of 1987, tariffs will be significantly lower, and estimates of nontariff barriers to Canada-U.S. trade have been reduced since 1976. Finally, the deterioration in Canadian terms of trade has resulted in a lower Canadian dollar vis-à-vis the U.S. currency, which has had the effect of enhancing Canadian industrial competitiveness. Even with these qualifications, however, the numbers are quite sensitive to assumptions about export elasticities. Brown and Stern have produced estimates that suggest a loss to Canada of real income from bilateral free trade.[6] These estimates, in a quite different economic model, assume that the demand for Canadian exports is fairly insensitive to price changes. I believe this assumption is inappropriate.

Bilateral free trade and employment

A fairly common way of analyzing labor market adjustment problems uses an input-output framework appended to a conventional Keynesian macro model with rigid nominal (or real) wages and a fixed exchange rate. Using the GET model, I have addressed the question of the short-term employment effects of an immediate and complete reduction of trade barriers between Canada and the United States, assuming both the structure of nominal wages and the Canadian exchange rate are held fixed. Surprisingly, the answer is an increase in aggregate employment of about 5.5 percent. Out of twenty-nine industries, eighteen expand in employment and eleven contract. These results depend on assuming export and import elasticities of moderate values, and on assuming that capacity constraints do not bind in the expanding industries within the time horizon of slightly under three years. If capacity constraints do bind, the aggregate employment-creating effect is smaller. This result points out the importance of the export sector as a job creator in Canada. Even though fairly significant amounts of import substitution occur, bilateral free trade creates jobs on balance, even in the short run. (Of course, moving labor from one industry to another is not costless, and therefore one must be careful not to understate the short-run problems of adjustment.)

These results are not atypical of those produced by other economic models designed to analyze trade policy. For example, a similar model of the Australian economy asks what would happen to short-term employment with implementation of a 25

6. Drusilla K. Brown and Robert M. Stern, "Evaluating the Impacts of U.S.-Canadian Free Trade: What Do the Multisector Trade Models Suggest?" paper presented to the Fourth Annual Workshop on U.S.-Canadian Relations: Perspectives on a U.S.-Canadian Free Trade Agreement (University of Western Ontario, April 4–5, 1986).

percent cut in domestic tariffs, holding real wages constant.[7] It indicates that cutting domestic tariffs would leave aggregate employment virtually unaffected, with a rise of about 0.05 percent. (These results are much less favorable for employment than those of the Canadian case under a bilateral trade agreement which also reduces barriers to Canadian exports to the U.S. market.)

What about exchange rate adjustments in response to bilateral free trade? Given a flexible exchange rate, the response to the initiation of trade liberalization is a powerful determinant of employment in the short run. The possibility that the Canadian exchange rate might appreciate, making exports more expensive and imports relatively cheaper and thus leading to a decrease in employment or an increase in aggregate unemployment, has been addressed by a number of analysts, starting with Robert Mundell.[8] They have used theoretical models that emphasize short-run rigidities in the labor market as the principle source of unemployment. All come to the conclusion that lowering the trade barriers of a small country, given sluggish nominal or real wages, causes a depreciation of its currency in the short to medium run. This assists in lowering unemployment beyond what would occur if the nominal exchange rate were unchanged.

Unfortunately, no empirical work exists on this aspect of the problem, since there has been no significant trade liberalization by a small industrial country in the period of floating exchange rates. Yet there is no evidence to suggest that Mundell was incorrect in his basic conclusion regarding the short-term response of the exchange rate. (In the case of Canada-U.S. trade, the Canadian exchange rate would do most of the adjusting in the short run, given the dominance of the bilateral trade in total Canadian trade compared to its share of total U.S. trade. Indeed, one would expect little impact on the U.S. dollar vis-à-vis other major currencies.)

The employment impact results using static Keynesian assumptions are probably much too optimistic, notably because labor constraints could show up quickly in export industries and export price elasticities could conceivably be quite low in the short run.

An alternative dynamic industry model, constructed to focus on the medium-term adjustment issues, was applied to the province

7. P. B. Dixon, A. A. Powell, and B. R. Parmenter, *Structural Adaptation in an Ailing Macroeconomy* (Melbourne, Australia: Melbourne University Press, 1979).

8. "Flexible Exchange Rates and Employment Policy," *Canadian Journal of Economics,* vol. 27 (1961).

of Ontario, where much of the adjustment in manufacturing is predicted to occur. The model has a medium-term horizon of ten years; federal and provincial tax, expenditure, monetary, and exchange rate policies are held constant; unemployment is industry-specific in the short run (an unemployed automobile worker is not considered to be immediately available for work in the rubber manufacturing industry, for example); nominal wages adjust sluggishly to increases or decreases in labor demand; and industry supply is limited in the short run by capacity constraints. The latter features are Keynesian in nature as they emphasize quantity rather than price adjustments to changing demand and supply forces. Employment can thus be affected in a number of ways in response to a bilateral trade agreement.

In the short run, stimulation of exports in a wide range of industries will increase employment. Increased access to the U.S. market will also stimulate investment in some industries and thus may cause employment to rise in the industries producing capital goods. Also, the reduction of protection on a wide range of intermediate goods industries will encourage expansion of output in those industries as cost of their inputs is reduced and they are able to take advantage of economies of scale. At the same time, however, employment will fall as imports are substituted for some domestic goods in both consumption and production. And those industries that experience a loss of product demand with the reduction in protective tariffs will also reduce investment and hence the demand for output and labor in the capital goods industries. It is a quantitative matter which of these various effects will dominate.

It is important to note that reported results are relative to a situation in which unemployment is frictional or associated with natural turnover in the labor market; the unemployment rate in the benchmark, or status quo, situation is that rate that leaves the inflation rate unchanged in the face of neutral aggregate demand policy. Projections are generated by shocking the model relative to the status quo path without trade liberalization. Both the U.S. and the world rate of economic growth are assumed to be unchanged by the free trade arrangement. The set of assumptions used to determine the effects of bilateral free trade produces conservative forecasts of increased employment or reduced unemployment. That is unavoidable because in the short run (one year) all industries are presumed to be operating near normal capacity, and inelastic supply in the export industries means that the possibility of increased exports is slight.

Table 4. *Change in Key Variables of the Economy of Ontario under Bilateral Free Trade Relative to 1987 Barriers*
Percent

Variable and time span	Difference in cumulative growth, by industry sector[a]				
	Primary	Manufacturing	Transportation equipment	Service	All
Gross provincial output					
After 5 years	0.280	1.258	0.161	0.671	0.886
After 10 years	0.341	3.248	3.107	1.241	1.791
Employment rate					
After 5 years	−0.006	0.598	0.295	0.169	0.263
After 10 years	−0.329	0.840	0.576	−0.064	−0.130
Value of investment					
After 5 years	1.792	4.395	2.042	2.639	2.953
After 10 years	1.164	3.463	4.474	1.252	1.569
Number of unemployed					
After 5 years	−0.984	−4.834	−3.960	−1.937	−2.541
After 10 years	−2.154	−2.674	−4.005	−1.857	−2.020
Value of exports					
After 5 years	4.627	7.100	8.475	0.141	6.823
After 10 years	5.458	11.050	12.947	0.675	10.518
Value of imports					
After 5 years	−1.813	11.686	12.836	3.415	9.206
After 10 years	−2.501	13.163	14.110	5.678	10.998

Source: R. Harris, "The Adjustment of the Ontario Economy to a Canada-U.S. Free Trade Arrangement," prepared for the Select Committee on Economic Affairs of the Ontario Legislature (February 1986).

a. The percentage change under bilateral free trade less the percentage change under 1987 conditions. For example, if primary industries grow 15.253 percent under bilateral free trade and 15.000 percent in its absence, the difference is 0.253 percent.

The results can thus be thought of as providing upper-bound estimates of the unemployment consequences of a bilateral agreement, when the economy is assumed to be operating initially at normal capacity, macroeconomic and tax expenditure policies are held constant, and no external shocks occur. Obviously if the agreement were initiated in a period of world recession, the unemployment rates would be different from those predicted in the model. The methodology isolates only the effects of bilateral free trade on the economy, independent of other possible domestic or international economic developments.

Table 4 presents the results of simulations of the impact on the Ontario economy of a bilateral agreement initiated in 1984 and running to 1993. Both the United States and Canada are assumed to eliminate tariffs and nontariff barriers to trade linearly over a five-year phase-in period. The barriers to trade in the primary industries are left unchanged. This exception is considered to be justified because of the relatively small size of Ontario's primary sector. Furthermore, both countries have numerous and intricate nontariff barriers in this part of the economy that cannot be reliably depicted in equivalent ad valorem tariff rates. Trade barriers used in the calculations are those assumed to prevail in 1987.

The impact of various policies can be most easily appreciated by considering aggregate industries. Thus agriculture, forestry, fishing and trapping, and mining are defined as the primary industries. Manufacturing industries, a subset of all manufacturing industries proper, includes primary metal products, metal fabricating, machinery, transportation equipment, and electrical products, which account for approximately half of the manufacturing sector output in Ontario. Transportation equipment is considered separately since the automotive industry is especially important. The service industries include transportation, communications, and utilities; wholesale and retail trade; community, business, and personal services; financial services, insurance, and real estate; and public administration. Finally, an aggregate of all industries is used to form results for the total provincial economy.

Table 4 shows the relative changes in some key economic variables after five and ten years have elapsed. The number in the table is the difference between the percentage change under the status quo and the percentage change under bilateral free trade policy. Thus after ten years, the total economy (all sectors) will have expanded output by 1.79 percent more with a five-year phase-in of a bilateral agreement than if no free trade agreement were implemented.

The following general observations on what happens in five years can be made from the results in table 4: (1) output expands in all sectors; (2) investment expands in all sectors; (3) exports expand in all sectors although only slightly in the service industries; (4) imports expand in all except the primary sector; (5) employment expands in all but the primary sector. Conversely, the number of unemployed persons is reduced and the unemployment rate is reduced in all sectors. Both employment and unemployment in the primary sector are reduced as labor shifts away from primary industries toward manufacturing and service industries.

Although the level of trade with the United States and the rest of the world is increased, net exports, or the value of exports less the value of imports, is reduced after ten years. However, the reduction in net exports for the total provincial economy after ten years is slight, estimated at under $10 million (in 1983 Canadian dollars).

During the transition, changes in employment do not mirror changes in output. In the primary sector, employment falls beneath the control case in year five, but there is a relatively small absolute number of jobs lost in the sector (less than 700 total in year ten). The manufacturing industries are winners in terms of job creation—the five-industry composite shows a steady increase in the number of jobs, with 4,500 new jobs created by the end of ten years.

After ten years, employment falls in the service and primary sectors but rises in other sectors. In fact, the positive impact of the five-year phase-in policy is the creation by the end of the tenth year of about 6,000 jobs in industries other than the service and primary sectors. In the middle of the transition in the fifth year, approximately 12,000 additional jobs will have been created.

Absolutely, the number of jobs created is not large. The surprising result, however, is that net job creation is positive during the entire adjustment period. Fears of large-scale job losses under bilateral free trade seem unfounded on the basis of this analysis. Indeed since the aggregate unemployment rate for the province falls throughout the adjustment period, the tentative conclusion is that aggregate adjustment costs in terms of forgone income to unemployed workers are minimal and that the demands on broadly based support programs like unemployment insurance will be correspondingly minimal. This is not to deny that some workers may lose their jobs because of increased competition from U.S. imports, but rather to suggest that these workers will be a small fraction of the total work force, and that in aggregate terms their loss will be offset by other workers' gain of employment.

Recall that an important short-run consideration with respect to the employment effects of a bilateral arrangement is the extent to which it induces additional investment. An increase in investment contributes to an increase in aggregate demand and thereby increases employment. Table 4 indicates that investment in Ontario increases by a significant amount in all sectors over the ten years. In both manufacturing and transportation equipment the percentage increase in investment is greater than the percentage increase in output by a substantial margin. This provides some support for the proposition that bilateral free trade will lead to a minor investment boom, which in turn will lead to increased employment in capital-goods–producing sectors, and notably in construction.

U.S. protectionism and market access

Recent debate in Canada on the costs and benefits of free trade with the United States has focused on the relevant consequences of U.S. protectionism for Canadian employment and income, or the costs and benefits of "market access." The issue arises in comparisons of the status quo with a bilateral free trade alternative. For the simulations in table 4 the status quo is defined as "no increase in U.S. barriers." If the status quo is instead defined as some escalation of barriers by the United States against Canadian exports, the estimates of how important the potential barriers might be to the Ontario economy change.

Table 5 reports the results of two simulations. One involves raising U.S. tariff barriers on the exports of all manufacturing and service industries, first to 15 percent in year two, and then to 25 percent in year three, where they would remain permanently. As most U.S. tariff and nontariff barriers are below the 15 percent level, this would be expected to have considerable effect on Ontario exports—particularly in the automotive sector. Obviously such a scenario entails an abrogation of the Automotive Agreement of 1965 by one of the two countries. The second form of U.S. protectionism focuses on the automotive industry. Sectoral protectionism of this sort might come about for a variety of reasons, including large-scale unemployment in the U.S. automotive industry, or initiation of a trade war between Japan and the United States.

Not surprisingly the impact of across-the-board U.S. protectionism is substantial. My simulations indicate that in the first year of the broad policy the unemployment rate increases by 0.6 percent, and thereafter it rises steadily so that after five years it stands 1.3 percent higher than it would have been; after ten years the unemployment rate has decreased slightly to a 1.2 percent increase relative to the base case.[9] Within the first five years the biggest effect is felt on the transportation equipment (automotive) industry, where the unemployment rate rises by 2.3 percent. The effect on employment is considerable. Total job loss in Ontario from protectionism is estimated at approximately 79,000 jobs after

9. R. Harris, "The Adjustment of the Ontario Economy to a Canada-U.S. Free Trade Arrangement," prepared for the Select Committee on Economic Affairs of the Ontario Legislature (February 1986).

Table 5. *Change in Key Variables of the Economy of Ontario under U.S. Protection of the Automotive Industry and of All Manufacturing and Service Industries Relative to 1987 Barriers*
Percent

| Variable and time span | Difference in cumulative growth, by industry sector[a] | | | | |
	Primary	Manufacturing	Transportation equipment	Service	All
	Protection of automotive industry only				
Gross provincial output					
After 5 years	0.070	−1.524	−4.893	−0.252	−2.380
After 10 years	0.107	−3.408	−10.239	−1.203	−1.335
Investment rate					
After 5 years	−0.036	−4.979	−13.145	−2.775	−2.638
After 10 years	3.639	−4.316	−13.489	0.140	0.101
Number of unemployed					
After 5 years	0.311	4.983	15.567	1.605	1.793
After 10 years	1.532	4.096	−8.102	3.404	3.213
Value of exports					
After 5 years	1.034	−12.012	−16.565	0.206	−8.061
After 10 years	2.930	−16.482	−23.059	1.297	10.734
Value of imports					
After 5 years	0.450	−4.031	5.509	−0.406	−2.500
After 10 years	−1.538	−4.727	−5.856	−1.689	−3.470
	Protection of all manufacturing and service industries				
Gross provincial output					
After 5 years	0.717	−5.886	−3.075	−4.104	−4.223
After 10 years	1.724	−11.169	−11.056	−7.768	−7.961
Investment rate					
After 5 years	5.038	−12.516	−7.020	−16.072	−14.224
After 10 years	20.424	−10.881	−19.615	−0.428	0.014
Number of unemployed					
After 5 years	4.021	20.873	26.263	15.059	14.896
After 10 years	12.549	13.834	13.883	17.372	16.458
Value of exports					
After 5 years	13.236	−19.557	−22.147	−28.398	−17.118
After 10 years	28.511	−25.979	−29.753	−31.661	−21.797
Value of imports					
After 5 years	−5.180	−16.672	−20.491	−7.408	−12.596
After 10 years	−9.683	−21.215	−24.603	−13.846	−17.789

Source: Same as table 4.

a. The percentage change under protection less the percentage change under 1987 conditions.

ten years. Not surprisingly the least impact in Ontario is felt in the primary sector. These results may be optimistic as wages are assumed to fall in the face of an excess supply of labor. In heavily unionized industries, were wages to remain rigid in the face of unemployment, the burden of adjustment would be felt in the first instance in the form of reduced employment.

At the same time that unemployment rises, output falls. After five years, as reported in table 5, the manufacturing industries have experienced a 5.9 percent reduction in output relative to the status quo, and after ten years an 11.2 percent fall. Output reductions of a similar magnitude occur in the transportation equipment industries. It is clear that increased unemployment is one cost of U.S. protectionism, but at the same time decreased production of this order of magnitude costs the economy as a whole dearly. Indeed, the simulations at the Canada-wide level show that real growth would decline by close to 2 percentage points for the first three years after the imposition of the U.S. tariffs and would start to increase only gradually thereafter back toward its long-run trend.

With the exception of the primary industries, net exports fall quite drastically in all sectors, in the range of 20 percent to 30 percent. As the simulation does not involve raising tariffs against primary exports, net exports from that sector actually rise relative to the base case. The explanation here is that the unemployment caused within the other sectors lowers the average wage in the economy considerably. In five years the average nominal wage in all industries falls by 4.3 percent and after ten years by 8.6 percent. This reduction in wages allows exports to increase in those areas where trade barriers were assumed to be low—in this case the primary industries. A fall in wages of this order highlights the fact that the principal loser from U.S. protectionism is the Canadian labor force. Either by reduced jobs or by reduced wages, workers bear the burden of an abrupt decrease in exports to the United States. The model predicts that after ten years total wages to employed workers fall by 10.1 percent relative to the status quo.

As the automotive industry (transportation equipment) is the largest manufacturing industry in Ontario, it is interesting to examine the impact of a U.S. policy directed only against this industry. A relatively pessimistic policy scenario that stresses the importance of this industry to the provincial economy poses that the automotive pact is shelved and the United States increases the tariff rate to 10 percent and 15 percent in years two and three, respectively (to remain at 15 percent), on Canadian automotive exports only. All other tariff and nontariff barriers remain unchanged. The results indicate that the effects on the automotive industry are severe. The rate of growth of output is 4.9 percent less over the first five years of U.S. protection and 10.2 percent less over the ten-year period (see table 5). Unemployment rises by 1.39 percent in the automotive industry after five years and by 0.15 percent in the entire economy. The job loss within the automotive sector in Ontario after five years of U.S. protectionism would be approximately 3,000 jobs. After ten years some 16,000 jobs in all sectors would be lost, most of the losses occuring in manufacturing.

The other effects of this selective sectoral protectionism in the United States are uniformly negative. Investment, net exports, output, and employment fall. On the other hand, the U.S. policy cuts the growth rate by 0.5 percent for only five to six years. The results suggest the economy has the ability to move its resources, albeit slowly, into other areas. The principal cost of such a policy is borne by those in the automotive sector who lose their jobs or have their wages cut. The simulation results suggest that after ten years real wages in the automotive sector would decline by 9.6 percent relative to the status quo in Canada-U.S. trade. Ontario would accordingly be significantly poorer.

In my judgment these results are optimistic, as they assume relatively low degrees of import substitutability in U.S. export demand functions. Raising these elasticities has dramatic negative effects on Canadian exports. As I am basically inclined to be a long-run "elasticity optimist," this leads me to even more pessimistic conclusions as to the consequences for Canada of U.S. protectionism against Canada.

Conclusion   What does the evidence reported here and elsewhere suggest about the benefits to Canada of a free trade deal? First, there appear to be some significant gains in terms of productivity that could be realized by a simultaneous reduction of Canadian and U.S. tariff and nontariff barriers. The range of these productivity gains is anywhere in the neighborhood of a 5 percent to 20 percent increase in labor productivity in manufacturing. These gains might lead to an increase in the level of aggregate real income over a range of 3 percent to 7 percent. This is the positive aspect of the deal that economists are prone to emphasize. Furthermore, the adjustment costs as measured by an increase in unemployment seem to be small; while the ultimate reallocation of the labor force might be as much as 4 percent, the move will take a number of years and the disruptions should be small.

The broader questions, and ones that occupy much of the public debate in Canada, relate to the structural adjustment due to technological change and increased international competition. I believe that the adjustment required on these fronts will be much larger than any that would occur as a result of a Canada–U.S. free trade arrangement. Indeed if Canadian manufacturing is to survive, it must at a minimum be able to compete in cost with comparable U.S. producers. An important benefit of a free trade deal would be the elimination of any disadvantage attributed to the small size of the Canadian market. In terms of comparative advantage, Canadian industry should look much like U.S. industry in the presence of a free trade deal. Specialization across the border would be even greater than it is today, and productivity correspondingly higher.[10]

Unfortunately, the debate on trade liberalization has taken a new tack in the last year. Specialization to a small country brings great risks if the major export markets are subject to disruption. It is this risk of losing the U.S. market that has all observers, both for and against free trade, expressing alarm. There is very little that can be said here on the positive side. The cost to Canada of a trade war with the United States would be prohibitive. While unilateral protectionism by Canada against the United States is unlikely except as a retaliatory gesture, protectionism by the United States in the form of a 15 percent across-the-board duty, were this to happen, could easily reduce Canadian real incomes by 5 percent to 8 percent, with the immediate adjustment in the form of dramatically increased unemployment. The outcome is clear. Many now view a free trade agreement as one means, perhaps the only one, of avoiding such an outcome at some point in the future.

10. I summarize debate on the impact of technology and foreign competition on Canadian manufacturing in R. Harris, *Trade, Industrial Policy and International Competition,* prepared for the Royal Commission on the Economic Union and Development Prospects for Canada (Toronto: University of Toronto Press, 1985).

Impact on the United States

PETER MORICI

FOR MOST AMERICAN policymakers, businessmen, and students of the international system, a free trade agreement with the United States' largest trading partner and recipient of foreign direct investment has attractions. It would make rules of access and participation in the Canadian market more certain and stable and encourage a more efficient organization of production in North America. Bilateral free trade would also affirm the often stated American goal of achieving international rules for trade and investment that encourage the allocation of productive resources among countries on the basis of market forces.

This paper assesses bilateral negotiations from an American perspective and asks what the United States has to gain from them. Past and present relations are important in evaluating potential U.S. benefits. But the fact that the government of Canada has taken the formal initiative in the current bilateral trade talks raises further questions. Why is a country with a somewhat different economic system and a population and gross national product one-tenth those of the United States taking the initiative? What are the talks really about? Answers to these two questions provide a context for discussion of the potential benefits of a bilateral free trade agreement for the United States.

What the talks are about

For over a century, the desirability of bilateral free trade has been periodically debated in Canada and explored with U.S. administrations. This enduring Canadian preoccupation stems from the tensions created by the attraction of the large, affluent American market, on the one hand, and the pervasive influence of U.S. investment, culture, and politics on the Canadian economy and social institutions, on the other. Free trade is a facet of the broader debate about how Canada can maximize the benefits it obtains from the world's largest bilateral trade and investment relationship.

The views expressed in this paper are those of the author and do not necessarily represent those of the National Planning Association or its members.

Among the issues are how much the patterns of industrial specialization, ownership and investment, and trade between the United States and Canada should be determined by market forces and regional comparative advantages, and how much by federal and provincial policies. What costs should Canadians bear for policies that seek to ensure a national presence in selected industries and to promote Canadian cultural and economic institutions and preserve the national identity?

The interface of two distinctive systems

Canada's view of government's role in shaping the national economy and international trading relationships is broader than the United States'. In effect, two differing economic systems have developed north of the Rio Grande—one a mixed economy which nevertheless emphasizes market forces and the other an economy with more proactive federal and provincial governments. These underlying philosophical differences, and the different economic policies they have fostered, have given rise to trade and investment disputes that seem to grow in length and intensity with the volume of bilateral commerce. Yet any bilateral negotiations between the two countries must go beyond the concrete issues—foreign investment performance requirements, subsidies, dumping and countervailing duties; services and intellectual property rights; and government procurement—and establish a set of rules that permits a smoother interface of these two national economic systems.[1]

Thus, the talks must center on nontariff practices that benefit export and employment opportunities in one country at the expense of the other. The U.S. side is reasonable in stating that everything should be on the table—it is expected and prudent that each side should request broad and far-reaching concessions. Realism requires, however, that the two sides be prepared to exchange commitments to limit and constrain national economic policymaking prerogatives in a manner neither will find entirely comfortable.

All international trade agreements, by their nature, involve some sacrifice of national sovereignty if they are adhered to and respected. Like contracts between individuals, agreements among nations constrain their signators to undertake or abstain from actions even if circumstances should unexpectedly change. Countries accept constraints on future policy options in return for anticipated benefits.

1. Professor J. H. Jackson discusses the problems that arise when countries with differences in their economic systems become involved in intense trade, in "Achieving a Balance in International Trade," *International Business Lawyer* (April 1986), pp. 123–28.

How much Canada and the United States are willing to limit the use of policies that give rise to nontariff barriers depends on the concessions each party receives from the other. The costs to each country represent its assessment of the economic, social, cultural, and political effects of the overall agreement. A substantial factor in this calculus is each country's perception of the global challenges it faces and how changes in the bilateral regime will affect its ability to meet those challenges and promote the economic opportunities and corporate welfare of its citizens.

The global environment

During the late 1960s and the 1970s, U.S. competitive performance waned in a succession of mature industries, and the U.S. economy became increasingly dependent on trade. Imports captured growing shares of U.S. markets, initially in labor-intensive industries, such as apparel and footwear, and later in capital-intensive industries with standardized production technologies, such as automobiles and steel, and resource-based industries, such as copper and basic chemicals. To the extent permitted by domestic politics, the United States sought to rely on exports of services, agricultural products, and high-technology industries to pay its way.

In services, U.S. export growth has been constrained by a maze of foreign trade barriers lying outside the jurisdiction of the General Agreement on Tariffs and Trade (GATT). In the merchandise sector, agriculture's contribution to merchandise exports grew from 18 percent to 23 percent from 1972 to 1974 but then declined to about 18 percent again from 1982 to 1984. This share had dropped to 14 percent in 1985, as demand for food imports grew more slowly in many middle-income developing countries (owing to debt problems and sluggish overall growth) and agricultural productivity increased in many developing economies (stemming from both improved technology and shifts toward rural development strategies). Subsidy programs and protection in the European Community and Japan, and in the United States, further exacerbated agricultural problems.

In high-technology industries, such as commercial aircraft, advanced electronics, and industrial machinery, the United States is being challenged by escalating competition from Japan and Western Europe. These developments are rooted in a general leveling of technological capabilities among the advanced industrialized countries[2] and to some extent the aggressive use of

2. During the 1960s and 1970s, the greatest relative decline in the U.S. endowment of research and development scientists and engineers was vis-à-vis Japan, Germany, and the United Kingdom, followed by France and Canada. See John Mutti and Peter Morici,

industrial and trade policies to improve competitive performance vis-à-vis the United States.[3]

If the United States is to avoid macroeconomic adjustments that will substantially lower long-term growth in domestic living standards, it needs to maintain and improve its capabilities in high-technology industries, increase the high-technology content of its mature manufacturing activities, and negotiate better rules of access and competition in foreign markets for U.S. services, agricultural products, and high-technology products. Those are issues that the United States worked hard to put into the agenda for the eighth GATT round of multilateral trade negotiations. The difficulties it encountered at Punta del Este and the meetings preceding it indicate that multilateral progress will be limited and slow. Therefore, a comprehensive bilateral trade agreement with Canada could be an important part of the effort to improve U.S. access to foreign markets.

Canada is, after all, the United States' largest export market. Rules in difficult areas such as trade in services, procurement, intellectual property rights, and foreign investment can probably be negotiated more easily and rapidly with Canada than multilaterally. Bilateral agreements might then set a standard for agreements with Japan, the European Community, and other important U.S. trading partners. Conversely, failure to conclude successful negotiations with Canada, the trading partner with whom the United States has the most in common, could be seen as a signal that significant trade liberalization is not in the cards at this time.

Canada faces many of the same competitive pressures in manufacturing as the United States. It must improve the productivity performance of its mature industries, strengthen its capabilities in high-technology activities, and export more services, or it must face declining living standards. But for Canada, additional competitive pressures make the adjustment problems more severe and increase its interest in a bilateral trade agreement.

Changing Patterns of U.S. Industrial Activity and Comparative Advantage (Washington: National Planning Association, 1983), pp. 8–9.

3. Macro studies by Gary R. Saxonhouse, "What's Wrong with Japanese Trade Structure," Discussion Paper 166 (University of Michigan, December 1985), indicate that Japan's trade results are consistent with patterns of comparative advantage. Michael Borrus and John Zysman, "Japan's Industrial Policy and Its Patterns of Trade," in Joint Economic Committee, *Japan's Economy and Trade with the United States,* 98 Cong. 2 sess. (U.S. Government Printing Office, 1985), attribute Japanese predominance to the strategic use of trade and industrial policies. I have argued that the facts indicate both explanations have their merits; Peter Morici, *The Global Competitive Struggle: Challenges to the United States and Canada* (Washington: Canadian-American Committee, 1984).

First, Canada is the only major advanced industrial country heavily dependent on exports of nonagricultural as well as agricultural natural resources, although this has moderated in recent years. Forest products, petroleum and natural gas, other minerals, and basic metals accounted for 65 percent of Canada's total merchandise exports in 1960, 47 percent in 1970, and 36 percent in 1984. Much of this decline was caused by the growing importance of automotive products in bilateral trade facilitated by the 1965 Automotive Agreement with the United States. But in recent years the primary causes have been weakening global demand for natural resource products and a shrinking Canadian share of these markets. In many commodities, Canada will continue to face soft prices and intense competition from developing countries, problems that are exacerbated by protectionist pressures on the Congress from similarly stressed U.S. industries. Actual or threatened loss of access to the U.S. market in forest products, steel, and nonferrous metals is a major concern for Canada.

Second, Canada's manufacturing sector requires much greater adjustment than much of its U.S. counterpart. While a strong advocate of the GATT process, Canada entered the 1980s with higher average tariffs than other advanced economies. Its high tariffs date back to the National Policy of 1879, which encouraged production of a much wider range of manufactured goods than would have been the case had Canada been more open to imports.

In the twentieth century, high tariffs attracted many foreign firms, which established production facilities in Canada to serve the country's small but affluent domestic market. These firms typically maintained product development, international marketing, and other major functional responsibilities in their home countries. Thus Canada's manufacturing sector was overdiversified and truncated, producing a wide variety of products on short (and thus inefficient) production runs. Of course there were notable exceptions in products such as refined nickel in which Canada's natural resource base allowed it to establish a strong position in world markets, utility aircraft and telecommunications equipment in which Canada's physical circumstances gave rise to a large internal market, and motor vehicles and parts in which Canada has enjoyed tariff-free access to U.S. markets. In response to the Tokyo Round of tariff cuts (completed in 1987), Canadian-based manufacturing firms began rationalizing, but more needs to be done.

Third, Canada's strong position in natural resources, coupled with tariffs and nontariff barriers in other industrialized countries that rose with the level of processing and manufacturing value added, helped skew the pattern of Canadian manufacturing development away from high-technology industries dependent on human capital toward resource-based manufacturing dependent on financial capital. Canada's historically proportionately smaller presence in the more technologically intensive industries, and consequently smaller research and development (R&D) infrastructure, make it more difficult for Canada to increase its emphasis on high-technology exports than for other major industrialized countries to do so.[4]

Canada thus faces pressures not only to meet competition from the newly industrializing countries but also to bring the productivity of many of its mature industries up to U.S. levels. Similarly, it must increase its capabilities in technology-intensive activities, but it begins in a less advantageous position than the United States. The best way for Canada to achieve these objectives is to negotiate free access to the large, affluent U.S. market and to accept for Canadian industries unimpeded competition from U.S.-based production facilities. And it must secure continuation of access for its highly efficient resource-based manufacturing industries, such as nonferrous metals, and regain access recently lost in forest products.[5] Altogether, Canada has a great deal to gain from a comprehensive reciprocal trade agreement that provides assured, as well as free, access to markets. It has strong incentives to resist nationalist pressure for inward-looking policies and to make substantial compromises to gain these terms in a bilateral agreement.

4. Canada devotes a smaller share of gross national product to R&D than do its major high-technology competitors, the United States, France, Germany, and the United Kingdom; this is often cited as evidence that Canada devotes "inadequate" amounts of resources to R&D. However, Kristian S. Palda and Bohumir Pazderka, *Approaches to International Comparisons of Canadian R&D Expenditures* (Ottawa: Economic Council of Canada, 1982), have found that when factors such as the industry structure of the Canadian economy are taken into consideration, the gap between Canada's R&D performance and that of its major competitors is somewhat reduced.

5. On May 22, 1986, following the recommendations of the U.S. International Trade Commission, President Reagan imposed a 35 percent tariff on imports of Canadian wood shakes and shingles. On October 16, 1986, the U.S. Commerce Department announced its preliminary finding that Canadian softwood lumber producers receive a net subsidy of 15 percent ad valorem from provincial pricing practices for stumpage in Alberta, British Columbia, Ontario, and Quebec. Subsequently the government of Canada agreed to impose a 15 percent export charge.

Principal
trade
agreements

Trade relations between the United States and Canada are principally governed by the GATT and several formal or informal sectoral arrangements. With the Tokyo Round tariff cuts completed, about 80 percent of Canadian exports enter the United States and 65 percent of U.S. products enter Canada duty free.[6] A Defense Production Sharing Agreement provides for cooperation in weapons development and production, and trade in agricultural machinery has long been duty free.[7] A lion's share of the duty free trade, in the range of 45 percent, is accounted for by the Automotive Agreement of 1965.

The Automotive Agreement provides for duty free trade between the two countries. But it is not a sectoral free trade agreement because production safeguards obtained by Canada seek to manage the allocation of production, investment, and employment between the two countries. The United States admits all Canadian vehicles and original equipment parts (excluding tires) with at least a 50 percent mix of U.S. and Canadian content. In contrast, Canada only admits vehicles and parts produced in the United States by firms that have vehicle production facilities in Canada and that meet certain domestic content equivalents. The agreement is thus limited to the four major North American producers.[8] When the agreement was signed, the American negotiators understood that these "safeguards" would be temporary ("transitional"), but they have turned out to be permanent. Clearly they are contrary to "the development of conditions in which market forces may operate effectively to attain the most economic pattern of investment, production and trade," an objective stated in article 1 of the agreement.

Before the arrival of substantial imports from Europe and Asia, the safeguards assured Canadians that the level of production in Canada would be linked to the volume of car sales there. Canada's duty remission program, as amended in March 1985, absolves foreign producers from 70 percent of the duty on the value of cars shipped to Canada up to the value of parts purchased in and exported from Canada; companies establishing substantial pro-

---

6. Ministry of External Affairs, *How to Secure and Enhance Canadian Access to Export Markets,* Discussion Paper (Ottawa: The Ministry, January 1985), p. 20.

7. The United States eliminated duties on farm machinery in 1913 and Canada in 1944.

8. Because the Automotive Agreement was contrary to the most-favored-nation requirements of the GATT, the United States requested and received a GATT waiver. Canada did not seek a waiver. Instead, it opened the agreement to companies in other countries that would meet the performance requirements—none has ever done so.

Table 1. *Canadian Merchandise Imports, Various Years, 1965–84*

Product	1965 imports Total	U.S.	1970 imports Total	U.S.	1975 imports Total	U.S.	1980 imports Total	U.S.	1984 imports Total	U.S.
	Billions of Canadian dollars									
Total merchandise	8.6	6.0	13.9	9.9	34.7	23.6	69.2	48.6	95.4	68.1
	Percent of total									
Fuels and lubricants	7	3	6	2	12	3	12	6	6	4
Industrial materials	27	26	23	22	18	19	22	24	21	21
Construction materials	4	3	2	2	2	3	2	2	2	2
Motor vehicles and parts	14	17	25	31	25	33	20	26	29	36
Other transportation equipment	3	4	3	4	3	4	3	4	3	4
Industrial producers' equipment	25	30	22	25	21	24	22	26	20	22
Food	8	6	7	4	7	5	6	4	5	4
Consumer goods	10	7	10	8	10	8	10	7	12	6

Source: *Bank of Canada Review*, various issues.

duction facilities in Canada may qualify for full duty exemption. Qualifying purchases need not be incorporated in cars sent to Canada; thus parts or vehicles exported from Canada to the United States can be used to gain remission of duty on cars imported into Canada from Japan and Germany.[9] The program has the potential to substantially increase the share of new North American automotive production in Canada, extending the kinds of production and employment benefits obtained by Canada from the four major firms through the safeguards to include the activities of the Asian and European automakers.[10] This further influences patterns of trade and investment in automobiles.

The nature of bilateral trade

In 1986, Canada purchased about 24 percent of U.S. exports and the United States about 80 percent of Canadian exports. The structure of this trade has been largely determined by evolving patterns of comparative advantage and the Automotive Agreement.

Canada is an important market for U.S. automotive products, other transportation equipment, and capital goods, which includes the full range of producer-durables, electrical and nonelectrical machinery, computers, and the like. In 1965, these products accounted for over half of U.S. northbound exports. As table 1 indicates, the Automotive Agreement caused a shift in emphasis from capital goods to automotive products in 1970, but export

9. From 1980 to 1985, Orders in Council establishing duty remission agreements with individual offshore producers did not grant duty remission for exports to the United States.

10. The automotive duty remission program and its potential impact are discussed in Paul Wonnacott, *United States–Canada Interdependence: The Quest for Free Trade* (Washington: Institute for International Economics, 1987).

shares have been fairly stable since then. Canada's large purchases of U.S. capital goods clearly indicate the importance of continued secure access to the Canadian market for U.S. technology-intensive industries.

Before the Automotive Agreement, Canadian exports to the United States were dominated by natural resource products and primary manufactures, such as basic steel and copper. Specifically, forest products, petroleum and natural gas, minerals, and basic metals accounted for 75 percent of Canadian exports to the United States in 1960 and 65 percent in 1965 (see table 2). The Automotive Agreement radically altered the statistics. By 1970, automotive products accounted for 31 percent of Canadian exports. The shift was dramatic, but it tends to overshadow the gradual change in emphasis in Canadian exports from raw materials and resource-based products, such as ores and concentrates, steel products, and copper, to secondary manufactures, such as machinery. From 1960 to the early 1980s, the share of Canadian exports contributed by nonautomotive secondary manufacturing increased steadily from 12 percent to about 20 percent. The latter trends reflect the gradual weakening of Canada's comparative advantage in minerals and natural resource products, its improved capabilities in secondary manufacturing, and the gradual lowering of U.S. tariffs on many manufactured goods.

Principal barriers to trade

The principal barriers to bilateral trade are tariffs, nontariff practices, and prospective measures, which impose uncertainty about future trade.

Since over 70 percent of bilateral trade is already duty free and another 15 percent is subject to tariffs of less than 5 percent, why

Table 2. *Canadian Merchandise Exports, Various Years, 1960–84*

Product	1960 exports Total	1960 exports U.S.	1965 exports Total	1965 exports U.S.	1970 exports Total	1970 exports U.S.	1975 exports Total	1975 exports U.S.	1980 exports Total	1980 exports U.S.	1984 exports Total	1984 exports U.S.
						Billions of Canadian dollars						
Total merchandise	5.2	2.9	8.5	4.8	16.4	10.5	32.4	21.0	74.4	46.9	109.4	82.6
						Percent of total						
Farm and fish products	19	10	20	8	11	5	13	3	12	3	11	3
Forest products	30	43	25	33	18	19	16	16	17	17	14	14
Petroleum and natural gas	2	4	5	8	5	8	13	20	9	15	7	10
Metals and minerals	33	28	27	24	24	16	18	12	20	16	15	11
Chemicals and fertilizer	5	3	4	4	3	3	3	4	5	5	5	4
Secondary manufactures	12	12	20	23	38	49	37	46	36	44	48	58
Automotive products	1	*	4	5	22	31	20	28	15	22	28	36
Other	10	12	15	17	16	18	17	17	21	22	21	22

Source: *Bank of Canada Review*, various issues.
* Less than 0.5 percent.

all the fuss about tariffs? The first reason is that trade tends to flow through duty free holes. The amount of potential trade that does not take place in sectors where at least some tariffs remain high in one or both countries is unknown. These include apparel, textiles, leather, footwear, furniture, petrochemicals, plastics, nonferrous metals, telecommunication equipment, home appliances, cosmetics, paper products, recreational boats, and fish products. Second, from an American perspective, much more trade passes duty free or at low tariffs into the United States than into Canada, and average Canadian tariffs on dutiable items are higher than the U.S. average.[11]

Each country has in place many long-standing nontariff practices, and some fairly recent policies and practices that are viewed by the other as inhibiting or distorting trade. The following areas are of principal concern.

Procurement preferences. The principal Canadian practices of concern to the United States are federal and provincial procurement policies—for example, the activities of the Canadian Oil and Gas Leasing Administration; Treasury Board federal purchasing guidelines (Procurement Review Mechanism) intended to encourage technology-intensive industries, such as computers, and provincial preferences for local suppliers; and discriminatory listing, markup, and purchasing practices for wine and beer by provincial liquor boards. The U.S. practices of concern to Canada are federal and state procurement preferences (such as Defense Department purchases that are not covered by the Defense Production Sharing Agreement); and federal laws conditioning funds granted to the states on domestic procurement preferences (for example, the Surface Transportation Act of 1978 and the Public Works Act of 1977).

Product standards. Areas in which differences in product specifications and requirements between the two countries can unnecessarily work to the detriment of producers in one or the other country include forest products, agricultural products, and food containers.

Subsidies. In the United States, industry and the Congress are concerned about foreign governments' use of direct and indirect financial incentives to maintain employment in mature industries and to target areas of traditional U.S. strength in high technology. Canadian federal and provincial industrial aids intended to foster

11. Canadian tariffs on dutiable items average 9–10 percent, U.S. tariffs 4–5 percent; see Clayton Yuetter, "Testimony before the Senate Finance Committee on U.S.-Canada Trade Negotiations" (April 11, 1986), p. 3.

industrial adjustment and regional development, such as assistance for the Atlantic fish products industry, have become the focus of U.S. attention.[12] Canadians for their part believe the United States may be going too far in assertion of its rights under the GATT subsidies code.[13]

Services. Clear rules of market access are needed in areas such as accounting, insurance, investment and commercial banking, trucking, and information services. Thorny issues include rights of establishment and national treatment, which usually are reserved for negotiations concerning foreign investment. Absolute equity in these areas is no more possible than is absolute free trade in goods. But U.S. service industries are anxious to achieve better access and less discriminatory treatment and in some cases national treatment.

Intellectual property rights. Closely related to service issues, and equally important to American negotiators, are patent and copyright issues such as greater patent protection for drug producers and copyright protection for U.S. broadcasters.[14]

Safeguard actions. Particularly important to both countries are the problems associated with the application of safeguard or escape clause protection under article 19 of the GATT. A better understanding is required of what is expected of each country when the other takes action against third-country imports (as in recent U.S. actions in steel).

Prospective barriers to trade

Probably the most important issues for the negotiators and the most difficult areas to resolve are prospective barriers to trade. The troubling area for Canadians is U.S. contingent protection and for Americans Canadian administrative protection.

U.S. contingent protection. Canadians have repeatedly asserted that the U.S. application of countervailing duties against subsidies and alleged dumping—known as contingent protection—has become a tool for harassing Canadian industry. They argue that

12. In January 1986, the U.S. Commerce Department levied countervailing duties on imports of Canadian Atlantic groundfish in response to various federal and provincial industry and regional assistance programs.

13. For example, see testimony of Donald S. Macdonald, in *United States/Canada Economic Relations*, Hearings before the Subcommittee on Economic Stabilization of the House Committee on Banking, Finance and Urban Affairs, 99 Cong. 2 sess. (GPO, 1987), p. 326.

14. American pharmaceutical producers are required to grant licenses to Canadian manufacturers of generic drugs for a 4 percent royalty—suppressing the prices they obtain in Canada and their returns on investments in R&D; Canadian cable companies are not required to pay royalties on the transmission of U.S. television signals.

Canadian firms, lacking the financial resources of their larger U.S. competitors, can less afford to undertake expensive legal battles. Canadians maintain that U.S. firms bring frivolous suits as a way of discouraging fair competition when it hurts them. Also, they claim that Americans define as subsidies what Canadians view as legitimate regional and industrial assistance programs and disagree about what constitutes optimal charges for scarce public resources (as in the softwood lumber case). In addition, Canadian firms are more vulnerable to legal action in highly competitive U.S. markets than American firms because definitions of dumping by foreign firms are more easily met than definitions of price discrimination by domestic firms.

An important concern for Canadian policymakers is that the threat of U.S. countervailing duty cases constrains their ability to undertake regional development and industrial adjustment policies and discourages small Canadian firms from exporting to or pricing aggressively in the U.S. market. A genuine concern for American policymakers is that Canada assists industries more frequently than the United States, and that this can work to the detriment of U.S. firms and workers. Clearer, more rigorous, and mutually acceptable definitions of what are countervailable practices are urgently needed, as well as more certainty in their application.

Canadian administrative protection. Americans are concerned that future Canadian governments will impose more performance requirements on U.S. firms seeking to invest in Canada, seeking to sell goods and services there on competitive terms, seeking access to Canadian resources, or wishing to sell in Canada products that require government protection of their integrity (for example, patent protection in the drug industry). Performance requirements can include goals for exporting, local sourcing, investment, employment, and domestic R&D. Such protective practices can cause U.S. and other foreign firms to locate activities in Canada that would normally be located in the United States, distorting patterns of trade.

From 1973 to 1984, Canada's Foreign Investment Review Agency (FIRA) sought to ensure benefits for Canada by seeking such undertakings from U.S. firms wishing to establish or acquire facilities in Canada. These undertakings had precedents in the 1965 Automotive Agreement and the duty remission programs that preceded it. In addition, Prime Minister Pierre Trudeau's 1980 National Energy Policy (NEP) sought to achieve similar benefits from U.S. oil and gas companies seeking leases on federal lands.

Prime Minister Brian Mulroney has renamed the FIRA Investment Canada and changed its mandate to encourage foreign investment. Generally, Investment Canada does not seek restrictive undertakings from foreign investors, a change welcomed in the United States. In establishing Investment Canada the Mulroney government reserved the right to review new investments and acquisitions in cultural industries. Current policy requires forced divestiture of foreign-owned book publishers if they change hands as part of a larger acquisition. This policy has raised concern in Washington that Ottawa may use the umbrella of cultural policy to limit U.S. participation in the distribution and dissemination of cultural products, going beyond the intention of cultural policy to assure an adequate market for Canadian cultural products.

Americans are concerned that future Canadian governments may return to the FIRA-style policies in other industries and, by so doing, compromise or reduce the benefits Americans receive through the elimination of Canadian tariff and nontariff barriers. Recent initiatives taken by the Mulroney government have given Americans cause to view experiences with the Automotive Agreement, the FIRA, and the NEP as part of a continuum of Canadian actions and to consider seriously the possibility of future actions placing performance requirements on U.S. and other foreign firms doing business in Canada. In March 1985 the automotive duty remission program was expanded to include exports to the United States. And in November 1986 legislation was proposed that would offer patent protection more consistent with the practices of other industrialized countries and in return require manufacturers of ethical drugs to increase R&D in Canada from 5 percent to 10 percent of sales there. The proposed law also provides other incentives for the production of generic drugs in Canada.

Clearly, just as Canadians require more certainty in the application of countervailing duties, Americans need assurances that efforts to manage the distribution of production, investment, R&D, and jobs through administrative protection will be ended.

Canada's interest in trade talks

Free trade is one of the oldest issues in U.S.-Canadian relations. With the end of British imperial preferences in 1846, the British North American colonies looked to the United States to market their resource products. At first, the Americans expressed little interest in a preferential agreement but accepted a limited reciprocal agreement in exchange for resolution of an Atlantic fishing rights dispute. The Elgin-Marcy Treaty of 1854 provided for free trade in animals; agricultural, fish, forest, and other resource products; and a few manufactures (dyestuffs and rags). Over the life of the treaty, these products accounted for about 55 percent of U.S. merchandise exports to Canada and about 90 percent of Canadian southbound goods.[15] Either party could abrogate by giving one year's notice, and the United States did so in 1866. Among the reasons cited by historians are British support of the Confederacy and increased Canadian tariffs (the Cayley-Galt Tariff of 1858–59) on products not covered by the agreement.[16]

The new Canadian Confederation made attempts in 1869, 1871, and 1874 to negotiate a new treaty but protectionist sentiments were strong in the United States. In response, Canada turned to the National Policy of 1879, which included high tariffs and construction of a trans-Canadian railway, measures intended to encourage the development of Canadian manufacturing and east-west commerce. In the late 1880s, U.S. protectionism subsided but, with the National Policy firmly in place, Canada was less interested in an agreement. Talks were held in 1891, and Canada expressed further interest in 1896 and 1897. Among the reasons given by historians for the failure to reach an agreement then was the U.S. preference for a customs union as opposed to Canada's desire for a more limited agreement.[17]

In January 1911, Canadian Finance Minister W. C. Fielding and U.S. Secretary of State P. C. Knox negotiated an agreement eliminating tariffs on many goods and lowering them on many others. The agreement was approved by the U.S. Congress, but the Canadian Liberals were defeated in the 1911 election by the Conservatives in part on the slogan "No Truck nor Trade with the Yankees."[18]

15. Anna Guthrie, "A Brief History of Canadian-American Reciprocity," in Sperry Lea, *A Canada-U.S. Free Trade Arrangement: Survey of Possible Characteristics* (Washington and Toronto: Canadian-American Committee, 1963), app. A, pp. 84–85.

16. J. L. Granatstein, "The Issue That Will Not Go Away: Free Trade Between Canada and the United States," in Denis Stairs and Gilbert R. Windham, eds., *The Politics of Canada's Economic Relationship with the United States* (University of Toronto Press for the Royal Commission on the Economic Union and Development Prospects for Canada, 1985), p. 14; Guthrie, "Brief History," p. 87; Richard G. Lipsey, "Canada and the United States: The Economic Dimension," in Charles F. Doran and John F. Sigler, eds., *Canada and the United States: Enduring Friendship, Persistent Stress* (Prentice Hall for American Assembly, Columbia University, and Council on Foreign Relations, 1985), p. 73.

17. Guthrie, "Brief History," pp. 87–88.

18. D. Muncton and D. H. Poel, "Electoral Accountability and Canadian Foreign Policy: The Case of Foreign Investment," *International Journal of Opinion and Policy,* vol. 33 (Winter 1977–78), p. 220; John Robert Colombo, ed., *Colombo's Canadian Quotations* (Edmonton, Alberta: Hurtig Publishers, 1974), pp. 200–01.

Postwar Trade Policy

The next serious attempt came when Canada encountered serious balance of payment problems in 1946 and 1947. A free trade agreement permitting development of Canadian industry in a manner more complementary to the U.S. economy was one long-term solution considered. In early 1948, the concept of a free trade area emerged in secret negotiations but Prime Minister Mackenzie King decided against such a bold step. Canadian balance of payments problems subsided, partly as a result of Canadian participation in Europe's use of U.S. Marshall Plan credits, and both countries turned their energies and attentions to the multilateral approach under the newly formed GATT.

After 1948, the only other major bilateral talks before the current negotiations were those to establish the Automotive Agreement. These were precipitated by the Canadian duty remission programs of 1962 and 1963, which were in danger of being declared an export subsidy under the U.S. countervailing duty law.[19]

While formal discussions to establish a comprehensive free trade agreement were not held after 1948, at various times scholars, public agencies, and leaders in the public and private sector studied and discussed the benefits and costs of such an arrangement. Advocates generally focused on the efficiency gains of rationalizing Canadian manufacturing and improving international competitiveness by restructuring the Canadian economy along lines more consistent with its comparative advantages.

During most of the Trudeau years, Canada pursued a two-track approach to international trade and economic policy generally. Since World War II Canada has recognized the important benefits of market entry and the rules of access it receives through participation in the GATT, and it has been one of the strongest advocates and defenders of the multilateral system. As a small country, it can ally itself with nations having common interests and achieve more leverage than it might hope to have in direct negotiations with larger trading partners. Also, as a small country, its concessions are less significant to making multicountry agreements and packages work—for example, a package of multilateral tariff reductions in which the United States, Japan, and the European Community (EC) are the other principal players. Indeed, Canada did perceive across-the-board tariff reductions of the kind

---

19. The events precipitating the Automotive Agreement negotiations are summarized in Peter Morici, Arthur J. R. Smith, and Sperry Lea, *Canadian Industrial Policy* (Washington: National Planning Association, 1983), app. 1, pp. 99–102.

agreed to in the Kennedy Round as not serving its interests and did not fully participate in these tariff cuts. When the Kennedy Round cuts were completed in 1972, Canada still had much higher average tariffs than the other major advanced industrialized countries. Under Prime Minister Trudeau, though, Canada agreed to full participation in the Tokyo Round of across-the-board tariff reductions but, having started from a higher base, Canada's tariffs still remain above those of the United States, Japan, and the EC.

Prime Minister Trudeau's so-called Third Option sought to lessen Canada's dependence on the United States and to influence patterns of economic development through the implementation of nationalist foreign investment and industrial policies.[20] The goals of this industrial policy included increased national benefits from the development of natural resources, rationalization of manufacturing to meet increased international competition, greater Canadian participation in high-technology industries, and greater Canadian ownership and control over the means of production, especially in the resource sector. The tools included extensive financial incentives to promote industrial adjustment and regional development, R&D, and technology-intensive activities; stringent monitoring and screening of new foreign investment with the establishment of the FIRA; aggressive procurement and energy policies; and establishment of the quasi-public Canada Development Corporation (a holding company which for a time amassed the largest pool of venture capital in the country).

During the 1970s, Canadian optimism about these strategies was buoyed by strong markets for its energy and other resource-based exports. Indeed, the October 1980 federal budget introducing the National Energy Policy and the November 1981 federal budget included plans to use the rents from high energy prices to provide increased industrial, regional, and R&D incentives.[21]

The Third Option did not work; the U.S. share of Canadian trade actually grew, and the industrial policies failed to appreciably improve Canadian competitiveness. During the final Trudeau years, as the world economy became gripped in a major recession and the outlook for Canada's resource exports weakened, Canadians began to look for alternative approaches to economic policy. Two important investigations were initiated that set a new agenda

20. For background on the Third Option, proclaimed in 1972, see Anthony Westell, "Economic Integration with the USA," *International Perspectives,* November–December 1984, pp. 4–26.
21. Morici, Smith, and Lea, *Canadian Industrial Policy,* pp. 24–25, 48–50.

for the discussion of Canadian trade policy and economic development options.

Meanwhile, with the Tokyo Round negotiations concluded, the Congress and the U.S. administration expressed interest in identifying additional ways to liberalize trade with Canada. In announcing his intention to seek the Republican nomination in 1979, Ronald Reagan called for a North American accord. The implementing legislation for the Tokyo Round, the Trade Agreements Act of 1979, directed the president to study the desirability of entering into trade agreements with other countries "in the northern portion of the western hemisphere." In 1981 a report from the president concluded that with respect to Canada "further opportunities to rationalize industries through freer trade should be explored on both sides."[22]

Another Chance

In August 1983, the government of Canada revived prospects for free trade with the publication of *Canadian Trade Policy for the 1980s: A Discussion Paper* and *A Review of Canadian Trade Policy: A Background Document to Canadian Trade Policy for the 1980s.* The two documents, usually referred to as the *Trade Policy Review,* recognized the considerable economic benefits that could be achieved through a comprehensive free trade agreement but also acknowledged the strong reservations of opponents, especially on the consequences of free trade for political sovereignty, increased Canadian dependence on natural resource exports, and dependence on U.S. technology.

The *Trade Policy Review* suggested that many of the benefits of free trade could be achieved through sectoral agreements.[23] Canada and the United States held preliminary talks and early in 1984 began a joint program to study steel, urban transportation equipment, agricultural equipment and inputs (including agricultural chemicals), and computer services and informatics. Formal negotiations awaited the outcome of the 1984 elections.

During this period, in discussions with Canadians, U.S. officials indicated American flexibility in the types of agreements—either sectoral or more comprehensive—that could be achieved. Being concerned about Canadian sensitivities, they were careful not to

---

22. President of the United States [Ronald Reagan], "Report on North American Trade Agreements Act of 1979" (U.S. Trade Representative, August 4, 1981).

23. See Ministry of External Affairs, *A Review of Canadian Trade Policy: A Background Document to Canadian Trade Policy for the 1980s* (Ottawa: Ministry of Supply and Services, 1983), pp. 209–12.

be out in front on (or to suggest publicly) broadening the agenda to include a comprehensive agreement, even though U.S. policymakers would be quite receptive to a Canadian initiative.

In January 1985, the new Conservative government shifted the agenda with the release of a discussion paper, *How to Secure and Enhance Canadian Access to Export Markets*. The paper recommended keeping all options open but articulated the difficulties likely to be encountered when seeking to balance benefits and costs to both countries within particular industries. It asked "whether sufficient political and private sector support could be mustered for individual agreements on a step-by-step basis or whether a comprehensive approach would better ensure positive results."[24] Subsequently, at a summit meeting in Quebec City in March, President Reagan and Prime Minister Mulroney agreed "to give the highest priority to finding mutually-acceptable means to reduce and eliminate existing barriers to trade in order to secure and facilitate trade and investment flows."[25]

On September 5, the long anticipated report of the Macdonald Royal Commission recommended that Canada give high priority to negotiating a comprehensive free trade arrangement with the United States.[26] In response to Prime Minister Mulroney's request for negotiations, the president sought and received authority from Congress to negotiate an agreement under the "fast track" provided for in the Trade Act of 1984. The authority, which expires in January 1988, provides for an up or down vote on a proposed agreement, without amendments, within ninety days of its submission to Congress.

Canadians and Americans each have their motivations for entering into a comprehensive bilateral agreement at this time. In Canada, even among some of the advocates of the more nationalistic policies of the 1970s and early 1980s, there is a strong realization that the country's natural resource wealth, while not running out, can no longer assure Canadians of rising incomes and protect an inefficient secondary manufacturing sector. The Tokyo Round tariff reductions have removed a substantial measure of the protection Canadian manufacturing once enjoyed. Canada needs to adopt outward-looking policies that will assure that the

24. Ministry of External Affairs, *How to Secure and Enhance Canadian Access to Export Markets*, pp. 25–26.

25. "Declaration by the Prime Minister of Canada and the President of the United States of America Regarding Trade in Goods and Services," March 18, 1985.

26. *Report of the Royal Commission on the Economic Union and Development Prospects for Canada* (Ottawa: Ministry of Supply and Services, 1985).

access it gained to the U.S. market through the Tokyo Round is secure against rising protectionist pressures in the United States.

As Donald Macdonald testified in September 1986, the Royal Commission's decision to recommend free trade with the United States

> was inspired by two convictions. Firstly, that the world trading environment in which Canada had enjoyed a substantial comparative advantage based upon its natural resource endowment is changing and that Canada cannot depend upon the same economic growth from development of its natural resources as has occurred over the past four decades. In short, Canada is going to have to become much more competitive on world markets in trade in manufactured goods and services. In order to achieve that, Canada will have to engage in a substantial restructuring to meet world competition. The second of the convictions is that tariffs in themselves have ceased to be either a principal obstacle to, or a principal defence of, Canadian industry. Rather, it is in the area of non-tariff barriers that Canada faces the greatest obstacles abroad.[27]

The benefits for the United States

Article 24 of the GATT requires that parties to a free trade area eliminate "duties and other restrictive regulations to commerce . . . on substantially all the trade." The common expectation is that to satisfy the GATT, a U.S.-Canada agreement would eliminate duties on (virtually) all industrial (mining and manufacturing) goods and possibly some agricultural commodities. In other areas, GATT-approved instruments provide little guidance. The critical factor is what will be necessary to balance issues important to each side. Canadian objectives emphasize doing something about U.S. contingent protection and improving Canadians' access to federal and state procurement contracts. For the United States, key concerns include services, the scope of subsidies, government procurement, intellectual property rights, and foreign investment. Differences in national priorities stem in large part from differences in economic conditions—where each country's bilateral and multilateral comparative advantages lie and how they are evolving—and to a lesser extent from differences in the foreign protectionist threat each sees to its national interests.

Canada's bilateral comparative advantages remain primarily in goods. Its industrial base is in transition, but adjustments (and subsequent bilateral trade opportunities) depend largely on shifting reliance from primary resources to secondary manufactures, rationalizing manufacturing to increase productivity, and cultivating

27. *United States/Canada Economic Relations,* Hearings, pp. 361–62.

major technology-intensive industries, such as machinery and drugs. Generally, Canadian interest in services is more oriented toward third countries with whom Canada has more of a comparative advantage than with the United States. Hence, Canada's critical bilateral objectives are fairly straightforward: eliminate U.S. tariffs and achieve in essence national treatment for Canadian products under those U.S. practices (trade laws and procurement regulations) that are most likely to threaten tariff-free access once it is obtained. Unlike U.S. concerns, these Canadian concerns are highly focused and essentially goods-related problems with which negotiators have experience from previous multilateral trade negotiations.

National treatment for Canadian goods in the United States (and vice versa) is conceptually the simplest solution to Canada's problems, but it does not appear to be politically feasible. However, given adequate restrictions on subsidies in both countries, it should be possible to craft approaches to contingent protection and procurement that give Canada what it needs and that are acceptable to the United States if U.S. concerns on other issues are met.

The objectives of the United States also relate to its changing competitiveness and, as a consequence, are much less goods-based. While the United States must increasingly rely on its technological base and expertise in services to pay its way in the world, there are structural limits on how quickly domestic labor and capital can make this transition, and U.S. adjustment problems are exacerbated by foreign governments' practices. In mature industries, foreign subsidies are often perceived to impose an unrealistically rapid transition of workers and capital to attractive, postindustrial occupations, giving rise to the American preoccupation with a "level playing field." In more technology-intensive activities and services, in addition to subsidies, foreign regulatory and administrative practices, discriminatory procurement, inadequate protection of intellectual property rights, and the intrusion of regulation of foreign investment into trade management are perceived to be particularly threatening to U.S. interests. Other than subsidies and procurement, these are relatively new areas for trade negotiations; nevertheless, they are of central concern to the United States, both bilaterally and multilaterally.

In the United States, new Canadian rules governing investment, intellectual property, or specific service industries (such as commercial banking or securities) are not likely to be perceived as having the same significance as major U.S. concessions in the most central area of Canadian concern—contingent protection. Considering the lack of experience in trade negotiations with many of the U.S. concerns, achieving agreement in any one of them may prove as intellectually and conceptually difficult as reaching an agreement on contingent protection. In the end, a bilateral agreement that includes substantial progress on contingent protection will have to address these diverse U.S. concerns to make economic sense for the United States, to be perceived as balanced, and to have the political support necessary to sell the agreement to the Congress. Thus I assume in discussing the benefits of a broad agreement to the United States that it will encompass contingent protection and subsidies, procurement, and many major U.S. concerns.

What the economic models reveal

Economists have sought to analyze the benefits of a U.S.-Canadian free trade area by estimating the welfare gains that would be created by removing trade barriers. This is an ambitious task owing to the many changes in prices and goods and services traded, and the resulting positive and negative effects on the efficient allocation of resources, that would follow from a preferential trade agreement. Generally speaking, the economists' models indicate some net welfare gains but their findings are limited by the lack of adequate data on some important trade flows (particularly services), the restrictive effects of many nontariff trade and investment barriers, and the diversity of production structures among and within individual North American industries, owing to the already generally high but uneven amount of industrial integration.

Economists are strong advocates of multilateral free trade. A basic tenet of international trade theory is that the elimination of all trade barriers will lead to the most efficient allocation of resources, increasing each country's gross national product. Certainly, removing trade barriers will impose adjustment costs on individual workers and firms, but the theory maintains that the gains outweigh the costs. The important exception to this conclusion is the case where a country is large enough to influence its terms of trade by regulating its volume of trade. The large country by erecting trade barriers can raise its welfare at the expense of its trading partners but only if its trading partners do not or cannot (because of their smaller size) effectively counter.

Economists are more ambivalent about preferential free trade areas because, in addition to the terms-of-trade question, elimination of barriers among a subset of countries discriminates against those countries left out of the arrangement. This creates the potential for trade diversion—for a gain in trade among members of the free trade area at the expense of nonmembers. It imposes costs that may somewhat, or more than, offset the benefits achieved by countries inside the agreement through preferential liberalization. Hence, whether or not a bilateral trade agreement will improve the static welfare of both the United States and Canada is an empirical question.

Econometricians have analyzed the static benefits of a U.S.-Canadian trade arrangement under a variety of assumptions about supply and demand, including the impact of the two countries' trade barriers on the bilateral terms of trade and on North American terms of trade vis-à-vis the rest of the world, the potential for trade diversion, whether intraindustry trade is dominated by like products or differentiated products, the potential for economies of scale in Canadian manufacturing, and the possibility that Canadian protection permits oligopolistic pricing behavior. These studies focus on the elimination of tariffs, and only to a limited degree do they capture the effects of nontariff barriers.

In a survey of these studies, Drusilla Brown notes that two generalizations emerge. First, depending on the assumptions chosen, either the United States or Canada could experience a welfare loss while the other gains. But in no case is either country's loss very large; losses never exceed 0.4 percent of GNP for the United States or Canada. Second, the models indicate large potential benefits for Canada—estimates range up to 9 percent of GNP—and small potential benefits for the United States—estimates are about 0.1 percent of GNP.[28]

What the models do not reveal   The potential impact of bilateral free trade has also been analyzed with computational trade models that provide useful insights into where and how large the adjustments will be.[29] They verify that Canada has more to gain than the United States because, as the smaller of the two countries, it has greater untapped economies of scale and is less able, alone, to influence its terms of trade. General findings indicate that potential gains will be much larger

28. Testimony of Drusilla K. Brown, in ibid., pp. 281–82, which summarizes a survey in Drusilla K. Brown and Robert M. Stern, "Evaluating the Impacts of U.S.-Canadian Free Trade: What Do the Multisector Trade Models Suggest?" paper presented to the Fourth Annual Workshop of U.S.-Canadian Relations: Perspectives on a U.S.-Canadian Free Trade Agreement (University of Western Ontario, April 4–5, 1986).

29. Unlike econometric models, which fit economic structures to data, computational trade models use assumptions about elasticities and other parameters and examine economic data for some benchmark year.

than potential losses—that the potential effects of trade creation may outweigh those for trade diversion. While these results are useful, they tend to understate the potential benefits in several ways, particularly for the United States.

First, the computational models provide estimates of the static long-term benefits and costs and generally do not give an adequate picture of the dynamic gains from free trade. A more efficient, larger, faster-growing Canadian economy will provide compound benefits over time to U.S. exporting industries.

Second, many of the facilities to be rationalized in Canada are owned by Americans. While the efficiency gains in U.S. subsidiaries increase Canadian incomes, and are scored as a benefit to the Canadian economy, these gains also would increase the profitability of U.S.-owned companies and the wealth of Americans.

Third, the models usually evaluate free trade on the basis of the price and quantity effects of removing tariffs and selected nontariff barriers (which are analyzed in terms of their tariff or quota equivalent), using estimated supply and demand relationships. Many of the distortions imposed by the current trade regime are not easily susceptible to this kind of analysis. These include efforts by U.S. subsidiaries operating in Canada to increase domestic content and exports because of their commitments undertaken to satisfy performance demands by the FIRA and other government agencies. In addition to lost opportunities to exploit comparative advantages, those commitments have resulted in organizational inefficiencies in the allocation of management responsibilities between U.S. and Canadian subsidiaries and sometimes in the location of R&D facilities in Canada simply to satisfy the goals of government officials. They also have imposed unnecessary overhead costs for negotiating, lobbying, and legal representation to influence government policy regarding basic business decisions about where and how products are to be produced. The same may be said about Canadian firms and entrepreneurs that have located activities in the United States because of concern about U.S. protectionism or about the costs of defending against countervailing duty suits. These are the hidden costs of Canadian administrative, and U.S. contingent, protection.

Fourth, from a strictly U.S. perspective, the computational models, being somewhat aggregate in their industry coverage, may be missing potential economies of scale for the United States that could be created for industries within some sectors by expanding their tariff-free market by 10 percent through assured access to Canada.

Fifth, these models do not give adequate consideration to the barriers to trade in services, such as banking, insurance, and professional services, whose removal is of greater interest to the United States than to Canada. Nor do they indicate the contribution to services exports that could be made by improved treatment of U.S. intellectual property rights.

A final, significant shortcoming of econometric estimates arises from the fact that, given the current environments in Washington and Ottawa, barriers to bilateral trade are likely to grow if a bilateral agreement is not negotiated, further reducing economic efficiency and real welfare in both countries.

Greater certainty in foreign trade

Some of the most important benefits of free trade to the United States would emanate from greater certainty and from improved rules governing the conditions Canadian governments may impose on U.S. and foreign firms seeking to sell products, develop resources, or otherwise invest in Canada. Many businessmen have indicated the importance of achieving access to Canadian markets for their goods and services on an equal footing with Canadian producers, and of having stable and predictable rules for investment and for treatment once they have established facilities. From the point of view of trade policymaking, an effective bilateral trade agreement not only must eliminate tariffs and achieve compromises on federal and provincial procurement preferences, subsidies, product standards, intellectual property rights, and other nontariff issues. It also must embody provisions assuring that the free flow of goods and services is not hampered by administrative protection. An agreement should assure that:

1. U.S. or other foreign firms seeking to establish distribution systems or product service facilities in Canada would not be subject to performance requirements that (a) require or encourage the manufacture of products in or exporting of products from Canada, or (b) in any other way, explicitly or implicitly, encourage the purchase of Canadian products to the prejudice of U.S. products. (This requirement would not address the issue of right of establishment for foreign investors in Canada and hence would not infringe on Canada's basic right to screen foreign investments; however, it would constrain Canadian options with respect to some admission criteria and the treatment of foreign investors once they are admitted.)

2. U.S. firms seeking rights necessary for effective sale and protection of their products' integrity in Canada on the same basis as Canadian firms (for example, U.S. firms seeking guarantees that the value of their products sold in Canada is not eroded by inadequate patent or copyright protection, as in the case of ethical drugs and television signals) would not be subjected to similar performance requirements.

3. foreign firms seeking duty-free access to Canada on terms similar to those accorded U.S. firms under the trade agreements (overseas automobile producers, for example) would not be subjected to performance requirements or be offered incentives that may cause these foreign firms to purchase Canadian-made, as opposed to U.S.-made, goods for use in Canada, the United States, or third countries.

4. admission requirements for foreign investors would be transparent, consistent, and stable over time; areas of specific exceptions or special rules, such as cultural industries, would be well defined.

5. in service industries, where right of establishment and national treatment are often critical to market entry and competitiveness, these rights would not be denied merely for the purpose of protecting Canadian suppliers.

With respect to the first and fourth points, by establishing Investment Canada in 1985, Prime Minister Mulroney took an important step in communicating to U.S. and other foreign businesses the new Canadian policy of welcoming foreign investment. As a matter of policy, foreign investment is now generally presumed to benefit Canada unless proven otherwise, and not vice versa. There are exceptions, most notably cultural industries. Investment Canada is, generally speaking, not aggressively seeking local content and employment, import replacements, exports, or similar activities in evaluating mergers and acquisitions outside of sensitive industries. This is a major change for the better. However, this is the policy of one of the most pro-American prime ministers in Canadian history, and it could easily be reversed by the next government. Accordingly, Americans must be cautious and consider how this policy could change if the bilateral trade talks should fail and a consensus coalesce in Canada that a more interventionist, inward-looking national industrial policy is preferable to the status quo.

With respect to cultural exclusions, Americans are becoming aware of Canada's need for independent, effective vehicles of Canadian cultural expression. But Americans need a better definition of Canadian cultural policy, with those industries and activities that require special treatment specified and their limits circumscribed. A good case can be made for Canada's need to subsidize Canadian arts even if the consequences are to preempt some U.S. products in the Canadian media. However, the protection and promotion of Canadian cultural vehicles does not require, for example, inadequate copyright protection for U.S. television signals or exclusion of American products from the development of Canada's cable television infrastructure (Canadian companies may own U.S. systems).

With respect to the second and third points, recent Canadian actions have given U.S. businesses and government policymakers reason to believe that performance requirements, while not currently used to ration access to investment opportunities in Canada, are still viewed as a legitimate instrument for assuring benefits to Canada when firms seek other kinds of market access. The domestic manufacturing requirements and preferential patent treatment for drugs discovered in Canada contained in the pharmaceutical patent legislation proposed in November 1986 directly speak to point two. The aggressive use of duty remission as modified by the government of Canada in March 1985 to encourage sourcing of automotive parts from Canada and the establishment of automotive production facilities in Canada speaks directly to the issue raised in point three. The continued use of these kinds of practices imposes considerable risk that the benefits the United States has already achieved through the seven GATT rounds and the Automotive Agreement could be seriously impaired. A bilateral trade agreement could eliminate this uncertainty.

With respect to the fifth point, complete national treatment is not feasible. However, a comprehensive bilateral trade agreement should begin with the premise that each country will afford market access to service companies of the other in a manner that is "no less favorable" than that afforded to its indigenous companies. While each country's domestic regulations, policies, and practices would continue to differ, each country would undertake to modify those that deny such national treatment, except in strictly defined areas and for selected industries.

The states and provinces play an important role in the regulation of some services and in the provision of others (through state and provincial enterprises). Each federal government should undertake primary responsibility to ensure equal market access for providers of services in both countries and to ensure that suppliers of goods and services have equal opportunity to compete for the procurement of subnational governments and state enterprises. When the regulations, policies, and practices of a Canadian (or U.S.) subnational government discriminate against U.S. (or Canadian) service providers, the Canadian (or U.S.) federal government should be required to seek, through consultation, appropriate modifications in the regulations or practices of the subnational government. In this way a bilateral trade agreement could bring more predictability and accountability to the actions of states and provinces.

The effect on GATT negotiations

Canada has at least as much in common in terms of culture and historic circumstances with the United States as any U.S. trading partner. Certainly, differences in the two countries' approaches to industrial development and trade policies are important. But such differences are much greater between the United States and other countries. This presents both an opportunity and a hazard.

The bilateral talks provide an important opportunity to work out agreements in subsidies, services, trade-related investment issues, and other nontariff problems that will be much more difficult to achieve in multilateral negotiations. This may be especially true in services such as insurance and commercial and investment banking, and in the activities of professionals. Bilateral agreements could serve as models or starting points for discussions with other countries and in the GATT. Successful elimination of major trade barriers on a bilateral basis would demonstrate the seriousness of U.S. intentions to overcome protectionist pressures at home and to open U.S. markets to competitors that provide free and fair access to their markets for U.S. goods and services. Also, some issues are of greater interest in a bilateral than a multilateral context—important aspects of U.S. contingent and Canadian administrative protection, for example—and may be best addressed in bilateral negotiations.

However, given the extensive bilateral and investment relationship, and the similarities between the Canadian and American cultures and economic systems, especially as seen by Europeans and Asians, failure to achieve some compromises on the difficult negotiating issues could send a pessimistic message to American negotiating partners abroad (and to critics of the GATT process at home) about the prospects for consensus in important areas. Failure to achieve a bilateral agreement would reduce the United States' leverage in efforts to persuade other, more reluctant, trading partners to participate in multilateral discussions of difficult issues.

*Political
pressures at
home*

It is fair to say that both federal governments are committed to the modernization of their national industrial bases and to reducing their relative dependence on mature industries for employment. Nevertheless, both governments have taken a variety of protective steps to cushion adjustments. Some measures have permitted modernization and gradual decline of domestic employment, while others seem less justified on such grounds. Regardless of their effects and merits, these measures have been motivated by domestic political pressures. They have created substantial tension, however, in U.S.-Canadian trade relations, jeopardizing past achievements and future progress. The U.S. actions in regard to forest products and Canadian initiatives on automobiles and prescription drugs are notable examples.

A bilateral agreement could include provisions that offer some measure of temporary relief for workers injured by import surges caused by bilateral liberalization and provide a better legal basis for both countries to resist permanent and more onerous measures advocated by domestic interest groups. By placing binding limits on policymakers' options, a bilateral trade agreement would constrain each government from providing excessive or unwarranted protection from the competitive imports of the other country. Also, an agreement regulating the application of U.S. contingent protection and Canadian administrative protection should reduce the incidence of frivolous complaints on both sides. Put more plainly, a bilateral trade agreement protects both sides from some of their own worst inclinations.

*Facing the
future*

As architects of the postwar international system, American policymakers are among the principal advocates of trade liberalization, accustomed to taking the initiative in trade negotiations (even when domestic political pressure requires action inconsistent with stated internationalist goals). This was most vivid at Punta del Este, where the U.S. administration managed to have all of its priority issues put on the list for the Uruguay Round. Concern among U.S. trading partners that the status quo could not continue, because of the strong protectionist sentiment in the Congress, helped American representatives stand firm on the inclusion of services, agriculture, and other important subjects.

In contrast, the bilateral negotiations are, at least at the formal level, a Canadian initiative born of a conviction that Canada cannot continue on its present course, either in the types of products it makes and exports or in its trading relations with the

United States. Canadian negotiators have strong incentives to go further in committing to constraints on Canadian policymakers' future prerogatives than they have had in a long time—if American policymakers are willing to do the same.

For the United States, the current environment offers the opportunity to negotiate rules governing the full range of U.S. concerns. A broad agreement could expand the market available to U.S. firms by as much as 10 percent—an additional market the size of California. A comprehensive agreement would provide for faster and more orderly resolution of disputes. Moreover, success in bilateral negotiations will send a clear signal to other trading partners that the United States is serious about stemming protectionist pressures and opening its market to products from countries that are willing to take on the tough negotiating issues and offer comparable access for competitive U.S. goods and services in their markets.

If either side fails to display adequate flexibility, efforts to bring nontariff practices under control will fail, along with hopes for a comprehensive agreement. Canadians will have to look for ways other than preferential access to the U.S. market to modernize their economy and insulate their citizens from the effects of American trade policy. More interventionist, inward-looking industrial policies could become the chosen strategy, greatly increasing U.S.-Canadian tensions. If Americans do not recognize the substantial benefits that may be achieved from a comprehensive bilateral agreement and conclude that it is not worth trading the status quo for some constraints on U.S. trade policy options in exchange for the same from Canada, they had better think again. The status quo is not an option.

General Discussion

MORDECHAI KREININ said the papers presented had covered most of the issues and, in his view, had done so competently. He noted some questions that had not been covered that required attention. First, exchange rate issues were barely mentioned. How would free trade affect the exchange rate, and what, if anything, should be done about it? Would management of the exchange rate become necessary, even for a transitional period? He thought not. Did the calculations of economic gains and losses take possible exchange rate effects into account?

Second, would the free trade arrangement supersede existing sectoral agreements, notably the automotive pact, and what effect would this have?

Third, how would a free trade area affect investments and other capital flows, both between the two countries and from third countries?

Fourth, are there lessons to be learned from the European Free Trade Area? For example, what rules of origin will be needed in respect to the re-export of products imported from third countries?

Fifth, what will be the effects of Canada-U.S. free trade on other countries, especially the developing countries in Latin America? Might it be harmful to them, exacerbating their export problems and debt positions? Would compensatory provisions be necessary, similar, for example, to the special arrangements the European Community made with the Mediterranean countries?

Sixth, is sufficient attention being given to the interaction between policies? For example, abolishing or tightening the policy on countervailing duties would require changes in policy on subsidies. In general, a free trade area may force coordination of a variety of domestic measures.

Julius Katz argued that in negotiating a comprehensive free trade arrangement there was no reason to view countervailing duty and subsidy practices in either country as inviolate. He asked why changes in these practices should not be subject to negotiations. It would be necessary to define what a subsidy is—that is,

73

which subsidies are legitimate and which are illegitimate. That would be part of the examination of countervailing duty law and practices in both countries.

Katz also took exception to Macdonald's use of the term *contingent protection* as leading to misunderstanding. Escape clause actions are intended to apply temporary additional protection to relieve or prevent serious injury. Countervailing and antidumping duties, on the other hand, are intended to offset unjustified actions by other countries—that is, to make trade fair. Lumping these different kinds of actions together does not contribute to an understanding of the issues.

Furthermore, Katz took issue with Macdonald's characterization of U.S. negotiations with the lumber interests as being highly prejudiced. Both governments, he said, had decided to put aside the results of the statutory proceedings, which would have resulted in a finding of dumping and injury and the imposition of a duty. It was appropriate, therefore, for the U.S. government to negotiate with the U.S. lumber producers, just as the Canadian government negotiated with the Canadian lumber producers and the provinces to reach agreement on a settlement.

Kyle, representing Senator Baucus, agreed that it is important to distinguish between the countervailing and antidumping laws and the escape clause laws as having different origins and purposes. As to whether the countervailing duty and antidumping laws should be subject to the negotiations, he said that several senators, to his personal knowledge, do not want them exempt.

To go from there and speculate about what might be done, Kyle remarked, points to a number of problems that are far from resolution. For example, if a bilateral commission were to be established in lieu of the trade remedy laws, its operation would require agreement on a definition of what constitutes a subsidy, on what would be done in case of a tie vote in the commission, and other questions that in effect amount to how much sovereignty the two governments were prepared to relinquish. Merely to list these issues indicates how very much would have to be accomplished before the end of September.

Macdonald agreed that antidumping duty laws should be reexamined if tariffs on both sides go down or are eliminated. Increased competition provisions may be adequate to deal with the problem. He also agreed with Katz that subsidies and countervailing duties are counterparts; if an effective agreement on subsidies is achieved, the need for countervailing duties recedes, although he could understand why the United States might want to keep them in the background.

In regard to the secretary of commerce's negotiations with the U.S. lumber producers, he said his comment was in no sense meant as a personal criticism. As far as he is concerned, the whole process for deciding the lumber case took on the character of a kangaroo court. The whole issue had been tried on identical facts in 1983 and had come out the other way. This was not an objective determination in the circumstance. He believes it was bizarre to conduct the trade relationship between the two countries in a way in which the most prejudiced viewpoint could set the pace for everybody else.

Andrew Kniewasser asked what might be done in the United States and Canada if the September deadline is not met.

Kyle thought several possibilities exist. First, achieve a comprehensive agreement in time. Second, reach an agreement that is less than comprehensive. Third, at least on the American side, ask the Congress to extend the fast-track authority so the negotiations could continue. And fourth, continue the negotiations without the fast track. He did not think the prospects were strong that the Congress would be willing to extend the deadline, first because of a belief that the deadline had a healthy influence on negotiations, and second, because, at the moment, the lack of consultation might have a negative influence. Once the relationship is strengthened, the answer might be different. Whether a partial agreement would be acceptable would depend entirely on what that agreement contained.

Bruce MacLaury asked whether a contingency plan existed on the Canadian side.

Macdonald thought it did not. He said if Congress extended the timetable, that, to a certain extent, would be acceptable to the Canadians. He suspected that the present government in Canada is going to be nervous if this issue is not decided before the next election is called, so that for the government 1988 is the year to complete the agreement.

In his view, continuing the negotiations in the absence of a fast-track procedure would be a nonstarter for Canada. That leaves reaching an agreement by September as the best option. Some critical elements could be left out of that agreement. To an outsider, it appears that much work remains to be done on the question of services; conceivably that could be left on the table. On the more traditional trade questions, a resolution would have to be reached if the agreement is to succeed.

Morici was doubtful about the strategy of a partial agreement. Apart from tariffs, the Canadian list is very short—contingent protection and government procurement. A great deal of negotiating experience about these issues has been gained from the GATT rounds. They present difficult political, not intellectual, problems. Solutions are pretty much at hand; the problem is selling them. The American list is long—services, foreign investment, performance requirements, intellectual property rights, and so on. These are very far reaching and difficult issues to negotiate. They reach deeply into the regulatory structures in both countries.

The real gains to Canada from an agreement on contingent protection are fairly large; the real gains to the United States, Morici argued, are reasonably comparable only if agreements are achieved in these other areas. For the United States to concede on contingent protection without having assurances that these other concerns are addressed creates a package that Morici thought would be difficult to endorse. An agreement in principle, reached before the deadline, on standards of access for American firms, which would be worked out in 1988 and 1989, might be workable. But he thought that a partial agreement, without these agreements in principle, would put the United States in a position of giving up its largest chip without having achieved progress on its full agenda of objectives.

Edward Cowan thought Macdonald's statement that Americans did not understand Canadian sensitivity and anxiety about cultural independence was well put. When Cowan had been a correspondent in Canada, he had difficulty in understanding the Canadian position. He did not see significant employment consequences involved. Could Macdonald elaborate and explain how this concern fits into the free trade negotiation and what Canada may want with respect to cultural independence?

Macdonald replied that it is not an employment question at all, but is a matter perceived by most Canadians as being politically significant and fundamental to having an independent political community. It is visceral concern of Canadians to preserve a political decision taken by people on their behalf two centuries ago.

He contended that the issue could be managed relatively easily by concentrating on a number of Canadian cultural measures that he believes the government in Ottawa would be prepared to address—for example, the failure to pay royalties with respect to some of the cultural assets of the United States that are being used. These could be negotiated.

Beyond that, he said, leave it alone. Adjustments have been made in Bill C-58 regarding tax treatment of Canadian business advertisements in U.S. media. An equilibrium has been reached regarding Canadian rules governing periodicals and newspapers, as well as for Canadian rules governing the broadcasting industry. Why, then, insist that all of these issues be put back on the table and started afresh?

MacLaury said that in fact Macdonald was suggesting a standstill on cultural issues, to which Macdonald agreed.

*Barriers to Cross-Border Trade
and Security of Market Access*

Barriers That Must Be Attacked

FRANK STONE *and* TOM BURNS

IN MARCH 1985 at a meeting in Quebec City, Prime Minister Brian Mulroney and President Ronald Reagan launched an initiative for a bilateral trade agreement between Canada and the United States with the goal of removing all or most remaining barriers to cross-border trade in goods and services, and creating agreed rules to govern this trade. In March 1986 in Washington the prime minister and the president reaffirmed the intentions of the two governments to enter into a comprehensive trade agreement. Negotiating teams were appointed by both governments, and negotiations have been under way since the spring of 1986. They hope to draw up an agreement by early autumn, for consideration under the respective legislative processes in the two countries and formal approval by the end of 1987.

Both governments have made it clear that they will proceed with their bilateral negotiations within the framework of their obligations under the General Agreement on Tariffs and Trade (GATT), the main agreement that has governed trade between Canada and the United States as well as the trade of each with other GATT member countries since 1948. The GATT rules, under article 24, permit the two countries to enter into a free trade agreement, provided that the agreement removes customs duties and other restrictions on substantially all bilateral trade within a reasonable length of time.

This paper reviews briefly the tariffs and other barriers to Canada-U.S. trade that would have to be removed and how that might be accomplished to fulfill the mandate announced jointly by Prime Minister Mulroney and President Reagan.

Previous efforts to remove barriers

As noted in the earlier discussion, this will not be the first time that Canada and the United States will have removed, or attempted to remove, tariffs and other barriers to their cross-border trade. For a decade in the middle of the nineteenth century a so-called

Tom Burns presented the paper and represented the authors in the discussion.

reciprocity treaty was in force that removed tariffs on most of their bilateral trade at that time. After its abrogation by the United States in 1866, a number of unsuccessful efforts were made to restore free cross-border trade. For seventy years trade relations were distinctly unneighborly, with each country applying its highest tariffs to the other's exports. This situation came to an end with the passage of the Reciprocal Trade Agreements Act by the United States Congress in the mid-1930s. Canada was one of the first countries to respond to this initiative; in 1935 a bilateral trade agreement was concluded between the two countries. This agreement, renegotiated and extended in 1938, substantially reduced many of the high import duties that had blocked or impeded cross-border trade.

The two bilateral agreements were suspended when the GATT came into force at the beginning of 1948. (It is relevant that Canada gave strong support to the American initiative that resulted in the GATT, in part because of the implications for future Canada-U.S. trade relations.) Since then, the GATT has provided a framework for the impressive reduction of tariffs on trade between its Contracting Parties, the United States and Canada included. Equally important, the GATT has provided a valuable set of rules that govern the use of tariff and nontariff barriers, and GATT procedures have been used many times by the two countries to resolve bilateral disputes over trade policy.

But it has come to be recognized on both sides of the border that the GATT has provided an incomplete and inadequate framework for managing the massive, intricate, and unique bilateral trade relationship that is of great importance to both Canada and the United States. Successive GATT negotiations have left in place a number of relatively high tariffs which impede the flow of goods across the border and reduce economic efficiency, productivity, competitiveness, and growth in both countries. The GATT rules and codes have proven to be inadequate to deal with recurring trade problems between the two countries, as experience in the past several years demonstrates. And the GATT does not provide the kind of institutional framework needed to manage policy issues that are unique to trade between the two countries. Nor does it cover trade in services or the flow of private investment, both of which are of great bilateral importance.

The multilateral negotiations under the GATT that were launched in September 1986 will provide further opportunities to reduce barriers to trade, strengthen GATT rules governing trade, and extend the rules to cover new areas such as trade in services.

Successful conclusion of a Canada–U.S. trade agreement would offer useful precedents and models for the multilateral negotiations and generally encourage progress in trade liberalization. The multilateral negotiations, however, are not likely to lead to the comprehensive removal of barriers to Canada–U.S. trade, or to the introduction of the kind of rules needed to govern some aspects of this trade. Past performance suggests, moreover, that these multilateral negotiations are not likely to be concluded for a number of years.

Indeed, Canada and the United States have already gone beyond the GATT to put in place several purely bilateral arrangements to reduce barriers and deal with unique trade problems. Foremost among these are the Automotive Agreement of 1965, the arrangements for bilateral trade in defense products, removal of each country's import duties on agricultural machinery, and arrangements covering Canada's use of seasonal duties on fresh fruits and vegetables. Even so, remarkably few purely bilateral trade arrangements have been created between these two neighboring countries with close and extensive economic ties.

Gains from removing barriers

The need for a comprehensive bilateral trade agreement, and the mutual benefits that would flow from it, have been better recognized on both sides of the border in recent years—most notably in Canada. While integrated North American markets already exist in many areas, their efficiency is reduced by barriers of one kind or another. The value of bilateral trade is larger than between any other two countries and continues to increase, amounting to over $120 billion in 1986 (in U.S. dollars). Each country is the largest trading partner of the other, as well as the location of the largest share of its foreign direct investment. The two countries, moreover, have a heritage of shared values, geography, and language, which together have nurtured the evolution of common economic goals while preserving each country's cultural identity.

The removal of barriers to trade across the common border would be large and permanent, promising to stimulate investment, productivity, competitiveness, employment, and growth in both countries. The impact on the Canadian gross national product would be greater proportionately although not necessarily greater in absolute terms. At the same time, while new opportunities for enterprise would be opened in both countries, the problems of adjusting to the new free trade condition undoubtedly would be more difficult on the Canadian side and persist for a longer period, principally because bilateral trade represents a larger proportion of the total Canadian economy. Anticipation of these problems has given rise to opposition to opening the border for trade among certain groups and in certain regions in Canada.

To achieve the full benefits that both countries seek and to establish a useful precedent for the multilateral negotiations, the bilateral trade agreement will need to be comprehensive in scope and innovative in design:

—Tariffs and other barriers should be removed immediately or at specified times, with a minimum of exceptions; for excepted areas, the agreement should set in motion processes aimed at opening the border over a period of time.

—Measures to liberalize cross-border trade should cover barriers to agricultural as well as to industrial trade.

—The agreement should build on, improve, and enlarge the GATT rules, including the revamping of the so-called trade remedy systems of both countries, as these would apply to cross-border trade.

—Effective rules or guidelines governing trade in services, intellectual property rights, and trade-related investment should be included.

—The agreement should create new joint institutional arrangements, including rules and procedures to resolve disputes, to assist in the dismantling of barriers to trade, to help avoid the establishment of new barriers, and otherwise to contribute to the operation of the agreement.

Removal of tariffs

Contrary to common perceptions in both countries, tariffs remain a significant barrier to cross-border trade. Both countries have indeed removed or reduced tariffs in successive rounds of GATT negotiations. The average level of U.S. duties on dutiable imports has been reduced from roughly 30 percent at the end of the Second World War to 5 percent, and the Canadian average from around 20 percent to 8 percent. But these averages mask much higher tariffs on a significant number of products. The 20 percent or higher tariffs on many textile and clothing products applied by both the United States and Canada are extreme examples, but both countries still have many tariffs in the 10–15 percent range. Moreover, many tariffs are higher on processed and manufactured goods than on the materials from which they are made, which results in exceptionally high levels of effective protection for some processed and manufactured products.

Both countries probably will need time to phase out some tariffs, and it is likely that their timetables for staging reductions will differ. A case might be made for allowing Canada a somewhat longer time than the United States to dismantle tariffs, since the larger role of imports in the Canadian economy is likely to give rise to greater difficulties in adjusting to the removal of tariffs. On the U.S. side the dismantling of tariffs may need to include the so-called customs user fees which were introduced recently, as well as the tax placed on oil imports in 1986 to help finance the clean-up of hazardous wastes, as these apply to imports from Canada.

There will undoubtedly be difficulties in the way of removing some of the tariffs in the agricultural sector. While the most visible barriers in this sector are nontariff measures, there is nevertheless a significant number of primary and processed food products on both sides that have been protected principally by tariffs. There should be substantial scope for reducing and removing these tariffs—a process that has been an important feature of successive negotiations between Canada and the United States in the GATT framework. On the Canadian side, the seasonal tariffs on horticultural products have been justified by the shorter and later growing season in Canada and may have to be accommodated in the new agreement.

The tariffs in the automotive sector present another special case. Under the 1965 Automotive Agreement, U.S. tariffs were removed on imports of Canadian motor vehicles and original parts, while Canada allowed tariff-free imports only to producers of motor vehicles that met certain performance requirements. As it stands, the Automotive Agreement has worked well for both countries and has been supported by their automotive firms. Certainly, the termination of the agreement in the context of a new trade agreement would present difficult political and economic problems on the Canadian side. Perhaps means can be found to modify the Automotive Agreement in ways that would liberalize its operation and provide for a continuing review of its special features to determine when and how they could be terminated or phased out.

The new trade agreement will need to contain provisions for rules of origin, because duty free treatment will doubtless be limited to goods with an agreed level of Canadian or American content. Also, rules of origin will be needed because the tariffs of the two countries are different on imports from third countries, and each will remain free to change these rates on third-country imports.

The removal of tariffs would in itself simplify the administration of the customs systems of the two countries, as applied to cross-border trade, and would reduce costs and other burdens on shippers in the two countries. The agreement could contain special provisions designed to reduce to a minimum the remaining administrative obstacles to clearing goods through customs at the border.

Whatever problems stand in the way of removing tariffs on cross-border trade, it will be essential that these be removed on a comprehensive basis over a reasonable length of time, if the agreement is to meet the requirements of article 24 of the GATT and is not to be challenged on these grounds by other GATT member countries.

The removal of tariffs on cross-border trade would provide a useful precedent for negotiations in the broader GATT framework and create additional leverage for Canada and the United States in the new GATT round. Further reductions on cross-border trade would prepare the two countries for tariff reductions on a broader, multilateral basis in the future.

Traditional nontariff barriers

A wide variety of nontariff barriers impede or distort cross-border trade in goods and services. Some are highly visible, such as U.S. quotas on imports of sugar and sugar products and Canada's prohibitions on imports of used automobiles and margarine. Others are much less visible, such as those arising from differing product standards or those embodied in differing regulatory regimes. A variety of nontariff barriers to trade across provincial and state boundaries can prevent imports (as well as domestic products) from moving freely within national Canadian and U.S. markets.

A number of the nontariff barriers to trade are not in place primarily to provide protection, but rather to support political, strategic, social, or cultural objectives. Some of these barriers may be particularly difficult to remove or to modify, at least in the short run, without abandoning the domestic policies they are designed to serve. In this category fall certain areas of defense purchasing, especially in the United States, and certain Canadian programs that support domestic cultural industries or promote development in disadvantaged regions. Programs in both countries that support farm prices and incomes are also in this category.

Whatever the practical effect of nontariff barriers in cross-border trade terms, the objective of the new agreement should be to relax or remove them as a way of achieving agreed economic objectives. Some can presumably be removed or relaxed at once, and processes could be established to remove others within agreed time frames, with the assistance where appropriate of new joint institutional bodies; others might have to remain for the foreseeable future. In some cases, the goal may be to achieve compatibility or harmonization of approach in the two countries.

A partial catalog of nontariff barriers to Canada-U.S. trade in goods and services would include the following:

—Purchasing policies and practices by governments in both countries at the federal, provincial, and state levels that extend preferential treatment to domestic or local suppliers. Examples are policies that give preferences to minority group enterprises and small businesses, buy-national types of legislation and practices, and purchasing by defense departments and agencies and by utilities and other enterprises owned or controlled by federal and subnational governments.

—Import restrictions that are integral elements of domestic programs designed to support farm income or prices. Examples are prohibitions or restrictions in both countries on imports of dairy products, Canadian quotas on imports of eggs and certain poultry, U.S. quotas on imports of sugar and sugar products, the Canadian prohibition on imports of margarine, and the Canadian system of licensing imports of wheat, oats, and barley and their processed products.

—Government subsidy programs in both countries that have the effect of inhibiting or distorting the flow of cross-border trade. Examples are subsidies by the federal or subnational governments designed to attract investment and tax systems designed to assist exports.

—Certain purchasing and marketing practices of publicly owned monopolies, such as those operated by Canadian provincial and a number of U.S. state governments to market alcoholic beverages.

—Regulatory systems that have the effect of discriminating against foreign enterprises, or obstructing trade between and within both countries. These systems are numerous and often well entrenched, regulating water, rail, road, and air transportation, financial services, and communications; the regulations may often be changed, and they are not always transparent.

—"Domestic content" or other forms of performance requirements imposed by governments. These exist, for example, in

Canada to support broad cultural objectives; they are also a feature of Canada's foreign investment control system, although less important now than a few years ago.

—Restrictions on trade in services that are imbedded in immigration policies. These can prevent, for example, engineering consultants in one country from accepting contracts in the other, or prevent manufacturers from sending their nationals as technicians across the border to service their products.

Among these nontariff trade barriers, two categories would be especially important for the new agreement to cover. One consists of the barriers embodied in federal government purchasing policies. The commitments of the two countries under the GATT code on government procurement, adopted during the Tokyo Round and improved since that time, could be extended to cover all or most of the procurement by each federal government. Enterprises in the two countries should be put on an equal footing, and the new bilateral commitments should be extended into the large and important area of defense purchasing. It would, of course, be desirable to include procurement by provincial and state governments under the new arrangements, or at least to provide for processes by which that procurement could be added later. But a comprehensive arrangement involving only the two federal governments would, in itself, be a major move toward bilateral trade liberalization.

Agriculture is a second area where there is scope for the removal or relaxation of a number of nontariff barriers and initiation of a process for further liberalization. For example, even without significant changes in existing support programs but with some arrangements on the pricing of exports, barriers to cross-border trade in manufactured dairy products, such as butter and cheese, might be removed or substantially reduced. There may also be scope for liberalizing Canadian restrictions on imports from the United States of poultry and eggs as well as grains and their products, and restrictions on trade in red meat might be terminated. On the U.S. side, relaxation of restrictions on imports from Canada of sugar and products containing sugar, which have been intensified in recent years, would represent an important contribution to bilateral trade liberalization. The two sides should also look for ways of minimizing adverse effects on their trade with third countries as they search for means of limiting the impact of domestic and international agricultural policies—for example, the impact on Canada of the new U.S. farm legislation. Their objective should be to increase the competitiveness and efficiency of agriculture in both countries.

It is unlikely that all the nontariff barriers to trade in goods and services can be removed or relaxed in the short run. The experience of the European Community over the past twenty years demonstrates the difficulty and the delays involved in lowering nontariff barriers among the member countries. And the objectives of the Rome Treaty, which are to achieve a common market among its members, go well beyond the objectives of the Canadian and U.S. governments, which are focused on removing barriers to cross-border trade and introducing other joint arrangements to improve the functioning of the two economies. Moreover, the GATT rules governing the formation of free trade areas and customs unions are less demanding about removing nontariff barriers than about removing tariffs. Thus, in the bilateral negotiations, the removal of all cross-border nontariff measures should probably not be viewed as an end in itself. The objective, nevertheless, should be to remove or relax barriers that obstruct the broad purposes of the agreement.

Negotiations in other areas

It is generally recognized that the new agreement should go beyond the traditional areas covered by trade agreements and extend to trade in services, the protection of intellectual property, and trade-related private investment policies.

Trade in services has not, so far, been covered by GATT rules. Both Canada and the United States have called for its inclusion in the new round of multilateral trade negotiations. However, the process of these GATT negotiations and their outcome remain quite uncertain. Successful bilateral efforts to deal with this important and growing area of trade could be a model and precedent for the GATT negotiations.

There are recognized difficulties in approaching negotiations on trade in services. These include the large number of areas involved, the differing characteristics of trade and of the issues involved among these areas, and the lack of reliable data on which to base international rule-making. In these circumstances, the initial attempt should be to reach agreement on a set of principles or guidelines. These could then provide a framework within which action could be taken to liberalize trade in particular sectors of services and to reach agreement on rules covering trade in particular sectors. This appears to be a realistic approach.

In the light of the history of regulatory development in services sectors in the two countries, many of the practices of state and provincial governments will have to be included within the scope of the bilateral arrangements, as progress is made on the guidelines or on sector-specific agreements.

In regard to the protection of intellectual property, the United States has stated it will seek provisions in the bilateral agreement, as well as in the multilateral GATT negotiations, aimed at better protection of trade marks, patents, and copyrights, and against counterfeiting. One objective is presumably to reduce trade-distorting practices arising from the inadequate protection of intellectual property; another would be to give greater security of access to technology in the future.

Private investment is a third area in which the United States has expressed particular interest, in both the bilateral and the multilateral context. It hopes to establish a framework of rules within which private investment can flow with a minimum of interference by governments. Canada should also have a substantial interest in creating such new rules, because of the importance of two-way flows of private investment to the Canadian economy. One set of issues involves the use of "performance requirements" as a condition of approval for investment plans. Another involves the "right of establishment," which has particular relevance in many of the service sectors.

Trade remedy systems

The bilateral negotiations can hardly fail to cover the use by the two countries of their so-called trade remedy or contingent protection systems. These comprise legislation and practices governing the use of countervailing and antidumping duties to counter subsidized and dumped imports, so-called escape-clause or safeguard measures to limit sudden flows of imports that injure domestic producers, and other import-restrictive measures designed to counter damage to trade interests caused by the actions of other countries. Although these trade remedy systems are authorized and disciplined by GATT rules, their use to deal with cross-border trade—or their abuse—has given rise to serious friction between Canada and the United States in recent years. On the long list of heavily traded products that have been subjected to, or threatened by, penalties under these systems are lumber and other forestry products, corn, some steel products, hogs and pork, fish, and a number of manufactured products. In Canada, it is widely believed that the U.S. trade remedy systems are being used mainly for protectionist purposes, and to harass Canadian competitors. Some petitions are considered to verge on the frivolous—for example, complaints about exports of Canadian cut flowers and raspberries. It is evident that the very existence of these systems, and the threat of their use, can inhibit or distort patterns of investment; for example, Canadian firms may be induced to establish plants in the United States rather than in Canada simply to avoid the threat that exports from a plant in Canada could become subject to special duties or other restrictions at some future time.

Under conditions of free or nearly free trade, some of the measures provided by these systems would be used or threatened less often. For example, as customs duties are abolished, there should be fewer opportunities for firms to sell their products at dumped prices across the border, for the products could simply be shipped back at the lower price into the home market. Further, in the bilateral negotiations and, indeed, in the multilateral GATT negotiations the rules governing the use of subsidies and countervailing duties, antidumping duties, safeguard measures, and the like could be improved and elaborated so as to remove some of the uncertainties arising from these trade remedy systems and to further discipline their use.

One way in which this subject could be dealt with would be simply to abolish the use of trade remedy systems by both countries as they apply to cross-border trade. But that is an ambitious step, and U.S. officials have warned that it would be unrealistic to expect the Congress to agree to any kind of blanket exemption for Canada.

A second possibility would be for the two countries to set aside their current trade remedy legislation, identify jointly the kinds of problems that would arise on both sides of the border when a free trade agreement is in place, and then develop a completely new set of rules to deal with such problems in an effective and mutually satisfactory way. Such an approach would explicitly recognize that the current GATT-based rules would not be responsive to the circumstances of a free trade area to be established between Canada and the United States; it would recognize the unique size and complexity of the trade and economic relationships between the two countries. Because it would be focused on the particular features of cross-border trade, such a fresh approach would be likely to produce significant improvements over the arrangements now in place.

A third approach, although less wide ranging, would be to determine whether amendments to the systems could make them work better and reduce the severe friction in Canada-U.S. trade relations. The following could be considered:

1. One glaring flaw in the current system is the process by which decisions are taken about the existence of subsidization or dumping of exports, and determinations as to whether domestic producers are being injured. The systems of the two countries operate in similar but not identical ways. In the United States decisions about subsidies and dumping are taken by the Department of Commerce and determinations of injury by the International Trade Commission. In Canada they are taken by the Department of National Revenue and the Canadian Import Tribunal. In both capitals decisions are taken unilaterally by these government bodies, without any need to consult the other government or to take its views into account.

This kind of unilateral decisionmaking in the two capitals on trade matters of great importance would surely become intolerable, and indeed would probably not survive very long, under the kind of free trade conditions the new agreement is expected to achieve. Such decisions, we believe, could best be made by an independent joint trade commission that would be established by the agreement.

2. A second flaw in the present systems is that decisions as to whether the other country is subsidizing an exported product need not take any account of whether producers of similar products in the importing country are also being subsidized. It would seem almost essential that under the new conditions created by the agreement the concept of "net subsidies" be accepted.

Both unilateral decisionmaking and the absence of the concept of net subsidies are features of the existing systems that are consistent with the rules of the General Agreement on Tariffs and Trade and with the code on subsidies and countervailing duties adopted in the Tokyo Round. There may well be a need to correct the GATT rules in these respects, and changes achieved under the bilateral agreement could provide a useful model and precedent.

3. The new agreement could make other needed improvements in the trade remedy systems of both countries—for example, by redefining "injury" and what constitutes an "industry" in the context of Canada-U.S. cross-border trade.

With regard to countervailing duties, the bilateral agreement might also provide a clearer definition than is contained in GATT rules for those subsidies that a priori would not be subject to countervailing duties. Agreement might also be reached to increase the de minimus levels that are used to determine whether imports from the other country are being dumped or subsidized, and whether domestic producers are being injured by such imports. These and other changes in the present systems would probably call for amendments to existing legislation on both sides, which could presumably be embodied in legislation to implement the new agreement.

Alternatives to existing trade remedy practices will need to be found. An agreement that fails to change the present systems would be unlikely to find much support in Canada. Uncertainties about access to markets would persist that would seriously undermine the basic purpose of the agreement; and the kind of bilateral frictions over important trade issues that have existed over the past several years would continue, undermining other areas of Canada-U.S. relations.

New institutional arrangements

The process of removing tariffs and other trade barriers, assuring that they are not reinstated in the future, and avoiding the emergence of new barriers could be greatly assisted by the creation of permanent joint institutional arrangements. Such arrangements could also be helpful in the avoidance of future trade disputes and in resolving those that do arise. The creation of such new arrangements would form an important and key element in the new agreement.

The Joint Ministerial Committee on Trade and Economic Affairs, which was created in the mid-1950s, met annually until the early 1970s. Membership in the committee included some dozen Canadian ministers and U.S. secretaries concerned with trade and economic affairs. Its meetings were discontinued for a number of reasons, including the difficulty of assembling so many senior government officials at one time.

In the new trade agreement, political-level responsibility for operation of the agreement should be assigned to the Canadian minister of international trade and the U.S. trade representative, who carry primary responsibility for trade policy and negotiations in the two countries. They could keep in close and regular contact and consult together at short notice on emerging problems and issues. Also, focusing political responsibility for the operation of the agreement more narrowly would facilitate consultation on both sides with provincial and state authorities as well as with the private sector.

In addition, the new agreement could provide for the creation of an independent joint trade commission to assist in the implementation and operation of the agreement, and perhaps also in the management of trade-related issues outside the strict confines of the agreement. Such a body has been proposed by several authorities in Canada and the United States in recent years. Its creation would be in line with well-established patterns of Canada-U.S. cooperation in other areas, as exemplified in the International Joint Commission (IJC) whose functions, structure, and procedures could serve as a model. The IJC, created by the Boundary Waters Treaty of 1909, renders invaluable service in helping the two countries deal with problems arising from the use of boundary waters, as well as helping to protect the environment in boundary areas.

The proposed joint trade commission would function primarily as an investigative and advisory body, with an additional mandate to help resolve bilateral trade disputes and dispose of complaints under trade remedy systems. The commission might have no supranational or regulatory functions, except those that may be assigned to it in connection with the cross-border trade affected by trade remedy systems that emerge from the bilateral negotiations.

Its main tasks would be assigned to it under "references" which it would be given by the two federal governments jointly, although provision might also be made in the agreement for references to be sent to the commission by a single party in exceptional circumstances. The agreement might indicate the kinds of issues the commission would be asked to investigate.

These issues could be confined to matters covered by the provisions of the agreement; preferably, they would include a broader range of issues in trade and related areas, so as to enable the commission to investigate issues outside the agreement as they emerge. In response to a request by the two governments, the commission would then organize and carry out a process of collection of data, verification of facts, and impartial analysis and submit its conclusions and recommendations to the two governments.

The joint trade commission might also be given one or more "standing references" by the two governments, which would assign to it responsibility to monitor and report on developments in legislation, policies, and practices in the two countries relevant to the operation of the agreement.

Following precedents established by the Boundary Waters Treaty and the International Joint Commission, the proposed joint trade commission might be composed of six commissioners, three appointed by each side on the basis of their qualifications to deal with trade and related issues, including both the economic and the legal aspects of these issues. The commission could be headed by Canadian and U.S. cochairmen and maintain offices in the two capitals.

The cochairmen, following the IJC precedent, would need to be authorized by the agreement to appoint a small permanent professional and other staff. The main resources for conducting the commission's work, however, and again following the IJC precedent, would be provided by a standing joint advisory board.

The members of such a board would consist of specialists appointed by the commissioners and drawn from departments of the two federal governments, from provincial and state governments, and from the private sector. The board need not be large in number—say, eighteen in total—but its membership should be representative of the various functional, sectoral, and geographic interests involved in the Canada-U.S. trade relationship.

The joint advisory board would be assigned responsibility for investigating and analyzing particular bilateral issues, as these are referred to the commission by the governments, and advising the commission on how these issues should be resolved, as well as on other recommendations that the commission might make to the two governments.

If the commission and its advisory board are to perform an effective and credible function of investigating and advising on bilateral issues, they should operate to the maximum degree possible as collegial bodies, rather than along national lines. The commission should not become another body for bargaining and negotiation, but rather for the tendering of impartial, objective advice on issues in the bilateral trade relationship.

The trade agreement should establish, within the framework of the commission, procedures analogous to those in the GATT for setting up joint dispute panels, as the need arises. The panels, composed of, say, three or five specialists, would be appointed by the joint trade commission in consultation with the two governments to investigate and make recommendations regarding the resolution of particular disputes. As has been the experience in the GATT, the successful operation of such procedures would depend on the willingness of the two sides to make use of them, to cooperate in the panels, and to respect their findings and recommendations. In particular circumstances, by agreement of the two governments, the commission itself could be empowered to arbitrate disputes.

As noted earlier, some of the most difficult bilateral trade issues, especially for Canada, arise from the application of antidumping, countervailing duty, and "safeguard" import systems to cross-border trade. They have led to restrictive measures, or the threat of them, with serious consequences for production and trade. These systems probably represent some of the most important barriers to cross-border trade; they increase the risk of exporting, discourage exporters and potential exporters from seeking new international markets, and can distort decisions on the location of investment.

Going further toward reducing the size of the problem, it may be desirable for the new agreement to require joint investigation of allegations of unfair subsidization of exports and of dumping of exports, as well as joint determination of injury as a condition for imposing antidumping and countervailing duties or safeguard measures on exports of goods or services from one country to the other. This could involve establishing a joint import panel, drawn from the U.S. International Trade Commission and the Canadian Import Tribunal. The panel would conduct public hearings and carry out its own analysis of whether or not exports of the products concerned from one of the parties involve subsidization or dumping and are causing or threatening injury to producers in the other country.

Following the precedents in the existing legislation of the two countries, positive determinations by the joint import panel in regard to dumping and countervailing duty cases might be binding and automatically lead to the imposition of such duties on a definitive basis. On the other hand, positive determination of injury in regard to safeguard cases could be advisory, leaving to the government concerned, as now is the case, the decision as to whether to impose safeguard measures.

The joint institutional arrangements would have the following structure:

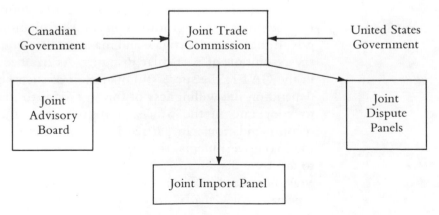

Accommodation to the GATT system

An agreement that led to the removal of tariffs and other barriers to cross-border trade between Canada and the United States could not fail to influence the new round of multilateral trade negotiations under the GATT. It would represent, in itself, a large step toward the liberalization of world trade, in view of the massive two-way flow of Canada–U.S. trade. It would also create a model and precedent for the improvement of the GATT rules that discipline the use of tariffs and other trade restrictive measures. But the removal of barriers to cross-border trade could give rise to difficulties in the two countries' relationships with their other trading partners, even though their actions might be perfectly compatible with the rules of GATT article 24 governing the formation of free trade areas and customs unions.

Article 24 gives Canada and the United States a clear right to conclude a bilateral agreement of the kind under negotiation. But the agreement must, among other things, result in the removal of tariff and trade barriers on a substantial proportion of cross-border trade, be implemented within a reasonable length of time, and not raise new tariff or other barriers to the exports of third countries. The two countries are thus obligated to design a bilateral agreement that is comprehensive in scope and not simply an exchange of preferential treatment in a few sectors.

Despite the restraints implicit in article 24, there could be concern in Canada and the United States as well as in other countries that a bilateral agreement could result in a weakening of the GATT system and cause damage to third-country trade relationships. To allay such apprehensions, the two governments should clarify at an early stage, jointly or separately, that it is not their intention to establish permanent or long-term tariff or trade preferences between them; that each stands ready to consult with third countries on trade problems that may be created for them by the agreement; and that during the new round of GATT negotiations, both countries would be prepared to exchange with other GATT members on a most-favored-nation basis many or all of the benefits exchanged bilaterally under the proposed agreement.

Further, during the GATT negotiations and on the basis of the arrangements they will have concluded between themselves, Canada and the United States might join in calling for a general review of the provisions of article 24, with a view to correcting and preventing abuses by other countries in the creation and operation of free trade areas, customs unions, and preferential trading arrangements. Among other things, the GATT rules should be strengthened so as to require closer monitoring by the Contracting Parties of the operation of regional trade groups, and also to elaborate and clarify the rights of other countries to seek remedies when their own trade interests are damaged by the operation of regional trade groups.

Conclusion   Removing tariffs and other barriers to cross-border trade in goods and services would improve the efficiency and competitiveness of the Canadian and U.S. economies, stimulate productivity and economic growth, and open new opportunities for enterprise and initiative. The process has been under way since before the Second World War, and particularly since then within the framework of the GATT. While the proposed new agreement would represent for both countries a momentous development in their trade relationship, it would represent an evolution of past policies, not a departure from them.

The removal of trade barriers will need to be comprehensive in terms of products and services in order to achieve the overall benefits of the agreement, to achieve a balance of mutual advantage from the agreement, and to satisfy the obligations of the two countries under the GATT. The process will be neither quick nor easy; and it would be unrealistic to expect, even in the longer run, total blanket removal of cross-border barriers. Some may need to be retained in order to support broader policies in place for political, social, cultural, or other purposes. One important objective of the agreement should be to avoid the erection of new barriers.

An agreement of the kind being negotiated can be expected to have particular characteristics reflecting close economic and trade links between Canada and the United States, as well as other special features of their relationship. It may not therefore be possible or useful to look to the experience of other regional trade arrangements, in Europe or elsewhere, for guidance in designing or operating the Canada–U.S. agreement. But a carefully constructed, outward-looking bilateral agreement requiring a comprehensive liberalization of trade could provide a needed example for the operation of regional groups elsewhere in the world.

To be successful, an agreement will have to be satisfactory to both countries, involving a mutual balance of advantage. Each will have to accept discipline and rules over its own trade and economic policies in exchange for the acceptance of similar disciplines and rules by the other. The resulting exchange of rights and obligations would extend beyond those contained in the

GATT and other agreements, but would not differ from them in their nature. It is difficult to see how a bilateral agreement of this kind, freely entered into, would represent a relinquishment of sovereignty by either country that would differ from the obligations they have accepted for many years under the GATT.

A combination of circumstances and events has raised an undeniable opportunity for concluding a comprehensive trade agreement between Canada and the United States in the mid-1980s. Outside North America, new developments in production and trade patterns have emerged that call for urgent, joint efforts by Canada and the United States to raise levels of productivity in almost all economic sectors. Both countries have experienced low economic growth and high unemployment in recent years. Neither can afford to neglect an opportunity to increase efficiency, enlarge markets, and open new avenues for enterprise. The removal of barriers to their cross-border trade on a comprehensive basis will also reinforce their parallel efforts in the new round of multilateral negotiations to achieve broader, global trade liberalization, improve GATT rules, and strengthen the GATT as an institution, to the benefit of all trading countries.

A new Canada–United States trade agreement must embody firm commitments by the two governments to ensure the long-term durability of the agreement and to prevent the erosion of its terms by subsequent action on either side. Canada has a particular need for certainty and confidence regarding the permanence of the new arrangements, given the extent of the adjustment that will be required in its economy.

At this point, failure to achieve a successful outcome of the negotiations could not fail to have serious consequences for broader Canada–United States relations. It would generate new protectionist trade measures on both sides of the border, and it would cast doubts on the eventual success of the broader multilateral negotiations in the GATT.

Establishing a Mechanism

JOHN J. LAFALCE

To DRAW ATTENTION to the importance of the current trade negotiations between Canada and the United States, I propose to outline some of the conflicting points of view concerning a free trade agreement between the two countries, and to address the issue of contingent protection and the need for a common treatment of subsidies. Finally, I shall suggest how a dispute settlement mechanism may be structured so as to reduce some of the fundamental economic and political objections to a free trade area.

Importance of the negotiations

In March 1985 it became evident that a Canadian government would once again brave internal Canadian politics to reopen the issue of free trade with the United States. At the so-called Shamrock Summit, Prime Minister Brian Mulroney and President Ronald Reagan signed a trade declaration that crystallized a political commitment to create "a more secure and predictable environment for trade." The declaration carefully avoided use of the term "free trade," in deference, no doubt, to Canadian sensitivities. But the intent of the Canadian prime minister was unmistakable. He demonstrated, at considerable political risk, that he was prepared to commit his government to comprehensive trade liberalization with Canada's major trade partner.

Under the Trade and Tariff Act of 1984, the president is required to notify the Senate Finance Committee and the House Ways and Means Committee of any request by a foreign government to initiate free trade negotiations with the United States. If neither committee disapproves within sixty days, negotiations may begin under the "fast-track" procedure, under which any resulting agreement can receive quick consideration. Both houses of Congress are committed to vote the agreement and implementing legislation up or down without amendment within ninety days after it is submitted for approval. Neither committee opposed the president's request for fast-track authority in April 1986, although it passed by only one vote in the Senate Finance Committee. Negotiations began formally in June.

It is not surprising that the world's two closest trading partners should have a great deal to discuss in these negotiations. The United States and Canada exchanged goods valued at almost $120 billion in 1986. The Canadians are our best foreign customers, purchasing U.S. products valued at $45 billion last year. In fact, every year Canadians buy U.S. goods worth as much as U.S. shipments to the entire European Community. We sell twice as much to Canada as we sell to Japan. Indeed, we sell more to the province of Ontario alone than to any other country. In all, exports to Canada in 1986 accounted for about 22 percent of total U.S. exports.

But, as critical as the Canadian market is to the United States, the American market, which accounts for over 75 percent of total Canadian exports, is even more vital to Canada. Canada's extreme dependence on the U.S. market also accounts, in large measure, for the different level of attention that the negotiations have received in the two countries. Yet I am confident that the focus on this issue in the United States will increase substantially as the negotiations proceed.

From a U.S. perspective, the trade deficit with Canada, which totaled about $23 billion in 1986 (but only $5 billion when services as well as merchandise are taken into account), is seen as part of our deteriorating trade position in the world. Our merchandise trade deficit increased during 1986 to $170 billion. The decline in the value of the U.S. dollar relative to the yen, the deutsche mark, and other major currencies has not yet had the hoped-for effect of reversing our declining trade fortunes.

In addition, during the past three years the U.S. dollar has fallen against the Canadian dollar much less than against other major currencies, which contributes to our trade deficit with Canada. These economic facts will not make it any easier for us to reach a mutually satisfactory agreement with Canada.

The United States is not, however, the only country in the world struggling to deal with a deteriorating economic situation. Pressure is also building in Canada that will make an agreement all the more difficult to achieve. Canada's current account deteriorated throughout 1986 and was in the red by more than $9 billion, compared with a break-even position in 1985. The root of that decline was a reduction in Canada's merchandise trade surplus from about $20 billion to about $10 billion.

Despite Canada's current account deficit with the world at large, its merchandise trade balance with the United States remained in strong surplus. One in five jobs in Canada depends on trade with the United States, compared with one in a hundred American jobs depending on trade with Canada.

These are the kinds of facts that describe the real trading relationship between the two countries. It is clear that both countries are suffering from the effects of deteriorating foreign trade balances and widening current account deficits, which tend to encourage unneighborly policy solutions. They also indicate that, while we may be each other's largest trading partner, Canada is much more vulnerable to changing trade practices than the United States.

This was made clear during the hearings of the Senate Finance Committee's Subcommittee on Economic Stabilization, which I convened in the summer of 1986 to educate myself and my colleagues on the main features of the U.S.-Canada economic relationship. Distinguished government officials, businessmen, and trade experts from both sides of the border testified as to their interest in a comprehensive trade agreement.

Canadian views on an agreement

One of the factors that have contributed to the reemergence of interest in a comprehensive bilateral trade agreement is Canadians' fear that the U.S. market is threatened by a tide of protectionism centered in the U.S. Congress. No country in the world has more to lose from American protectionism than Canada. Although the protectionist backlash is not aimed at Canada primarily, how long will Canada be able to escape becoming a major target? The threat is manifested in recent actions taken against Canada in the areas of softwood lumber, steel, pork, and fish. While a comprehensive trade agreement would not offer Canada full immunity from protectionist actions originating in the United States, those that developed would be better managed within a bilateral framework.

A second factor contributing to renewed interest in the free trade option was the realization that further liberalization of bilateral trade would yield concrete economic benefits on both sides of the border. Canada may be the more substantial beneficiary. Economists who testified before the Economic Stabilization Subcommittee concluded that the phasing out of Canada's tariffs on imports from the United States and of U.S. tariffs on Canadian exports would be more important to Canada than to the United States because of the great difference in the size of the two economies. Canada's exports to the United States account for about 20 percent of its gross national product, whereas U.S. exports to Canada are equivalent to only 2 percent of American

GNP. Because bilateral trade is so much more important to Canada, the benefits to Canada from the mutual removal of trade barriers would be of greater significance. Canadians have estimated that the income gains resulting from a free trade agreement are high—in the range of 5–10 percent of Canadian GNP, according to the Macdonald Royal Commission.[1]

A bilateral trade agreement that provided Canadian industry with assured access to a market of more than 250 million people would encourage many firms to invest in Canada to serve the American market. Currently, export-dependent firms in Canada have a major incentive to locate production in the United States so as to avoid existing and potential American trade barriers. This fear of being shut out of the U.S. market partly explains the large investment flows from Canada to the United States in recent years. During 1980–84, Canada experienced a net direct investment outflow of almost $14 billion, most of it destined for the United States. A comprehensive trade agreement assuring access to the U.S. market could remove this disincentive to investment in Canada.

These are the arguments that have the strongest support among Canadians who favor a comprehensive trade agreement with the United States. But there are many concerns about a potential agreement, some economic and some political.

A key economic issue is Canadian firms' fear of greater import competition from the United States. Some firms, especially those engaged in the textile, brewing, and agricultural products sectors, are doubtful that free trade will benefit them. Many of these firms will oppose steps to liberalize bilateral trade, although adjustment assistance may win their support.

A second major economic concern is that presented by Canada's largest trade union organization, the Canadian Labour Congress (CLC). A vice president of the CLC who testified before the Economic Stabilization Subcommittee argued that a comprehensive free trade agreement "would cause dislocation of 800,000 to 900,000 jobs in Canada" and give rise to a significant loss in Canadian economic sovereignty.

The fear of losing economic sovereignty is linked to the third dominant concern in Canada about a bilateral agreement—loss of political and cultural independence. Many Canadians are preoc-

---

1. *Report of the Royal Commission on the Economic Union and Development Prospects for Canada* (Ottawa: Ministry of Supply and Services, 1985).

cupied by doubts that Canadian cultural industries could survive in a free trade environment. This subject provokes strong emotions on both sides of the border, such as the conflict surrounding the nondeductibility as business expense of the cost of advertising placed in foreign media, or concern about the acquisition of Canadian publishing firms by large U.S. media companies.

The fact is that free trade in the cultural field, coupled with the elimination of certain investment regulations, would lead to Canadian-owned firms in this sector being put at a significant disadvantage. They would find it difficult to compete against American firms that operate with the advantage of greater economies of scale. I believe strongly that care must be taken to protect sensitive sectors that are key to the maintenance of Canada's political and cultural values.

U.S. views on an agreement

Partly because of the lesser American economic dependence on trade with Canada, most Americans, including members of Congress, have been indifferent to the trade talks. Some of the attractions of a bilateral comprehensive trade agreement will become evident to Americans as the talks progress.

Congress has shown much concern over the problem of competitiveness, and a good deal of trade legislation has been addressed to the issue, often proposing strictly protectionist solutions. Negotiation of a bilateral treaty offers Congress what should be a logical alternative: to tackle the competitiveness problem through trade liberalization, rather than restriction—that is, by reducing barriers that increase costs for U.S. firms doing business with Canada.

Since many large U.S. companies have Canadian subsidiaries, the greatest gains from a comprehensive trade treaty will result from moves that permit better utilization of Canadian facilities with corresponding benefits for U.S. plants. A key benefit will be the phased elimination of the Canadian tariff and the simplification of burdensome customs procedures. Average Canadian tariffs on dutiable trade are still about twice the U.S. level.

The phasing out of tariffs could open the way to an extensive reform of customs procedures on both sides of the border. Companies engaged in U.S.-Canadian trade would agree that cumbersome customs procedures are a major obstacle to the flow of trade and impose substantial costs which reduce competitiveness. Because of the vested interests of customs officials in maintaining the status quo, it has been difficult to streamline the customs procedure. As the representative of a congressional district with four international bridges to Canada and a substantial cross-border flow of goods, I am particularly sensitive to these problems.

An initial step in reducing costs could be an agreement on a single document that would serve as both an entry and an exit form and would be used by both governments. Aside from providing greater efficiency, customs simplification could stimulate smaller U.S. firms to consider selling in the Canadian market. These firms often shy away from exporting because of the complexities and high costs associated with shipping across the border.

Both governments agree that a treaty must include nontariff barriers, such as subsidies, safeguards, and government procurement. Government procurement in both Canada and the United States is restricted in many cases to domestic suppliers. The U.S. telecommunications equipment and power-generating equipment industries are particularly disadvantaged in this regard. A new trade agreement could open up a very significant government procurement market in Canada for the United States.

Establishment of new rules to regulate trade in services will be in the economic interest of both the United States and Canada. Services account for some two-thirds of GNP in both countries, and they are an increasingly important element of world trade. Trade in services is not currently subject to regulation by the General Agreement on Tariffs and Trade (GATT). The United States has a real opportunity to develop rules to govern trade in services in a bilateral context with Canada, which then could be a model for the Uruguay Round of multilateral negotiations getting under way in Geneva.

Subsidies and contingent protection

The issue of subsidies is perhaps the most important and the most difficult of the nontariff measures. Many of the trade disputes between the United States and Canada can be traced to disagreements over the use of subsidies. Since 1980 the U.S. International Trade Commission has conducted thirteen countervailing duty investigations involving Canadian exports, including potatoes, steel pipes, hogs, and lumber. This aggressive use of U.S. trade laws has alarmed Canadian producers, and Canadian negotiators are under strong pressure to win special treatment for Canada in the U.S. application of its trade laws.

The October 1986 decision to impose countervailing duties on softwood lumber, a vital industry in the province of British Columbia, is a case in point. The Canadians view that decision as a policy by the Reagan administration to regard as subsidies common Canadian practices and policies simply because they differ from the American norm. Whatever the merits of the Canadian interpretation, any economic and political bias in the countervail process works against a positive trading relationship between our two countries.

Moreover, emphasizing what Americans perceive to be improper subsidies can ultimately work to the disadvantage of the United States. For example, U.S. farm support programs have disrupted world markets for wheat and other agricultural products, causing economic hardship for Canadian farmers. And Canada has retaliated with a 67 percent countervailing duty against U.S. corn—the first time that another country has used a countervailing move against the United States. The Canadian action could well serve as a precedent for other countries that have trade complaints against the United States and should be of great concern to the United States.

Disagreement between Canada and the United States in many countervailing duty cases centers on differing perceptions about which government subsidy programs are "unfair" and distort trade. From the Canadian perspective this is the crucial issue in negotiating an agreement aimed at securing Canadian access to the U.S. market. If Canadian industry restructures to benefit from the advantages of free trade, only to find that the price of its success is to be shut out of the American market through protectionist actions by the United States, Canadians will question the advantages of a new treaty.

From the American perspective, the issue is a broader one. The Congress is concerned about the U.S. trade deficit of $170 billion. Getting Congress to exempt Canada from legislation that allows the United States to deal with government-subsidized exports would set a precedent that could be used by other countries in negotiations with the United States. No such precedent would be contemplated without a significant undertaking by Canada to restrict the use of industrial policies that might be countervailed by the United States.

One approach that merits careful consideration would be for both countries to agree to apply countervailing duties only to the differential between the subsidies available to firms in both countries. While this method takes into account the idea of the "level playing field," which figures prominently in congressional deliberations, such a calculation presents serious technical problems and would need agreement on what constitutes a subsidy. With respect to regional development subsidies provided by federal grants, it may be possible to place a realistic limit on the amount of a locational subsidy that would be allowed without being actionable. Incentives given by provinces and states to attract investment are difficult to place under discipline because of constitutional problems and regional considerations.

If the two countries' negotiators are able to find common ground in certain subsidy areas, a treaty could lay the groundwork for a joint attempt to get other trading partners to accept the approach in the multilateral negotiations.

One very important sector examined in the 1986 Senate hearings was automotive trade. Two-way trade under the Automotive Products Agreement comprised more than one-third of total U.S.-Canada trade in 1986. If the automotive pact were simply a sectoral free trade agreement, there would be no difficulty in fitting the automotive sector into a comprehensive trade treaty. But the pact as administered by Canada contains a number of features that do not easily fit into the definition of free trade. Only designated vehicle manufacturers may import duty free; and to be so designated, firms must meet certain production and content requirements. The United States has always argued that these requirements were meant to be transitional, but they have become a permanent feature of the arrangement.

Conditions in the North American automobile industry have changed radically since the pact was negotiated in 1965. The Canadian government has recently reverted to using a duty remission program, to which the United States has again objected, to encourage Japanese automotive investment in Canada. Since the program permits Japanese firms to use exports to the United States—which are duty free under the automotive pact—as a way to earn the rebate of Canadian duties on imports from Japan, this arrangement has already begun to raise political heat on Capitol Hill. These issues will need to be resolved, whether within the comprehensive trade agreement or outside it.

Prospects for success

What then are the prospects for success in the bilateral negotiations? The timetable for completing the talks is very short. If there is to be an agreement, then most likely it will have to be concluded before the present congressional authority for negotiations expires in January 1988.

With protectionist ferment bubbling to the surface in Congress, it is a difficult time to negotiate a deal that will further open the American market to foreign imports. While it is true that fast-track authority does not require formal Senate advice and consent, the final agreement must be voted up or down by both houses of Congress. Thus the administration will not sign any treaty with Canada that does not have firm political backing on Capitol Hill.

I understand that the Canadian government has put substantial emphasis on the negotiations. It has moved a large number of people into separate offices under senior leadership that reports directly to a cabinet-level trade committee in Ottawa. While the U.S. civil servants who are working on this matter are able, I am concerned that there are not enough of them to do the job and that the talks are not receiving the special emphasis they deserve from the administration.

I was pleased that Vice President George Bush and Treasury Secretary James Baker visited Ottawa in January to discuss the trade talks with Prime Minister Mulroney. And it is significant that President Reagan referred to the importance of the talks in his 1987 State of the Union Message. But the negotiations will need much more emphasis in order to win the support of Congress.

Nor can approval of a new trade agreement in Canada be taken for granted. The Conservative party's popularity is now limping along at 30 percent, the lowest poll results since its massive election victory in 1984. Despite the mid-1986 cabinet shuffle that saw Pat Carney replace James Kelleher as trade minister, an aggressive organized labor attack on the Mulroney trade strategy weakened Canadian public support for the initiative. The Liberals' position on the talks remains ambiguous. The Liberal party convention in December 1986 adopted two resolutions on trade, one that tacitly supported a bilateral free trade agreement as long as it met certain conditions, including the removal of countervailing actions, and another that called for a strengthening of multilateral trade ties and proposed that negotiations with the United States proceed only on a sectoral basis, within the GATT framework. Finally, obtaining provincial support for a trade agreement will be a difficult task indeed for Ottawa, given the disparate interests of the provinces and their key role in ratifying a treaty.

A joint trade dispute settlement commission

In light of the disagreement surrounding countervailing duties and subsidies, it is my feeling that at a minimum the negotiations should aim at agreement on a dispute settlement mechanism that would investigate national trade grievances. My suggestion is to form something like a joint Canada–United States trade dispute settlement commission. Its objective would be to see that each side looked at the same factors when determining criteria for trade remedy action, with each country adopting similar standards for measuring the degree of injury as the basis for determining the level of protective duty to be applied.

Such a commission might be structured as an independent agency, with commissioners appointed by the politically accountable institutions of government for fixed terms of office. The general role of the commission would be to mediate between the parties in trade disputes and to make findings and nonbinding recommendations to the governments. The issues under the commission's purview would be determined in practice by the trade treaty, the application of which would of course be open to interpretation.

The commission could send some of its cases to subcommissions or joint panels of experts for mediation and sometimes for proposals for settling disputes. Panels could be drawn from the two governments and from senior people working in industry on both sides of the border. If trade officials in each country were required to refer disputes to the commission before reaching a final decision, the panels could assist in the resolution of trade conflicts in their particular industries. The proposal is not to create a supranational authority that would bind the governments of either country. Rather, the idea is to provide a safety valve so disputes could be examined free from the pressure of narrow, sectoral interests which tend to dominate discussions on counter-vailing actions.

Even if the relevant panel were to reach agreement on only a few of the items in dispute, that much at least would be off the political table. And since panel members would include people on both sides of the border working every day in the relevant industry, they would have a better understanding of the problems specific to that industry. As they began to appreciate what they shared, cross-border tensions might ease.

Although the trade dispute settlement commission's findings and recommendations would not be binding, the settlement procedure would tend to give them standing with governments. It is likely that as the bilateral treaty matures, the opinions of the commission would have de facto acceptability, as has happened in the case of another bilateral institution, the International Joint Commission, which deals with boundary questions.

I want to emphasize that these steps are short-term. They should not be allowed to deflect from the long-term goal of establishing a comprehensive mechanism to stabilize and promote a trading relationship that has been beneficial to both countries and needs to be nurtured and further developed in an increasingly competitive world. It is time that businesspeople, academics, and union members on both sides of the border let their political leaders know that they see no profit in strict nationalism. We must work together to build a positive and fair trading relationship.

Canada and the United States should negotiate realistically about securing more assured access to each other's markets—for the real bottom line in the trade negotiations is not simply creating a dispute-settling mechanism. It should be possible to make real progress in developing common rules to ensure a more stable trading relationship, which is in each country's self-interest. Above all, each side should support initiatives to break down the barriers to trade that handicap efficient businesses on both sides of the border. If North America can lead the way with a comprehensive, ground-breaking bilateral trade agreement, the chances of widening trade opportunities with the rest of the world will be much brighter and more beneficial.

An Approach to Antidumping and Countervailing Duty Laws

ROBERT E. HUDEC

How SHOULD the United States respond to the collection of proposals that a free trade area agreement include some modification in antidumping and countervailing duty laws? Such proposals, largely from the Canadian side, are sketched out in the Stone and Burns paper. As one who is neither involved in the negotiations nor familiar with their day-to-day development, I believe the most useful contribution I can make is to help to define the general issue and evaluate the several kinds of proposals being made.

Current activity and prior practice

In a paper prepared for the *World Bank Economic Review*, J. Michael Finger and Julio Noguès offer interesting data on the volume of antidumping and countervailing duty activity in the world today.[1] In the six years 1980–85, the number of actions initiated by the United States, the European Community (EC), Australia, and Canada was as follows:

	Antidumping cases	Countervailing duty cases	Total cases
United States	280	252	532
Australia	393	18	411
European Community	254	7	261
Canada	219	12	231

It is evident that the application of this area of trade remedy law is large, and by no means an exclusive preserve of the United States. It has also been growing.

The issue of how to treat antidumping and countervailing duty laws has come up in every postwar agreement creating a customs union or a free trade area. Thus far, the practice has been mixed. To my knowledge, only the European Community has succeeded in eliminating the application of these remedies internally. The EC has a central antidumping and countervailing duty law

1. "International Control of Subsidies and Countervailing Duties" (forthcoming), table 1.

111

administered by the Commission of the EC. The law applies only to external trade, treating the Community as a single customs territory with communitywide standards of "industry" and "injury." Members are not allowed to use national remedies against each other.

In the Cartagena Agreement of 1969 establishing the Andean Common Market, members have preserved the right to apply "unfair trade" remedies against each other but have transferred jurisdiction for defining and administering such laws to a central board, or "junta." In 1971, the board issued a regulation defining its rather broad jurisdiction and procedures in this matter. The regulation mentions dumping specifically, but it applies to every measure that "can distort competition."[2]

In other major free trade area agreements, existing national antidumping and countervailing duty laws and remedies are preserved. Article 17 of the agreement governing the European Free Trade Association (EFTA) permits members to take action against dumped or subsidized goods. And similar provisions apply in the agreements between the EC and individual EFTA members. The provisions of the EC–Swiss agreement are typical—article 25 preserves dumping remedies; subsidies are dealt with in article 23:1(iii), which prohibits trade-distorting subsidies, but it is followed by article 27:3(d), which authorizes "measures necessary to remedy the situation." In the U.S.-Israel Free Trade Area Agreement, article 5 requires consultations, but otherwise permits each party to retain existing national antidumping and countervailing duty laws and remedies.

Two conclusions emerge from this survey of practices. First, the General Agreement on Tariffs and Trade (GATT) allows the members of a regional organization to treat antidumping and countervailing duty laws in any manner they choose—eliminating their internal applicability, retaining their internal applicability, or something in between.

Second, the degree to which members of regional organizations seem disposed to limit or modify these laws varies with the degree of integration they set out to achieve. The European Common Market is clearly the most far-reaching attempt at integration and the objectives of the Andean Common Market are nearly as broad. That such agreements have done the most in changing national

2. "Standards on Competition" (Decision 45 of the Commission, December 18, 1971). The Latin American Free Trade Area (LAFTA) and its successor the Latin American Integration Area (LAIA) appear to contemplate similar unification of administration, but I have found no evidence that this element of the trade union has been made operative.

laws is not surprising. The greater the degree of integration, the more anachronistic it becomes to deal with unfair trade practices by means of long-range artillery.

A common theme in all the proposals limiting or eliminating antidumping and countervailing duty remedies in Canadian-American trade is a new relationship that a free trade area will bring about. Usually the new relationship is simply assumed to be reasonable justification for change.

In fact, the proposals reflect a variety of different policy arguments, with different implications for how they might be justified. Some proposals rest on opposition to the antidumping and countervailing duty laws themselves, while others accept the stated purpose of the laws but argue that specific changes would make them more effective.

Opposition to the laws as such is widespread among academics and policy experts, who typically view them as an economically irrational, shoot-yourself-in-the-foot kind of protectionism. (Legitimate concern about unfair business practices, they argue, is already taken care of by existing national laws, such as the antitrust laws.) This kind of opposition seems to be fairly well represented in the proposals being made for the Canadian-American agreement. Proposals frequently use "contingent protection," "administered protection," and similar terms to characterize antidumping and countervailing duties, the terms typically used by the academic opposition to portray these laws as just another kind of trade barrier.

Arguments based on pure opposition to antidumping and countervailing duty laws probably do more harm than good. The recent history of such laws in the United States and data demonstrating their growing employment around the world show that these laws have become not only a hard fact, but an insistent political necessity. Arguments premised on the assumption that they are fundamentally wrong policy are simply no longer accepted by most legislators.

Moreover, proposals for change based on opposition to the very existence of these laws do not have much to do with free trade negotiations. If the laws are wrong, they are wrong in all circumstances. Nothing done in the free trade negotiations makes the wrong any greater, nor is there any reason why correction of the wrong should be more urgent in trade between these two parties than in trade generally.

Proposals that accept the stated purpose of antidumping and countervailing duty laws and claim to improve on them divide into two basic types. First are those that ask for elimination of this or that element of current law because it does not meet the stated purpose of the law. Proposals of this kind begin by offering "correct" definitions of the law's basic concepts—"dumping," or "subsidy" or "industry," or "material injury." They then suggest changing or eliminating certain rules in the current law that penalize practices not within the definition.

This type is probably the most common proposal being made in connection with the Canada-U.S. free trade agreement. All the good ideas about new standards of "industry," new de minimus standards, and new concepts of "net subsidy" fall into this category.

The main point to be made about proposals to reduce excessively broad antidumping and countervailing duty laws is that, no matter what negotiators may say, the problems are not peculiar to the free trade agreement itself. Overly broad laws are indeed a trade barrier, and free trade negotiations are supposed to remove all trade barriers, including this kind. But this issue is a general problem affecting the legitimacy of antidumping and counter-vailing duty remedies against all trade partners. If a claim of excessiveness is valid at all, it is equally valid for all trade affected. There is no evident reason why such laws should be changed for Canada and not for everyone else.

Stone and Burns appear to be aware of this point, stating that issues of this kind might well be addressed in the larger setting of the Uruguay Round trade negotiations. But they do not take the point far enough. Absent some better and more visible link to what is accomplished in the free trade area negotiations, demands to cure antidumping and countervailing duty laws will almost certainly be treated as something that does not belong in those negotiations. They will, to the contrary, be viewed as a topic that must be dealt with in wider, or more multinational, forums.

Is it possible to develop proposals for changing antidumping and countervailing duty laws that have a stronger link to the creation of a free trade area? One such approach rests on offering alternative solutions. Rather than try to limit the laws by showing that they are too broad, one can try to justify change by showing that the free trade area agreement will offer new and better ways to deal with the underlying problems of injurious dumping and subsidies—ways more suitable to the more integrated trade rela-tionship being created.

With respect to dumping, a free trade area tends to create an almost automatic self-help remedy. Stone and Burns point out that a duty free border will permit competitors in the importing country to ship dumped imports back to the point of origin. The prospect of "reverse dumping" could act as a deterrent to dumping in the first place.

The key is to make certain that this phenomenon is developed into a positive, purposeful element of the free trade area agreement—something that can be held out as a reason for doing something different with antidumping remedies. The free trade agreement should contain provisions explicitly addressed to promoting reverse dumping.

Both the EFTA Agreement (article 17[2]) and the EC Agreement (article 91[2]) do that through a "boomerang clause" which guarantees the right to return any exported good to the country of origin. Even where that right might automatically follow from the liberalizing provisions of the agreement, it makes sense to follow the EFTA and EC examples of repeating and emphasizing the point with a special clause attached to the treaty provisions that deal with dumping.

It should also be possible to enlarge the typical boomerang clause and include other types of barriers that might prevent reverse dumping—restrictions such as resale price maintenance laws, or laws enforcing exclusive licenses or exclusive distributorships. Ultimately, such a clause might be used to prevent price discrimination by establishing uniform application of antitrust and other competition laws.

Typically, free trade areas offer an alternative solution to countervailing duty remedies in the form of legal obligations and procedures that seek to regulate trade-distorting subsidies at their source. The EFTA Agreement (articles 13 and 24), the EC Agreement (article 91), the EC-Switzerland Free Trade Area Agreement (articles 23 and 27), and the U.S.-Israel Free Trade Area Agreement (annex 4), all have one or more subsidy-regulating obligations. Such obligations are, of course, an almost necessary part of any agreement to reduce trade barriers, for subsidies can be as trade distorting as tariffs and quantitative restrictions. But once in the agreement, such obligations perform the added function of making it easier to justify less reliance on conventional remedies for protection against subsidies.

The political effectiveness of offering this kind of substitute remedy was demonstrated in the 1979 U.S. legislation implementing the Tokyo Round agreements. Congress agreed to a significant liberalization of the existing countervailing duty law (the addition of a material injury test), but only after the administration offered, as a substitute for the lost protection, an improved GATT discipline over subsidies at the source (the 1979 GATT subsidies code adopted in the trade negotiations).

The joint commission proposal

If a Canada-U.S. agreement were to contain such alternative remedies for dumping and for subsidies, what kinds of changes in U.S. law could be anticipated? If it were possible to make a persuasive case that the alternative remedies would succeed in eliminating all dumped or subsidized imports from the partner country, it would be possible—in theory, at least—to justify exempting the partner country's trade from antidumping or countervailing duty remedies. At the moment, however, it seems unlikely that the U.S. Congress is ready to be persuaded, except after a substantial demonstration of the efficiency of such alternative remedies. Furthermore, it is doubtful that either Canada or the United States is ready to accept rigorous regulation of either its subsidy practices or its related competition laws. One has to think, therefore, of using the free trade agreement's provisions to justify proposals for more limited changes in national antidumping and countervailing duty laws.

What kind of changes could be achieved? The Stone and Burns proposal to shift administration of the laws to a joint commission would appear to be an appropriate first step. The logic of such a change could be stated as follows. The present situation involves an action-reaction relationship between two kinds of unilateral national behavior—subsidy or dumping practices by the exporting country, and protective measures by the importing country in response. The free trade agreement will be subjecting several aspects of the exporting country's behavior to a new discipline, under joint supervision in the new commission. A balanced agreement would require that the responsive practices of the importing country also be subject to the same new regime—a new discipline under joint supervision.

The joint commission could then serve as the vehicle for what comes next—a further evolution of joint discipline in parallel. Proposals for new rules limiting subsidy practices, for example, could be matched by proposals for new limitations on countervailing duty remedies. The joint commission would be ideally suited for this work, assuring that one institution would be in charge of enforcing both sides of the deal.

The key to any joint commission approach in this area is the requirement for parallel movement. One cannot ask for a bilateral "integrationist" approach to trade remedies unless one is willing to take the same approach to the underlying trade problems—the practices of the exporting nation to which the trade remedy laws are responding.

Indeed, that is the key to any kind of movement in the antidumping and countervailing duty laws. If the free trade agreement is to serve as a justification for reform of any kind, it must address both sides of the problem.[3]

Broadened powers for a joint commission

Does the Stone and Burns suggestion of a joint commission to serve a variety of purposes go far enough? I believe that, in general, the proposal is too modest. The major purpose of any international agreement is to create a new political force in support of its objectives. A joint commission that merely provides a place for governments to meet from time to time will necessarily be less effective in this regard than an institution with an independent personality and an independent commitment to the goals of the agreement.

The existence of an independent personality depends on staffing the institution with persons who are fully committed to its success. Staff placed on temporary assignment by the two governments will not have this kind of commitment. Both executive and adjudicatory functions should be handled by full-time career officials of the institution whose principal loyalty is to the commission rather than a member government.

On the adjudicatory side, this approach would require creating a permanent tribunal instead of ad hoc tribunals like the GATT panels for resolving disputes over treaty interpretation or like the mixed tribunal of officials from national decisionmaking agencies proposed to administer trade remedy laws. Ad hoc tribunals have several shortcomings. A tribunal modeled on the GATT panels would simply not provide enough continuity and accumulated legal expertise to administer the more rigorous legal structure needed in a regional integration agreement. As for administering trade remedy laws, it would not only be extremely difficult to

---

3. Given the general disposition to view a Canadian-U.S. free trade agreement as a precedent for the Uruguay Round of GATT negotiations, the parallelism suggested here might serve as a model for a multilateral settlement on subsidy and countervailing duty policy. The solutions provided in a Canada-U.S. free trade agreement would be distinctive only to the extent that those two parties are willing to go further than others toward the elimination of the underlying practices.

replicate the bifurcated (often trifurcated) U.S. procedures on an international level, but it would also be impossible to prevent the delegates' international role from interfering with their domestic legal responsibilities.[4]

Greater attention should also be given to the legislative side of the joint commission. Probably the best way to obtain legislative enactment of trade liberalization measures is through the device of harmonization, where each national legislature is asked to enact common rules for the two countries. Harmonization supplies an independent justification for change; in the United States, such a justification would find support in the strong "uniform law" traditions under which state laws have been harmonized in the name of economic unification. In addition, by requiring lawmakers to legislate for their own exporters at the same time that they legislate protection for import-sensitive industries, harmonization would offer the most balanced setting in which to consider trade issues generally.[5]

It is clear that neither the Canadian nor the U.S. government would be willing to give the joint commission power to legislate harmonized laws. The commission therefore should be given the power to draft legislation for consideration by the two national legislatures. A key element of such a procedure might be the creation of a legislative arm of the joint commission—a subcommission consisting of representatives from the two national legislatures who would advise on the substance of harmonization proposals and provide an informed link to each legislature when the proposals are considered.

This legislative dimension would be particularly important in establishing procedures to administer antidumping and countervailing duty laws. The joint commission could hardly carry out that function very long if it had to apply different national laws to the exports of each party. Eventually, it would be essential to

4. Efforts should be made to assure there would be enough work for a full-time tribunal. There would seem to be no a priori reason why such a tribunal could not handle all issues, such as rules of origin, arising at the Canadian-U.S. customs border.

5. Canadians may view harmonization as a species of legal imperialism since, as a result of the relative power of the two parties, the process is likely to end up requiring Canada to align itself to U.S. law. There is no satisfying solution to this problem, for there is no way of changing U.S. law in a certain area without at least opening the possibility of changing related Canadian law at the same time. The alternative to harmonization is no change on either side. Assigning a strong and conspicuous role to the joint commission will help to alleviate both the appearance of imperialism and the danger itself. Beyond that, the only real protection is to start excluding matters from potential harmonization. However, because there are no natural boundaries to trade, the price of reciprocal exclusions is likely to be quite high.

have a harmonized law applicable to all trade in either direction. In addition, any future improvements in trade remedy laws would almost certainly require enactment of common legislation.

Indeed, it is doubtful that Canadian objectives to improve U.S. antidumping and countervailing duty laws could be achieved without changing the substance of the current U.S. laws. This is evident in the ambiguity in most Canadian proposals for joint administration. On the one hand, the goal seems to be greater objectivity—as the many allegations of politically inspired decisions in recent cases suggest. On the other hand, there also seems to be a desire to allow consideration of the special trade relationship—in short, a thumb on the scale in favor of modified objectivity.

There is ambiguity because there is more than one problem. Objectivity—or at least the appearance of objectivity—is certainly one of the problems. It is simply not in the cards that Canada will be satisfied with the judicial neutrality of any procedure that is under the supervision of the official in charge of political relations with affected domestic industries. The United States would not accept a similar situation in Canada.

But objectivity is probably not the whole story. It is unlikely that any foreign government would want a completely objective and juridically accurate application of the present U.S. laws. So far, the Commerce Department seems to have been a good deal more liberal than the Court of International Trade, whose objectivity would be beyond question. Commerce has crafted more than a few "creative" decisions in order to keep U.S. laws from leading everyone over a cliff. It is difficult to know whether an international agency could apply these laws with the same creativity. In any event, a new, harmonized law would be a much safer basis from which to depart.

Challenges to a
Bilateral Association

CARL E. BEIGIE

THE Stone and Burns paper is a solidly reasoned call for the United States and Canada to launch a bilateral trade agreement patterned along the lines of a "GATT-plus" exercise.[1] The authors see such a bilateral accord, if it can be negotiated successfully, as constituting a productive stopover on the way to further progress toward multilateral trade liberalization.

For an economist, to be against the principles of the General Agreement on Tariffs and Trade or of a broadly parallel "GATT-plus" would constitute a violation of the creed of Efficiency Maximization—the economist's equivalent of the Hippocratic Oath. But the negotiations are now well along, and economic reasoning and logic are likely to be dominated by politics and political argument. This is not the comment of a cynic but of one who has spent his professional life observing economic issues moving from theoretical discussion to the arena of policy negotiation and implementation.

I was born, raised, and formally educated in the United States, but for most of my adult life I have lived in Canada. Now a Canadian, I have come to be frustrated by the arguments of most Americans with whom I discuss the Canada–United States economic relationship. To put the matter bluntly, there tends to be too much "warm feeling" in the United States toward its northern neighbor, which produces a certain fuzziness of thought. One of the great dangers in the current discussions between Canada and the United States is that what politicians—or the people in their employ—say is not always consistent with a neutral assessment of the facts.

Occasionally, the Stone and Burns paper drifts into sentimentality on trade liberalization. It is not true, for example, that the Automotive Agreement of 1965 is "working well for both

---

1. Atlantic Council, *GATT-Plus, A Proposal for Trade Reform* (Praeger, 1976), suggests an agreement supplementary to the GATT among the industrialized nations that would further liberalize trade in accordance with rules tighter than those in the GATT and provide for weighted voting in the administration of those rules.

countries." The combination of virtual productivity parity across the border made possible by the agreement, approximate nominal wage parity between the two countries' workers, and a Canadian dollar that has fallen in value to only three-quarters of the U.S. dollar in exchange markets has meant that Canada now has a distinct advantage as an automotive production location, at least in a North American context.

Despite this advantage, which was a direct outgrowth of the automotive pact, Canada retains certain "safeguards" even today when its bilateral automotive trade position is in substantial surplus. The Canadian automotive union, the premier of Ontario, and the federal New Democratic party have been adamant that these safeguards not be placed on the current bargaining table. This would be an unjustifiable position for the Canadian government to take. Yet the Big Three automobile companies apparently support this position, possibly because they see promise of this Canadian form of protectionism being applied forcefully to control the growing actual and potential penetration of cars produced by third-country suppliers into North America.

If developments in the automotive industry are a guide, it seems likely that a more comprehensive bilateral accord is going to raise tough challenges in terms of trade multilateralism and Canadian foreign policy independence. For example, if the United States decides to press its case against Japan to force an improvement in its trade deficit, then one has reason to ask what U.S. expectations would be of a trade-agreement-associated Canada in this matter. Obviously, there is no way that Canada and the United States can both improve their net bilateral merchandise trade balances via such an agreement. Canada could, however, be expected to lend support by helping the United States to improve its overall trade position by measures not unlike those Canada has practiced under the automotive pact. While such an implicit understanding might be acceptable to certain parts of Canada (especially Ontario), it would greatly upset western Canada, which sees Japan far more as a customer for its resources than as a competitor for its production.

A key feature of the traditional economic case for bilateral free trade is the opportunity it would provide Canada to gain scale economies. This argument should be looked at skeptically, primarily because growth prospects for developed countries are in services and in newer, niche-type products for which the emphasis is on speed and flexibility rather than on large-scale, standardized production. Where scale economies are still relevant, there has been a movement toward managed rather than toward freer trade, as demonstrated in steel and cars. In any event, the major gains for Canada from a bilateral agreement probably would come from dynamic factors that, while certainly posing large potential benefits over time, will also require fairly serious changes in the Canadian economic mentality to be realized fully.

Let me return, however, to the main point. It is inherent in the disparities of the Canada–United States relationship that a trade accord (what might be called a bilateral "association") will bring with it actual or perceived threats to Canada's political independence (and thus to its effective "sovereignty"). That is, the two countries are negotiating not merely a GATT-type trade liberalization but also, in effect, a form of "sovereignty-association."

That phrase, "sovereignty-association," is a familiar one to Canadians, having been the term René Levesque used to describe the goal of the Parti Québécois in the Quebec referendum debate of 1980. In that episode, Quebec was seeking a way to separate from the Canadian Confederation, whereas in the current context the goal is to find a politically acceptable way for two independent countries to formalize a closer economic partnership with a minimum loss of political flexibility for the smaller of the two economies.

Despite positive words from both the Reagan and the Mulroney administrations, prospects for pulling this off remain dubious, irrespective of the economic merits of trying to do so. The Stone and Burns paper asserts that a bilateral agreement would have to be quite comprehensive to be compatible with GATT rules. If that is so, then how is Canada going to be induced to go along with the package when there is still a widely held perception in the country that a significant range of issues will be left totally "off the table"?

The two countries' "national myths" are bound to be another complicating factor in these negotiations, which in any event have an intense political component. Canadians and Americans have certain beliefs not only about their next-door neighbors but also about themselves. For example, Canadians tend to the view that U.S. corporations act, effectively, as the economic agents of their federal government, whereas Canadian governments have either an essentially hands-off or a rather blundering approach toward corporations, whether domestic or foreign-owned. On the U.S. side, one encounters a belief that Canada, being a more "socialistic" society, subsidizes everything, whereas the United States is virtually faultless of such intervention. Such myths have emerged

often in the past and will in the future as the two countries'
politicians, media, and general public debate whatever emerges
from the current negotiating sessions.

One of the reasons for raising these kinds of politically oriented
points is that for Canada's prime minister to launch the request
to negotiate a bilateral agreement showed a certain amount of
courage and vision, although some might claim it reflected a
greater amount of political-economy naïveté. To continue with
his firm support might require Mr. Mulroney to accept exceptional
political risks. He is having serious problems in the opinion polls,
and U.S. trade actions on shakes and shingles and softwood
lumber, for example, have not helped. If the United States takes
the action it has threatened on any of a range of other products,
such as steel, potash, and uranium, Mr. Mulroney's ability to
carry the public of Canada (as opposed to the Parliament, where
he controls an overwhelming majority) will be severely tested.

On this point of the electorate versus the Parliament, the
primary issue may not be the specific agreement negotiated per
se but the ability to follow it through in Canada. Observers in
the United States should be aware that unless Mr. Mulroney's
government improves its popularity, the momentum for any
bilateral agreement it negotiates with the United States might not
be sustained. It is a definite possibility that a minority government
will follow the current one in 1989, with the balance of power
being held by a party that has strongly opposed such an agreement.

When economists move too far into the practical world of
politics, they tend to become depressed and depressing. So let me
comment on what I see as the most positive case for a bilateral
agreement for Canada and for the United States. It is my hope
that such positive considerations will dominate what comes to
pass in bilateral trade relations over the next year.

For Canada, the positive case centers on the ability to raise the
country's growth rate significantly above what it would otherwise
be for at least a decade and to retain a noticeably higher level of
output into the indefinite future. Furthermore, the opportunity
would exist to work out a "tailored" transitional adjustment
mechanism on a bilateral basis that would simply not be possible
on a multilateral basis. With faster, more efficient growth achieved
within a sympathetic adjustment period (although with a firm
cut-off point), Canada would have greater funding to meet its
unique social objectives without incurring massive and eventually
debilitating budgetary deficits.

Without going into detail, I would suggest that the transition mechanisms should reflect a clearer view of what the bilateral exchange rate should be than is now the case. Few persons seem to agree with me that this is a very important economic issue.

Finally, it has never been totally clear what the positive case in a bilateral trade deal with Canada is for the United States. Sentiment is fine, but it seems that Congress has little patience today for appeals to sentiment. Possibly a bilateral accord could provide a useful prototype for broader policy purposes, but this could well be stretching things. There is no clear evidence at this point of a strategic focus in U.S. policymaking that would give Canada the comfort of supplying something that the United States really wants.

When all is said and done, I suspect that Canada is going to be governed by a very simple motive: if U.S. trade barriers are going to go up, Canada wants to be on the American side of whatever "playing field" emerges. Mr. Mulroney has put up with many recent U.S. pressures and actions that have not made him popular at home, but he has at least kept the bilateral trade agreement "ball" in play.

General Discussion

LaFalce, referring to the earlier discussion, did not believe it was fair to charge that the administration has not discussed this issue adequately with the Congress. In his experience, Ambassador Peter Murphy has been more than willing to respond to requests for briefings, and he was sure the same was true for any other members or committees who took the same initiative.

In respect to whether the automotive pact was "on the table" for renegotiation, he emphasized it was important, as in some of the other issues, to get away from semantic difficulties. For example, the United States insists that "everything is on the table." A reporter then asks whether that includes the level of social welfare benefits. The U.S. negotiator replies that an issue that affects trade should be subject to discussion. This answer is then taken to mean that the United States is unfairly demanding changes in policies that are beyond the scope of the negotiations, an interpretation far removed from reality.

The fact is that trade in automobiles and parts constitutes one-third of the total trade between the two countries. Any aspect of the rules governing this trade would necessarily be subject to discussion and possible change at the initiation of either country.

Robert Dunn agreed with Beigie that by definition both countries could not improve their bilateral trade balance as a result of a free trade arrangement. On the other hand, the trade balance of North America as a whole could improve because of the trade diversion effects of the agreement. The United States could import products from Canada that otherwise it would have imported from a third country, and vice versa. He had no quantitative estimate of how large this trade diversion effect could be but believed it could be significant, and therefore a selling point for the agreement. In theory the exchange rates of both countries would appreciate as a result of such trade diversion but the net effect on the North American trade balance would still be positive.

Morici thought Canada would benefit much more from trade diversion than would the United States. To that extent Canada's exchange rate would appreciate by more than that of the United States, thus tending to reduce this present source of friction.

Leonard Weiss, commenting on the deadline problem, suggested that if necessary an agreement on trade alone, including agriculture, would be a logical stopping point for the present negotiation. Services, intellectual property, and investment would by agreement be deferred for subsequent negotiation.

He also pointed out that the emphasis on countervailing duties, antidumping duties, and escape clause actions in the discussion neglected the impact of section 301 in the U.S. trade legislation. Under this provision the United States can unilaterally decide what is unreasonable, unfair, or unjustifiable in the trade practices of other countries. How this provision would operate also deserves consideration in the negotiations.

A Canadian Official View

Negotiating an Acceptable Agreement

JOHN H. MCDERMID

ON JANUARY 27 the president renewed in strong terms his administration's commitment to a new trade agreement with Canada. In Ronald Reagan's words, "We will work to complete an historic free trade agreement between the world's two largest trading partners."

We in Canada needed to hear that. But words are not enough. We need to be sure that negotiations translate this political commitment into a mutually acceptable agreement. My prime minister and the president embarked on these negotiations more than a year ago. The pace so far has been slow, and I believe that we need to get on with it. Canada and the United States have the largest bilateral trade relationship in the world. Canada is not only the largest, but also the fastest growing export market for U.S.-made goods and services. These facts are well known to everyone in this audience, whether Canadian or American.

But I am a firm believer in making sure that the message is repeated time and time again. We hear much of America's trade deficit these days and of unfair foreign competition. I would remind you that while Canada enjoys a merchandise trade surplus with the United States, the United States enjoys a surplus on the services side. The result is that the trade relationship is far more balanced than most Americans realize. Canadians are fair traders and their relationship with the United States is justly seen as the envy of the world.

Of late, however, the indiscriminate, and I would say unfair, use of U.S. trade remedy laws has threatened this relationship. Canada appreciates America's need to become competitive. Canadians, too, are searching for new ways to become competitive. But the road to competitiveness is not through protectionism.

Protectionism only makes a bad situation worse. The road to prosperity lies in cooperative trade negotiations, like the one our two nations are pursuing.

For the past fifty years, successive Canadian and American governments have pursued trade policies that reflected the realities of the

129

day. Americans understand, as do Canadians, that trade is the basis of prosperity. Trade creates wealth, the wealth that pays for medicare, education, regional development, national defense, the institutions and the values that define a nation's way of life.

Canada's small population compels us to look outward. Unlike industries in nations with large domestic markets, Canada's industries require open and secure access to foreign markets to achieve competitive scale and volume. Part of the Canadian strategy lies in strengthening the General Agreement on Tariffs and Trade. Like you, we are determined to play a constructive role in using the GATT negotiations to prevent a return to the destructive beggar-thy-neighbor policies of the 1930s. The threat of a return to such policies is real—the rebirth of mercantilism and the drumbeat of protectionism are constant reminders. But in today's circumstances, the GATT is not enough, for Canada or the United States. The GATT has changed over the years. It now has many players, most of whom have free trade arrangements with their neighbors. But Canada does not and neither does the United States.

The pace of the GATT has slowed and the issues have become more complex. And the results of negotiations have become less satisfactory. It will be a while before the current Uruguay Round bears fruit; even the optimists talk about four years or more. Canada and the United States are working hard to advance the pace, particularly in the severely troubled agricultural sector.

Our two countries, therefore, are pursuing negotiations aimed at a comprehensive bilateral trade agreement, an agreement fully consistent with our obligations under the GATT. Our object is to achieve deep and broad reductions in trade barriers. This will create a more open and secure access to markets. We can do that jointly much sooner than will be possible in the multilateral framework of the GATT.

The bilateral and multilateral efforts are not alternatives. Rather, they reinforce one another. The bilateral negotiations, however, recognize the uniqueness of the relationship between our two countries and our requirement, as well as the opportunity, to advance mutual commercial interests.

In the early days of the GATT, the leading industrial powers negotiated and bound themselves to reduce the then-principal barrier to trade, the tariff. Tariff reductions were so successful that today tariffs are of relatively minor significance for much of what GATT members export. While trade may seem more open than in the days of high tariffs, it is in reality much less secure.

New investment aimed at growth requires a stable and predictable trading environment. Low tariffs help but they are of little practical value if the improved access they offer can be frustrated by other barriers at the border.

The protection formerly provided by the tariff has been replaced by trade remedy laws, such as antidumping and countervailing duties, emergency import restrictions, and so-called voluntary export restraints. They allow countries to exclude or penalize imports if they are tainted by claims of unfairness, whether justified or not. It is under these laws that American producers are seeking and finding protection through increased barriers against imports. Congress is prepared to expand and strengthen these remedies. Canadian exporters find themselves caught in this net.

These remedies erode the rule of law for which the GATT stands. They are based on unilateral determinations as to what is or is not an unfair import. They may find sanction in the letter of GATT law, but they are certainly contrary to the spirit of the GATT. Such a set of laws in the hands of a rich and powerful nation can be, and is proving to be, a dangerous protectionist weapon, a weapon that has been trained on Canada.

At the heart of the bilateral negotiations, therefore, is the issue of trade remedy laws. Canada has seen the capricious use of these American rules exercised in regard to U.S. imports of shakes and shingles, fish, and now lumber. Before Congress starts throwing up new barriers, its members have a responsibility to look squarely at the consequences of protectionism and make decisions that are in the long-term interest of their constituents. The combined effect of a 35 percent special tariff on shakes and shingles and the countervailing duty investigation on softwood lumber have brought home to many Canadians the dangers of Americans becoming economic isolationists.

The two countries were able to settle the softwood lumber issue by a government-to-government agreement. Canada agreed to impose an export tax of 15 percent in return for the withdrawal of the petition by the U.S. lumber industry for countervailing action. This was, for Canada, an exercise in damage limitation. We do not like it, and a better way to settle the problems has to be found for the future.

The export tax penalizes Canadian producers and consumers. Lumber helps build houses, U.S. houses, which means jobs, not just for the construction industry but for wholesalers, retailers, and transportation companies. Specifically, lumber imports from

Canada reduce costs to the consumer. Canada's export tax on lumber will cost Canadian jobs; it will impose costs on Americans as well.

What is the answer? It is not to wring our hands and to gnash our teeth. It lies in finding a better way to solve these kinds of problems, whether for lumber, fish, hogs, steel, or whatever. I have no quarrel with Americans who say they cannot accept dumped or subsidized imports from Canada. We do not want such imports either. We also do not want a situation where the determination of what constitutes dumping and subsidization is made unilaterally.

What the president said in his State of the Union Address on trade applies equally to Canada. We are willing to be trade partners but never trade patsies. A new bilateral regime will require major adjustments in Canada, adjustments that business will not undertake unless it is convinced that the agreement will lead to better, more secure, and predictable access to U.S. markets. Canada's objective is to restore predictability and stability to trade between the United States and Canada.

To achieve this, Canada wants a unique and clear set of rules to govern the issues that give rise to trade remedies. We want a set of rules that is consonant with free and open borders. We want rules that will provide a fair and equitable way to resolve differences with the United States. We do not want unilateral decisions.

There are real trade grievances on both sides but it should be possible to work out a better way of resolving them. If the status quo were working smoothly, neither side would want a change. It is not working, and that is why the two countries are trying to negotiate something better.

Let me leave no doubt. My government has made it clear that a new regime on trade remedy laws must be part of the agreement, not Band-aid solutions to the present laws. A new regime must reflect the special circumstances that would exist in bilateral trade and the new regime must also be consonant with other commitments in the agreement. It must provide for joint agreement on rules to define subsidization and other unfair practices that may distort trade, and joint determination of what constitutes breaches of the rules and appropriate remedies where such breaches occur. The key to a new set of rules will be meaningful commitments and disciplines on subsidy practices and strong, quick, binding dispute-settlement procedures.

I hope this dispels the myth that Canada is calling for a removal of trade remedy laws or exemption from trade remedy laws. What Canada wants is a meaningful and mutually beneficial replacement.

Over the past year, U.S. and Canadian negotiators have met once a month. These sessions have covered the full range of issues, including government procurement, trade remedy laws, agriculture, tariff and nontariff barriers, services, intellectual property, dispute settlement, and implementing mechanisms.

Now is the time to engage more fully and to step up the pace of negotiation. We have to do this if we are to meet the deadline imposed by the U.S. fast-track procedures. While negotiations are in progress, we still have to manage the specific irritants—that is, the polite words that our foreign ministries use to describe problems. They provide a good illustration of the need to reach a new understanding between us on the rules of the road.

But these irritants are not like an itch that needs to be scratched. Dealing with them influences how we are going to do business in the future and the environment in which we are trying to negotiate an historic agreement.

Let us look at steel. Last year American steel makers suffered a record $4 billion loss. Over the past five years steel mills in the United States have been shut down, and employment in the industry has been greatly reduced. Canada has had similar problems. Our steel industry rationalized, at great expense, because it knew that if it was to compete, it could not count on government subsidy and bailouts to keep it healthy. The biggest export market for Canadian steel is the United States. Now Canada finds itself under increasing pressure to agree to so-called voluntary export restraint, even though we are fair traders and our steel is being sucked into the U.S. market through the inability of the U.S. industry to meet demand.

Both countries benefit from trade in steel. One-third of U.S. steel exports goes to Canada, the largest foreign market in the world for the U.S. steel industry. Canadian steel mills buy over 95 percent of their coking coal and one-third of their iron ore from U.S. mines. That represents jobs for coal miners in Pennsylvania and ironworkers in Michigan. The steel goes into cars and industrial farm machinery made and used on both sides of the border. Disruption in cross-border steel trade will hurt both countries.

The manner in which irritants—big or small—are handled affects the climate as well as the political will for the negotiations. Americans in this audience are not unfamiliar with the fallout in

Canada over the restrictions placed on U.S. imports of shakes and shingles and softwood lumber. Such actions levy a heavy toll on Canadian public and political confidence.

Clearly the timetable for the negotiations is being set by the political calendars of both governments. The outcome of these talks will depend heavily on the commitment of the U.S. administration to the negotiations and the resolve of the administration to carry a deal through Congress. We have heard that many times at this conference from the American speakers. In this connection, last April's surprise comes to mind; for a dozen days, the U.S. Senate pondered its agreement to the administration's request for fast-track authority, and in the end went along by a majority of only one vote. Canada also recognizes, however, that a deal that does not carry the broad support of Americans, regardless of party, stands little chance of gaining the necessary support in Washington. We were encouraged by the reassurances of senators who visited Canada recently, led by Senator Lloyd Bentsen, and hope that the administration will be able to keep that support firm.

Similarly, whatever the Canadian government agrees to has to stand the critical test of gaining the support of Canadian public opinion, Parliament, and the provinces. It is essential, therefore, that whatever we craft together clearly serves the best interests of both countries. This condition is fully attainable because trade is not a zero-sum game. Both partners will gain from a good and fair agreement.

I am optimistic that a year from today both countries will be hailing an historic trade agreement and will be beginning to put in place a new system that will serve us well into the twenty-first century.

Policies toward Investment and Trade in Services

The Importance of Services

HARRY L. FREEMAN

THE FREE TRADE TALKS between the United States and Canada appear to be in trouble because of inattention and indifference by the American business community and the American media. The failure of these talks would be a major tragedy, with implications far beyond U.S. and Canadian relations. At American Express, we are actively supporting and promoting the U.S.-Canada trade negotiations, which we consider to be vital to the long-term economic and security relationships between the two countries. But much of the rest of the business community is apathetic, and the U.S. media's coverage of the talks does little to stimulate awareness.

Business has a very high stake in the outcome of these negotiations. Businessmen should be doing everything in their power to see that a good, workable bilateral trade agreement is reached. It is not enough for the two governments to be talking. They need the active support and interest of the politicians, the media, respected think tanks such as the organizers of this conference, and above all the community in both Canada and the United States.

One area that any trade agreement with Canada must address if it is to be acceptable to U.S. business and Congress is the liberalization of services. American Express would like to see an umbrella code or framework of rules and principles developed for the services trade, as well as sector-specific agreements that focus on trade obstacles in particular industries, such as telecommunications, information services, and financial services. This will be a path-breaking exercise since, for the most part, these issues have never been addressed in a systematic way in a trade negotiation.

Financial services in particular is a sector that is too important to be ignored, and it offers an excellent opportunity for making significant progress on liberalization. Rapid technological change and the spread of deregulation have helped to blur the line between domestic and international markets. Financial markets are becoming global and financial institutions are finding that to remain

137

competitive they must become strong internationally. Since the relevant market is global, not national, it is not in the interest of either Canada or the United States to shelter domestic financial institutions.

Let me dwell briefly on "competitiveness," the current Washington buzzword. We obviously have very serious competitive problems in manufacturing. What is little recognized is how competitive the financial services sector is on a global basis and how the United States is losing market share. Take our friends, the Japanese. Ten years ago, something like seven out of twenty of the largest banks were American. Seven out of ten now are Japanese. The largest bank in the world is not Citicorp; it is Dai Ichi Kangyo in Tokyo. In the securities field the top four Japanese securities firms, led by Nomura, earned just under $3 billion in their fiscal year ending in 1986. It would take the earnings of twenty-five to thirty American investment security houses to equal that figure.

For another statistic: Nomura has a market capitalization of about $35 billion. That is, taking its shares at market value and multiplying by the number of shares outstanding, that is the amount of capital they really have.

For comparison, American Express is the largest financial services company in the United States in terms of market capitalization at around $16 billion. The second largest U.S. firm is American International Group at $10 billion. Citicorp is probably about $6 billion or $7 billion. The next three American banks together would not add up to $15 billion.

Canadian banks are not small. The four or five chartered banks would be in the top fifteen to twenty if they were ranked with American banks. There are, of course, big banks and investment companies in France, Germany, and the United Kingdom.

So, speaking from an American financial services executive's point of view, it is becoming a very tough world.

Moreover, the competitive situation in the service sectors—financial services and advertising, for example—can change very rapidly. The technology is usually not patentable. The unique know-how we have often has a life of hours or a few days. In this kind of world the competitive balance can shift quickly. It is not a matter of "America is going to hell." It is rather the fact that the whole world of services is changing. The assumption that "we have this big advantage in services" cannot be taken for granted any longer.

In Canada, as recent moves toward deregulation demonstrate, there is rising concern that if business is denied access to competitively priced, innovative financial services from Canadian institutions, then business will simply move off shore. As the former finance minister of Canada, Donald Macdonald, has observed: "Only by developing world-scale capabilities among Canadian firms can we assure a continued Canadian presence in our own market. . . . Protectionism or delay will only assure a loss of competitive position for Canadian institutions both at home and abroad."[1]

As if in answer to this warning, the Canadian federal and Ontario governments announced major financial deregulatory reforms in December 1986—reforms that represent significant progress and demonstrate that the Canadian governments are well aware of the need to stimulate competition in the financial services industry.

Now, for the first time, Canadian banks as well as federally regulated trust, loan, and insurance companies will be able to own up to 100 percent of other types of financial institutions. This means that Canadian banks may own securities firms; nonbank financial institutions may engage in consumer lending; and all banks (including foreign banks) as well as trust, loan, and insurance companies may provide portfolio management services and investment advice. Securities firms will be opened completely to foreign ownership under parallel Ontario and federal deregulation plans. The one drawback to all this is that nonresident-owned firms such as foreign banks are forbidden to expand by means of acquisition into new (nonsecurities) financial businesses; the only way they can expand into these areas is by creating a new firm.

Still, these proposed changes will greatly enhance domestic competition among Canadian banks, securities firms, insurers, and trust companies. They will also position Canadian financial services firms to be competitive internationally and give them greater access to foreign sources of capital. American Express—as a diversified financial services corporation with a major payment systems subsidiary, a securities firm, an asset management company, and an international bank—is still looking carefully at the latest proposals to determine how we will be affected. Certainly Shearson Lehman, our securities subsidiary, is pleased; it has announced plans to increase its share in McLeod Young Weir to 30 percent, following the securities industry deregulation.

1. *The Macdonald Report*, vol. 1 (August 1986), p. 1.

I think the Canadian proposals furnish a good model for the United States, where financial services firms are still shackled, to an important degree, by regulatory barriers established long ago— barriers such as the increasingly outmoded and ineffective Glass-Steagall Act. Now that countries like Canada are taking resolute, even courageous, action to come to terms with new competitive realities, U.S. firms may begin to find themselves at a competitive disadvantage. One can only hope that the deregulatory developments in Canada, the United Kingdom, and elsewhere will galvanize the U.S. government into modernizing its own financial regulations.

Given all the changes in the financial services industry, I believe that the time is ripe to lay financial services on the table as an important sector to address in a U.S.-Canada services agreement. There are still major financial services issues that need to be covered in bilateral negotiations. And because services markets— especially the market for financial services—are changing so rapidly, a services agreement must be broad enough and flexible enough to cope with future, not just current, issues and problems.

Needless to say, it is unrealistic to expect that all issues can be addressed within the short time frame of the U.S.-Canada negotiations, especially if the negotiators keep to the September 1987 deadline. But at a minimum, it will be important to Congress and to U.S. business that the negotiators provide both a good framework agreement that lays out the basic principles governing bilateral services trade and a sectoral agreement that applies those principles to financial services and makes significant progress toward creating, over time, a free trade zone in financial services.

Immediate issues

What can be accomplished by this autumn and what will have to be addressed later, in a second phase of negotiations? I believe that four important objectives can and ought to be achieved in financial services within the present deadline:

—First, the development of a sectoral framework that would specify how the principles established should be applied to financial services.

—Second, the resolution of specific bilateral problems in financial services, either through a special financial services agreement or in other sectoral agreements (for example, on government procurement, or tourism).

—Third, the identification of longer-term issues to be addressed in a second phase of negotiations on financial services.

—And finally, the establishment of a mechanism for ongoing cooperation and consultation on financial services.

The framework of principles governing all services is especially important since it will lay the ground rules for continuing liberalization and negotiation well into the future. The draft framework developed by U.S. negotiators and proposed late in 1986 to the Canadian side contains many principles that could usefully be applied to specific barriers in financial services.

National treatment, for example, would entail eliminating the 16 percent limit imposed on foreign banks' share of total Canadian industry capital. It is still not clear whether, under the new regulations, foreign firms offering nonbank financial services will be allowed to provide investment advice and portfolio management in Canada. National treatment would ensure that they would be allowed to do so.

In cases where national treatment alone would be insufficient to guarantee market access, the right of market access should be considered paramount. This would include the right to have a commercial presence in the other country in order that services trade may take place.

One area where this is an issue for my company is access to specialized telecommunications networks in Canada—specifically, the payments and authorization system for credit card purchases. The Canadian Payments Association, which under the Bank Act runs the payments system, has made periodic rumblings about restricting access to the payments system to deposit-taking institutions—thereby threatening to exclude all nonbank issuers of cards. Should this threat ever become reality, it would pose a serious barrier to market access for my company and others.

Another example of market access problems is the Canadian regulation specifying that foreign-resident firms may only offer their financial products (for example, mutual funds) in Canada if they first establish Canadian subsidiaries. American Express believes that U.S. firms should have the right to offer their services either from within Canada or from across the border.

Another principle or guideline should provide for changes in laws and regulations that inhibit services trade. For example, Canadian pension funds are required, with few exceptions, to invest 90 percent of their assets in Canada, and some U.S. states impose similar restrictions. These restrictions should be eliminated.

A fourth principle would be the establishment of rules governing transactions between and competition between state enterprises and private corporations. For example, Air Canada, a crown corporation, operates a credit card service, Enroute, that is given all government and crown corporations' card contracts, regardless of how Air Canada's capabilities compare with competitors'.

Fifth, the guidelines should provide that local, state, and provincial laws comply with the terms of a trade agreement. This is an ever-present problem in negotiations between governments with federal systems. My company would like to see such laws made subject to specified notification, consultation, and dispute settlement procedures in the final trade agreement.

Finally, the agreement should establish formal mechanisms for coordination and consultation between the United States and Canada. These mechanisms would not only handle dispute settlement but would also lay the basis for continuing negotiation and liberalization beyond the formal conclusion of the free trade agreement. I envision that these formal mechanisms could be used to facilitate the convergence, over the long run, of the two nations' financial regulatory systems.

I am not advocating new rights for U.S. firms only. All rights should be fully reciprocal. Whatever U.S. firms can do in Canada, Canadian firms should be allowed to do in the United States.

Longer-term issues

Many issues related to financial services should be addressed in later negotiations. Financial services are undergoing massive changes around the globe. Institutional barriers are breaking down, and the ability to offer competitive services is heavily dependent on access to telecommunications and electronic delivery systems. One example is securities trading, which is heavily dependent on global telecommunications linkages and on complex computing capabilities. In consumer finance, linkages with automatic-teller-machine networks and point-of-sales networks are crucial for financial services companies. Because of this rapidly changing environment, whatever financial services arrangement U.S. negotiators propose must be open and flexible enough to accommodate change and to minimize barriers to innovation and efficiency.

The changing environment offers opportunities to explore ways in which the United States and Canada can bring about some measure of bilateral convergence of their financial supervisory and regulatory policies. I suggest that as the two governments grope toward better ways of regulating financial services, they take advantage of the opportunity to develop similar standards and modes of regulation—thereby moving closer to genuine free trade in financial services. Free trade in services would accelerate cross-border commodity trade and capital market development in both countries.

An example of such cooperation is the recent agreement between the U.S. and U.K. banking supervisors to develop common minimum standards. This agreement is an important step toward the worldwide application of common standards of banking soundness and prudence. The time has come for a similar agreement between the United States and Canada. In fact, I think the two governments should go even further and extend cooperation into nonbanking financial areas as well.

One idea might be for the United States and Canada to formally agree that each other's supervisory requirements are sufficiently rigorous that the financial institutions of one country may offer their services without restriction in the other country's market. The ultimate goal would be a convergence of domestic financial regulations in the two countries. I also think that a formal mechanism should be set up to promote bilateral consultation and cooperation on financial services.

Finally, there is the question of the relationship between the U.S.-Canada free trade negotiations and the multilateral negotiations now under way in the General Agreement on Tariffs and Trade (GATT). The Uruguay Round is arguably the most important multilateral trade round in decades, but tangible results will come slowly, over a number of years. In the meantime, bilateral negotiations can and should be used to set liberalizing precedents in both traditional and nontraditional areas—precedents that can serve as examples of what the United States and Canada want to achieve in the GATT.

It is possible that more can be achieved bilaterally than is now hoped for in the new round. An early and comprehensive U.S.-Canada agreement could serve as a goad to other countries, forcing them to reevaluate their positions on liberalization. The signing of a comprehensive U.S.-Canada bilateral agreement might force GATT negotiators to get down to brass tacks quickly, as the realization sinks in that if Canada and the United States do not obtain satisfaction multilaterally, they will continue to pursue their goals bilaterally. The other side of the coin, of course, is that if two nations as friendly as Canada and the United States cannot negotiate a comprehensive trade agreement, then how can the GATT negotiations be expected to get anywhere?

In short, I believe that the results of the U.S.-Canada negotiations will have a strong influence, either positive or negative, on what is possible in the GATT negotiations. Although this is true for all areas, the impact is likely to be especially strong in sectors such as services and investment where no international precedents exist.

As the U.S.-Canada negotiations proceed, therefore, proponents of a free trade system should be looking not just to the short political timetable under which the negotiators are operating, but also to the long-term future of both the bilateral relationship and the multilateral trading system.

Specific Objectives and Practical Solutions

JACQUES PARIZEAU

THE FIRST REAL STEP toward the establishment of the European Economic Community was the setting up of the European Coal and Steel Community in 1953. It is remarkable that what was in effect a free trade arrangement for a limited range of commodities implied from the outset an agreement on transportation rates. It was considered as inevitable that as soon as the trade of such goods was liberalized, a service such as transportation which has a major impact on price would be brought into the picture.

Until recently, U.S.-Canadian trade discussions have been conducted in a very different context. Services have never really been discussed in trade negotiations and the rules applicable to foreign investment have been kept in a separate box.

At the Quebec meeting between Prime Minister Mulroney and President Reagan in March 1984, the emphasis was still on tariff and nontariff barriers to trade, insofar as they hinder or prevent the trade of goods. Only recently in fact has the emphasis changed, with services and investment rules considered to be part and parcel of any free trade arrangement between the two countries.

The insistence of the United States at Punta del Este on having services on the agenda of the next round of negotiations under the General Agreement on Tariffs and Trade (GATT) gave a clear indication of what the next step would be. By then, it had become clear that the U.S. negotiations with Canada would be a test to see how far these issues could be defined, rules set, and progress made on the specifics. Thus besides progress in eliminating tariff and nontariff barriers on goods, the present bilateral negotiations are highly significant for what they can accomplish in the largely uncharted waters of the liberalization of services. And since the supply of services is frequently dependent on investment flows, rules for investment will also have to be covered.

One cannot escape the impression that Canada is gradually emerging from a quarter of a century of policies designed to control and restrict foreign and particularly U.S. investment. Canadians entered the 1960s with alarm. What has been called the "big takeover" of the fifties had left whole sectors of the Canadian economy in foreign hands. Studies conducted during this period, and particularly one undertaken by the U.S. House Committee on Energy and Commerce, showed how relatively modest foreign investments by multinational corporations could lead to large amounts of purchases by foreign subsidiaries from their parent companies. In addition, guidelines imposed by the U.S. government in 1965, which required that U.S. subsidiaries abroad remit more royalties and dividends to the parent companies, had a powerful impact on Canadians and Canadian governments alike.

It is possible to underestimate the scope and extent of the steps taken by Canadian authorities to protect Canadian-owned firms against foreign infringement and, therefore, because of the perceptions of the times, against trade diversion and financial decisions detrimental to the expansion of Canadian business. Establishment of the Foreign Investment Review Agency (FIRA) and the National Energy Policy (NEP) are well-known government moves. But others should be added. A prime example is the amendment of the Bank Act in 1967 that prevented a single shareholder from holding more than 10 percent of the capital stock of a bank and limited all nonresidents' ownership to a quarter of the stock. This so-called 10–25 rule was afterwards extended to nonresident shareholders of some other types of financial institutions. Provincial authorities instigated similar protective measures. Hence foreign financial institutions could enter the Canadian field by setting up their own subsidiaries, but incumbent Canadian institutions were still effectively protected. Other examples could be given. Protecting home-grown businesses against takeover became a national responsibility. These policies worked. In case they did not, the rapid development of public holdings in private businesses, particularly by Ottawa and by the province of Quebec, supplied levers of ultimate control.

Behind this protective wall, a massive concentration of economic and financial power was taking place in Canada. Helped by the tax reform of 1972 and by a rapid accumulation of institutional savings, the process of concentration inevitably led to an overflow of Canadian investment abroad. Most of it went to the United States. Eventually, yearly flows of Canadian direct investment in the United States became larger than those of U.S. direct investment in Canada.

Since the 1970s, the FIRA and the NEP have been watered down, deregulation in the financial industries has set in motion a general review of ownership regulations, and the first steps toward privatizing state corporations have brought about the sale of various businesses to U.S. interests. If the field is not quite leveled, the ballgame is certainly not what it used to be.

Thus, the setting is in place for a much broader discussion than simply getting rid of the remaining duties that are applicable to the trade of goods. Talks on bilateral free trade cannot be conducted on the basis of previous liberalization talks between Canada and the United States, nor can they be helped by past negotiations. The nagging suspicion still exists that in some matters the two countries do not know quite what they want, and when they do know what they want, they are not sure what the ultimate result will be.

Scope of the negotiations   A few things about the bilateral negotiations are clear, however. It is well understood in the United States that they represent a remarkable opportunity to test several principles. These include the "right of establishment" and "national treatment." The right of establishment, of course, has been confirmed, but only insofar as nonresidents are allowed to start from scratch. They are still not allowed to buy control of existing corporations. But what if the system were so organized that no single shareholder, whether resident or nonresident, could control certain types of businesses? This question is at the root of a number of discussions concerning Canadian financial institutions.

On the other hand, national treatment does not necessarily imply that all performance requirements are dropped. That impression is an overhang of the FIRA years. A wide variety of businesses belonging to resident interests are subsidized in one form or another, or have guaranteed contracts, and consequently are subject to performance requirements. Others still operate under what amounts to monopoly conditions established by regulatory authorities, and they cannot escape performance guidelines.

Inevitably, the creation of a code that would apply to subsidies should be of considerable interest to the United States, if only to serve as a stepping stone to further negotiations within the GATT framework or in bilateral negotiations with other countries. However, while both Canada and the United States recognize that some arrangement with respect to subsidies is called for, one does not get the impression that precise objectives have been defined. There is a vast range of ways in which, for instance, research and development can be helped—from straight subsidies to any number of fiscal breaks; from national defense contracts to university funding; and from manpower training to rate fixing by regulatory bodies. What exactly should be subject to a code of conduct remains unclear. And even assuming that a given code is adopted, will there not be innumerable ways to circumvent it?

Procurement policies too will come under scrutiny with respect to services as well as goods. There the issues are much clearer. Difficulties arise, however, from the special political organization of Canada. Ontario and Quebec make up two-thirds of Canada's population. With their state corporations and their municipalities, each of these provincial governments has, with respect to procurement, an importance so great in comparison to that of the federal government that a commitment by the federal government alone is not likely to satisfy U.S. interests.

Canada's interests in the bilateral negotiations are much more evident, and in a sense much simpler, than those of the United States. Besides the obvious drive to eliminate tariffs on trade, the main issue is and will remain countervailing action by U.S. authorities. The threat of countervailing duties, and their use in specific sectors of trade, is what started Canada's interest in a free trade arrangement. If for some reason the threat should vanish, that interest would probably wane. In fact, over the full range of goods and services, Canadians have done well for themselves in the U.S. market. Since the fall of the exchange rate, competitive conditions have been reestablished. Beyond the traditional exports of raw materials, beyond the automotive trade, indigenous Canadian companies in sophisticated manufacturing, in advanced technologies, and in financial services have fared well. Canadian investment in the United States in distribution networks has increased greatly. However, a problem remains in that a number of companies fear that success is dangerous, for it may spark countervailing action.

Fear of countervailing action affects the direct investment policies of Canadian companies in the United States. In fact, uncertainty may lead Canadian firms to choose to invest in subsidiaries in the United States rather than establish distribution networks there.

It is clear that the U.S. government will not renounce the use of countervailing action in a bilateral agreement. No country would. But as with respect to subsidies, and for many of the same reasons, an arrangement might be arrived at that would establish rules with some degree of permanency that would be applied in such a way that success in market penetration would not be a criterion justifying countervailing duties.

Procurement policies in the United States are also an issue. The use of such policies by state administrations and state regulation of service activities are impediments to trade. They may not be as spectacular as the practices of a few Canadian provinces, but their impact is nonetheless real. The consequences of the Buy American Act are not negligible. Yet it is the U.S. defense budget that offers huge possibilities for both product and technical service industries. Unfortunately, although justifiably, the barriers imposed to protect national security close much defense procurement to foreign bidders. But that fact does not cancel the consequences on Canadian regional development or research and development. Canadians should calculate the cost of their being shut out of defense possibilities and use it to counterbalance practices on their side that they feel must be protected. It is surprising that they have not raised procurement issues in their discussions of how to maintain cultural protection vis-à-vis the United States within the context of a free trade arrangement.

It is understandable that the Americans should fit bilateral talks with Canadians into a strategic design that eventually might lead to a broadening of the scope of the GATT. Canadians are looking for protection against uncertainty, as they have become more and more attracted by what U.S. markets can offer, and therefore have become more and more dependent on them.

Principles for agreement

In this maze of conflicting interests and diverging approaches, an attempt must be made to set a few principles with respect to ownership rules and national treatment, as they pertain to investment and services. Although Canada is withdrawing gradually from the protective measures of the 1970s with respect to non-resident ownership, no clear idea is emerging as to what kind of policy, if any, should be applied to foreign ownership. The debate over deregulation or "reregulation" of financial institutions is illustrative. After two years of discussion, a consensus has been reached to allow some overlapping of functions. It would permit the establishment of companies to purchase different types of financial institutions. Obviously this would permit further concentration among Canadian financial institutions. Some of these holding companies are already of international importance. Others could become so.

The question remains whether foreign interests could seize control of the financial superstructures that are being built up. The Canadian reaction is understandably that they should not be allowed to. Canadians cannot easily accept the idea that such companies could become wholly owned subsidiaries of large U.S. conglomerates. Thus, the most recent statement of federal intentions, the white paper presented to the House of Commons by the minister of state for financial institutions, retains the 10–25 rule as applied to nonresidents. Furthermore, while foreign financial institutions can be established in Canada, they must start from scratch and expand on the basis of their own merits.

There is, however, an alternative approach. No one, ultimately, resident or nonresident, should be in a position to control huge financial holdings or institutions. Beyond a certain size, open ownership should be favored. Following the spirit of this idea, the Finance Committee of the House of Commons has proposed that any financial group that controlled less than $10 billion of domestic assets could be wholly owned by a single shareholder or a group of shareholders. Then as assets grow, the company's shares would be gradually opened to outside ownership, so that by the time domestic assets reached more than $40 billion, no shareholder or group of shareholders could control more than 10 percent of the stock, which is the present rule applicable to chartered banks. These guidelines make no distinction between resident and nonresident shareholders. In other words, ownership rules can avoid discriminating according to place of residence while still preventing any form of wholly owned subsidiary from exceeding a certain size or scale of operation.

Rules that can be imposed on financial institutions to protect the public interest cannot, of course, be forced on all other types of businesses. Does this then mean that policies designed to prevent takeovers of Canadian firms by nonresidents should by and large be abandoned within the framework of a broad bilateral arrangement? Given the limitations raised with respect to financial institutions, and the exceptions raised for the cultural industries, the answer is probably yes.

In fact, developments in the relationship between the Canadian and provincial governments and business make it easier now than in the past for Canada to renounce its approach with regard to protection against foreign direct investment. During the past several years, this new state of affairs has attracted little attention and, yet, it is of considerable consequence to the present negotiations.

The privatization steps that are now being taken in Canada are subjecting state corporations to reexamination. Because these corporations have multiplied over the years, such reexamination was inevitable. After all, government cannot go on accumulating business ventures without ever getting rid of any of them. For some persons, a strong ideological view is added to the simple urge to clean up; for others, common sense seems an adequate justification for privatization.

Government intervention has not always taken the form of an outright purchase of private business or the establishment of crown corporations. So-called mixed enterprises, where governments or crown corporations own part of the capital stock of a company and often are in a minority position, have proliferated. In fact, government agencies are shareholders in hundreds of corporations in Canada.

All governments do not participate equally in such operations. The federal government has been fairly active. Quebec's government has been very active indeed and one of its agencies now handles the largest portfolio of company shares in all of Canada. Other provinces have been less intensive in their purchases, although Alberta through its Heritage Fund was, at one time, tempted to join the trend. It is interesting that the Ontario government has recently set up a task force to study the investment policies of its various pension funds. It is too soon to speculate whether the findings of this task force will lead to the use of these considerable funds for business financing. But the fact that the task force was set up is revealing.

Government agencies involved in mixed enterprises do not usually manage them or play an active role in their management. Sometimes, however, their clout can be felt when major changes are envisaged, particularly changes of ownership or management. One cannot, for instance, fully understand the power struggle within Canadian Pacific a few years ago, or the change of control in Noranda, without taking into account the role played by the Caisse de Depot et Placement of the Quebec government.

International tools are now available to influence what Canadians have tried to control through formal limitations and protective measures. In this new context, the old reactions have little to contribute and there is no reason why the Canadian authorities cannot enter into formal commitments.

National treatment is a much more difficult issue to deal with when it comes to services. This is due to the remarkable complexity of regulatory structures on both sides of the border. Trying to simplify or standardize regulatory structures and regulations is probably unrealistic. But it is not hopeless to expect progress. For example, the Statement of Principles Respecting Trade in

Services by Life and Health Insurance Companies between the United States and Canada, of November 28, 1986, is interesting. It was signed by the Canadian Life and Health Insurance Association, the American Council of Life Insurance, and the Health Insurance Association of America.

Bilateral trade in life and health insurance amounts to approximately $300 billion in policies in force annually. The trade is conducted by fourteen Canadian companies operating in the United States and eighty-six U.S. companies operating in Canada. The agreement establishes the principles of nondiscrimination between resident and nonresident firms in both countries. The accord is aimed at eliminating legislation, regulation, and administrative practices that discriminate by residency. However, no effort would be made to gain reciprocity of regulatory structures on either side of the border. Any moves toward deregulation or "reregulation" would be pursued as the individual government saw fit to proceed.

This so-called agreement has possibilities. In Canada life insurance is regulated by both the federal government and the provinces, in the United States for the most part by the states. Regulations can differ widely from state to state and province to province. When appreciable differences occur, as they have recently between Ontario and Quebec, companies are caught between difficult choices. What the agreement seems to say is let U.S. companies operating in Canada face those same choices that Canadian companies must make between the regulations of Quebec and Ontario.

A bilateral agreement that required national treatment for U.S. suppliers of services in Canada would imply that there is an existing national treatment for Canadian suppliers in Canada. This might be the case in areas that are under exclusive federal jurisdiction. But in a number of instances, provincial jurisdictions prevail and there is no national treatment in effect within Canada. In other cases, it does not matter very much that national treatment is nonexistent. For instance, security transactions and investment dealers are under strict provincial control and it never has been possible in Canada to set up the equivalent of a Securities and Exchange Commission. Yet as all investment dealers want to have access to the Toronto Stock Exchange, they will in practice follow Ontario regulations, even though in their respective provinces they might have access to somewhat more indulgent provisions.

In a number of other instances, there is in theory and in practice no such thing as a national treatment. Several ways have been suggested in public debate in Canada for handling these situations, which are akin to provincial or state procurement policies vis-à-vis other provinces or other states. One is to use the special circumstances of bilateral negotiations with the United States to try to convince Canadian provinces to relinquish if not some of their constitutional powers, at least the exercise of a few of them. At the time of the constitutional discussions of 1981 and 1982, the federal government made strenuous efforts to reduce the possibilities for provinces to discriminate against each other. In the end, these efforts were to no avail. Efforts today are not likely to be more strenuous, or the resistance weaker, or the result different. There would be even less probability that similar efforts made by the American government with respect to the states would succeed.

A second option is to recognize that provinces in Canada have the right to fragment their markets and therefore to operate on the principle that if true national treatment is to be granted to U.S. business, Canadian provinces must be an integral part of the negotiation process. They must be in a position to accept or refuse the proposals and, in the end, have a right to veto whatever package has been designed. While agreeing to consult provinces closely, the federal government has refused to bring the provinces into the negotiating team. Nevertheless, the Canadian position with respect to certain specific dossiers such as the beer industry grants what amounts to a veto to the provinces. But to accept provincial intervention throughout the process would scuttle the negotiations. The broadside launched by the Ontario government in December 1986 on the subject of national treatment should leave no doubt as to the outcome of this option. It is unfortunate that the test the U.S. government has tried to conduct with respect to investment and services has been with a federal country, and one of the most decentralized at that. Negotiations between unitary states would be simpler.

A third option remains. When a province or a state can and does discriminate with respect to other provinces or other states, national treatment would correspond to the conditions applicable to other provinces or other states. In other words, for U.S. companies to have access to national treatment in Ontario would imply that they would be dealt with as corporations from any other province. That principle is operable. It can be imposed by the federal government. Its possible applications would be numerous and would go far beyond trade in services. It would leave aside the difficulties of maintaining a true common market in each country. Realistically speaking, if those difficulties have not been cleared up after several generations, there is no reason to expect to clear them up in two years simply because the two central governments have decided to talk to each other.

If Canada and the United States want to achieve a comprehensive agreement, it is imperative that specific objectives be more clearly defined than they have been. Furthermore, negotiators should shy away from anything that would imply changes in the political framework of either country. Finally, the negotiations should aim for concrete, even limited, arrangements rather than broad statements of principles that may be satisfying for the soul but will have little chance of becoming operational.

The Hard Choices

WILLIAM NISKANEN

A FREE TRADE AGREEMENT between the United States and Canada is the sort of system that everyone would support behind a veil of ignorance, without thinking about the source of his own income or where he lives. In the real world, however, some groups know, or believe, that they will lose by broader trade. Indeed, it is often the case that the benefits of increased trade are fundamentally unpredictable or diffused while the costs are known and concentrated. As a consequence, the beneficiaries often seem poorly represented in the political process, and those who would lose most vocal.

This is the central political problem of preserving and extending free trade. That problem should be recognized in structuring a proposed trade agreement.

Three approaches have been suggested at various times to try to overcome this political dilemma. The most naive is that typically promoted by economists. They hope that, somehow, increased information—which, of course, they will provide—will increase the potential for agreement. One should be suspicious about this point of view. It suggests that the problem of disagreement on rules that everybody recognizes as good rules is a consequence of too little information. The discussions at this conference, for example, have included appeals for more information on the effects of free trade by region, or on countries other than the United States and Canada, or on exchange rates.

I see no reason why more information on the distribution of outcomes—even if one could be confident about those estimates—is likely to improve the prospects for agreement. In a fundamental sense, one should even question whether the marginal value of information, even if supplied free, is positive. There are a variety of things that I would just as soon not know—the day of my death, the details of my daughters' social life. My preference is not to publish the estimates of bilateral trade balances. In general, they are a source of more mischief than of understanding.

One should be, at least, very careful about the assumption that more comprehensive information on the various dimensions of the trade proposals is likely to improve the prospect for agreement, particularly if the information is about purported distributional effects. My point is that the benefits of good rules are fundamentally unpredictable. You do not know what kind of entrepreneurial activity will take place under a different rule regime. For example, the companies that thought that they would benefit from airline deregulation—United Airlines was the only major carrier that promoted deregulation—have not particularly benefited from it. One company that strongly opposed it—then called Allegheny, now US Air—has been an enormous beneficiary.

In retrospect, it seems quite probable that the United States would never have had airline deregulation if the airline unions had realized how much of their members' then-current salary was economic rent created by the regulatory structure. Possibly as much as 50 percent of the salaries of flight employees in the airlines in 1978 was economic rent of this kind. The unions, in fact, did oppose deregulation, but probably without knowledge about how much they had to lose. So, be careful about the proposition that increased information is somehow going to solve problems, particularly if it bears on distributional changes.

Generally, it is easier to identify losers than to identify gainers. Benefits may be more widely diffused and just lost in the noise of other things going on. More information is not likely, by itself, to bring much support to the table, particularly when, as now, the negotiators are under pressure to come to some kind of agreement they can present to Congress in September. In that time frame, there is no way—fortunately—to get all the information that somebody or other may feel is necessary.

There is another approach that on occasion has worked. Some of the more important changes in economic policy in the United States in the last decade have been a consequence of the convergence of elite opinion and political courage. That is the ideologue's ideal; somehow, an inspired idea that crosses party lines will converge with the courage of members of Congress and other politicians to rise above their parochial interests to support the idea and run with it.

That does happen. That set of conditions led to substantial deregulation of the older forms of price-and-entry regulation in the United States, primarily late in the Carter administration and to some extent in the Reagan administration. That process also led to the Tax Reform Act of 1986. It was not popular pressure, not a balancing of parochial interests, but the power of an idea, courageously supported by a few politicians.

One should not count on that happening, however. In the case of tax reform, it took something close to a religious conversion (with the help, apparently, of two pitchers of beer at a lunch at an Irish pub on Capitol Hill) to lead Senator Bob Packwood from being a defender of almost any kind of fringe benefit or tax preference into being an advocate of tax reform.

Happenings of that nature are rare events. They are not characteristic of normal political activities. I do not sense that there is a prospect for a convergence of elite opinion and political courage that can carry the day for a U.S.-Canada free trade agreement.

The third approach is to play the political game in a way that balances the visible, concentrated losses to some parties with visible, concentrated gains to other parties. If the political contest within the United States is between consumers in general and the steel industry, the consumers are going to lose, as they have on almost every trade issue. If the contest, however, is between the steel industry and the chicken or dairy farmers in the United States, it is not at all clear what the outcome will be.

The negotiating strategy itself must recognize that each party to the negotiation must give the other party enough visible, concentrated benefits to carry the day at home. In other words, the U.S. negotiators must create visible, concentrated benefits so that the Canadian negotiators can go back to the Parliament and say, "This is an example of the major benefits that we will get out of this." It is not enough to point to the very real but very diffused benefits of lower prices, increased efficiency, and so forth.

What does it take for this strategy to succeed in this particular negotiation? For the United States, I believe, it means that the U.S. negotiators must put some change in trade remedies on the table.

For Canada, I believe, it means that the Canadian negotiators must be willing to consider changes affecting agriculture, investment, and services, changes that have the greatest potential for creating major, visible, concentrated benefits in the United States. To that extent, my advice is directly contrary to that of Senator Baucus, which is, "Don't touch trade remedies," or of Donald Macdonald, which is, "Don't touch agriculture or raise any sensitivities about Canadian cultural nationalism."

Instead the strategy should be to counter the visible and

concentrated losses with visible and concentrated gains in each country.

Remarks in the earlier discussions have given me the impression that the existing negotiating strategy is likely to fail. Prospects for this strategy seem fairly pessimistic, given the apparent unwillingness of the political spokesmen to address those matters of greatest concern to the negotiators from the other country.

The strategy that I suggest may also fail, but I think it deserves attention for several reasons. One is that if it succeeds, the benefits will be large. And it is likely to attract other countries at some future time to make similar arrangements with either the United States or Canada or jointly through a multilateral arrangement. Finally, if it fails, it will fail for the right reason and the negotiators will have made the right points in both countries.

What does it take to follow this strategy from a Canadian point of view? I think that the concern that it will force a convergence of regulations is unfounded. What will be important from the U.S. point of view, as Jacques Parizeau has suggested, is a national-treatment standard that may very well be a provincial-treatment standard, but that does not necessarily require a convergence of U.S. and Canadian regulations governing certain kinds of business. It means that when a U.S. firm operates in Ontario, it will be subject to the same types of regulations as an Ontario firm operating in Ontario. It does not mean that the regulations to which that U.S. firm is subject in Ontario will necessarily be like the regulations to which it is subject in the United States. There need be no complex, probably politically infeasible, convergence of the regulatory structures, as long as equal access is protected.

Donald Macdonald was correct in saying that Americans do not understand the sensitivity of Canadians about their cultural nationalism. I certainly do not understand it. The novel that won the *Los Angeles Times*'s prize for the most important fiction of the year in 1986 was written by a Canadian. A Canadian movie with the rather provocative title *The Decline of the American Empire* is popular at the moment among cultural elites around the United States. I do not think that the Canadians have any reason to be apologetic for their cultural institutions or their cultural contributions.

The issue, in any case, is not ending subsidies but ending restrictions on access. A great many publications in the United States are heavily subsidized, particularly those of nonprofit institutions. Many cultural activities in the United States are heavily subsidized. Americans should not be asking Canadians to stop subsidizing cultural activities, many of whose benefits accrue to Americans, but to stop restricting access to American cultural contributions, including game shows and whatever else might be on television, in the Canadian market.

To repeat, the issue concerning trade in cultural activities is not subsidies but access. It may be important, for a variety of reasons, to transfer more of the subsidies from consumers to the budget, as a means of making those subsidies more explicit, but that is not an important aspect of the problem.

For the United States, as I have said, there is no meaningful prospect for a trade agreement to which the Canadians will agree and that has any prospect of being viable for long, unless U.S. negotiators are prepared to put on the table some change in the U.S. trade remedy systems, specific to trade within this agreement. That does not necessarily mean generalizing those terms to the rest of the world, and, in an important sense, it is probably better not to do so.

It should be possible to make a case, as Professor Hudec has done, for dropping the antidumping systems entirely, as long as a clear right to re-export exists. If Americans can send back to Canada products that are offered in the United States at a lower price than in Canada, there will be no way to maintain a two-price system. The two-price system will disappear if this kind of re-export or so-called boomerang provision is in the agreement.

As a further means of reducing the controversy over subsidies, it should be possible to move toward a net subsidy concept. This is often a complex determination, but it will appeal to a general sense of fairness. Existing American subsidy laws and counter-vailing duty laws do not recognize the concept of net subsidies. Regardless of whether there are major subsidies in the United States on a given product, subsidies by other countries on the same product are countervailable. The net subsidy concept, if administrable, would help to balance matters.

I want to see a good, durable, agreement—one that will serve as a model for the current round of negotiations under the General Agreement on Tariffs and Trade. If the multilateral negotiations are not successful, Canada and the United States could invite other countries to join the arrangement they had worked out together. Such an agreement will be possible only if each country is willing to address hard choices within its own area of political responsibility so that the solutions to key issues will be politically acceptable in the other country.

General Discussion

KNIEWASSER asked Freeman how an agreement on free trade in services would enable a bank-owned Canadian securities firm to have access to the United States market in view of the restrictions of the Glass-Steagall Act.

Freeman replied that it would require changes in the Glass-Steagall Act; he believes such changes will take place in the next one to three years. The United States has little choice. Both U.S. industry and the financial services sector realize that foreign competition is making the regulatory framework in the United States increasingly outdated. Companies are starting to be seriously hurt as a result.

Freeman said there are numerous political obstacles in the way of a complete overhaul, if not dismantling, of the Glass-Steagall Act. At the same time, a powerful coalition has been formed among industrial firms, banks, and nonbank financial service firms—large and small—to move in that direction. In this connection, Gerald Corrigan, president of the Federal Reserve Bank of New York, recently published his own proposal for an extensive overhaul.

In regard to the prospects for the trade negotiations, Freeman acknowledged the many problems brought out in the panel presentations and the note of pessimism they conveyed. However, there are forces on the other side, most notably the new political push at the highest levels in both governments to arrive at workable solutions to problems. He considered this attitude to be a new factor of major significance.

MacLaury asked Freeman what he had meant in asking for national treatment for certain financial services. Would he, for example, accept a situation where Canada chose as a matter of national policy to restrict access to officially backed electronic transfer facilities to deposit-taking institutions—that is, to banks? Access to these facilities by foreign nonbank entities, then, would not be possible, even though they had been accorded national treatment.

160

Freeman replied that he would not be satisfied; he would want both national treatment and reciprocity. His company wanted nondiscriminatory access to the payment systems of other countries just as American industrial companies want nondiscriminatory access for their products to markets abroad. As a matter of fact, he believes Canada is moving away from a policy of according access to the payment system to depository institutions alone.

Freeman added that in the U.S.-Israel Free Trade Agreement, which includes reference to services, his company is trying to work problems out pragmatically on a day-to-day basis. He believes the experience gained will be useful in the Canada-U.S. context.

Parizeau disclaimed pessimism about the outcome of the negotiations and he was certainly not negative about the benefits of a comprehensive arrangement. His concerns apply to the shortness of the autumn deadline, principally because he suspects that the discussion about such ideas as national treatment and nondiscriminatory access is still at the level of broad concepts. It is essential to get down to concrete issues and determine what can, or cannot, be done within the existing time frame. For example, as he had pointed out in his presentation, the life insurance companies of the two countries in discussing these questions decided it would be useless to try to merge the two regulatory bodies or harmonize their policy orientations. Instead, they defined national treatment in such a way as to make it possible to reach useful specific agreements affecting their operations in the other country.

Niskanen thought the two countries should be seeking a constitution-like agreement, rather than a statutory or regulatory agreement. Such an agreement should avoid excrutiating detail and great specificity. It should set forth agreed principles as the basis for working out problems and also establish a dispute-settlement mechanism. It should not attempt, between February and September, to settle detailed problems on trade between the United States and Canada. That probably is the only approach that is feasible between February and September, and may also be the most desirable. It should not be necessary to go back to a major agreement with Canada in order to change some minor U.S. provision, statute, or regulation, which happens to be covered by rules spelled out in the agreement.

A certain amount of specificity is necessary. The agreement must be specific enough to make sure that the Canadian and American negotiators are using words in the same way and that they are understood in the same way in Ottawa and in Washington when ratification is considered.

Macdonald returned to the cultural question. He said that during the first thirty-five years of his life there had not been a Canadian feature film industry, first because the funds were not available, and second because the foreign-owned distributors would not show Canadian films because they were not compelled to do so. Once they were compelled to do so by government policy, Canadian films were produced. Similarly, there was no Canadian popular music industry until the Canadian Radio and Television Commission required a minimum Canadian content. After that, Canadian singers appeared and subsequently became internationally popular. He repeated the figures he had cited earlier: 70 percent of the magazines and 80 percent of the prime-time content on English-language television are foreign, principally from the United States. Must the United States have 100 percent of the market before it agrees it has been fairly treated?

Niskanen replied it is unwise to specify what the percentages ought to be, in any case. The issue is an agreement on rules and not an agreement on outcomes. There is no basis for an agreement on outcomes—the preferences for outcomes in one country are not necessarily inconsistent with preferences in the other country. An agreement on rules by which this trade will be conducted means that both parties must be prepared to accept outcomes consistent with those rules.

Richard Dawson asked whether the U.S. Congress would be prepared to approve an agreement confined mainly to principles rather than one that specifically covers the main areas. Freeman said that most members of Congress are uncommitted on the question of Canada-U.S. free trade but a large reservoir of good will toward Canada exists in Congress. If a useful agreement is negotiated—whether emphasizing general principles or specific provisions—and active measures are taken to mobilize support, he believes the votes for passage will be there.

Parizeau said the main Canadian concern in the negotiations is to obtain some relief from U.S. protectionist actions, which Canadians see as a growing threat. If they were asked in return to agree on some statements of general principles, they would readily accept. However, Parizeau could not see how an agreement based on broad principles would be acceptable to the United States, either in satisfaction of its bilateral interests or to use as a model or pressure point for the GATT negotiations. Statements of principles would need some meat—at the least opening new vistas that could become operational for services and direct investment. Some minimum specificity is essential. Otherwise, the resulting free trade arrangement will consist of some reductions of tariffs, limited arrangements designed to stabilize the incidence of duties, and a few high-flying ideas. That will not be considered satisfactory. If Canadians want to get something concrete as far as countervailing duties are concerned, they will have to be concrete in other areas.

Niskanen predicted that Congress will not go along unless the agreement creates some strong vested interests in its coming into being. The only way to do that is to include agriculture, services, and investment in the agenda. It will be essential to have American businessmen and farmers testify strongly in its support so as to counter the predictable opposition by those who believe or know they will lose. Without the support of such newly created vested interests in the agreement, he did not believe the strong commitment of the president and the administration would be enough.

Openings in Agricultural Trade

A Canadian View of
Agricultural Issues

T. K. WARLEY *and* R. R. BARICHELLO

LIBERALIZATION of bilateral trade in farm and food products is widely acknowledged to be fraught with difficulties. The agrifood sector in both Canada and the United States is extensively regulated. And in both countries conflict exists between the attainment of the goals of national agricultural policies on the one hand and the obligation to open borders and create a "level playing field" of competitive conditions for production and exchange on the other. This paper identifies some of the more important agricultural and trade policy issues that are involved in the achievement of "the broadest possible package of mutually beneficial trade barrier reductions" to which the two governments are committed.

The conflict of interests unsettling the North American negotiations is also, of course, at the heart of global agricultural trade policy difficulties. Thus, its handling and resolution in the bilateral context has great significance for the multilateral trade negotiations on agriculture under the General Agreement on Tariffs and Trade (GATT) in the remaining years of the decade. As in the multilateral negotiations, bilateral negotiations on agriculture will have to grapple with the distortions in food production and trade that derive from such nontariff measures as price and income support and stabilization programs, economic regulations, market control arrangements, and technical standards.

The task will be exceptionally difficult for three basic reasons. First, national agricultural and food policies have important objectives and powerful constituencies. No one wishes to jeopardize those elements of public policy that are intended to correct for market failures, provide public goods, or promote development of the agrifood sector, and few politicians or bureaucrats are anxious to surrender protection provided to the less competitive firms and product groups in their national agrifood industries. Second, frontier measures and trade arrangements for farm and

T. K. Warley presented the paper and represented the authors in the discussion.

167

food products are simply external adjuncts of the interventionist policies pursued within national borders. It follows that the liberalization of cross-border trade entails changing and harmonizing domestic price support and stabilization programs, economic regulations, marketing arrangements, and technical standards. Third, the task is not only politically unpopular, it is also technically difficult because of differences in such matters as the extent of intervention, commodity coverage, assistance provided, the policy instruments used, and institutional arrangements in the two countries. For these reasons, even if there is the political will to create freer and fairer arrangements for trade in agricultural products, the practical accomplishment of that goal will not be an easy task.

Canada's agricultural trade

The Canadian agrifood system as a whole is trade-driven. Exports of farm and food products account for around 50 percent of aggregate farm receipts. The comparable figure for the United States and the European Community is around 20 percent. Grains, oilseeds, and red meats, which together account for around 64 percent of the gross value of Canadian farm output, are effectively priced in world and continental markets. The 15 percent of output represented by horticultural products, potatoes, and tobacco is partially protected. Only the dairy, poultry, and eggs subsectors (21 percent of gross output) are sized to satisfy domestic consumption at "made in Canada" prices and are fully insulated from world market conditions.

Since 1983 the United States has been Canada's largest, fastest growing, and most diversified export market for agrifood exports (see tables 1–3). In 1985, the United States took 27 percent of total Canadian agricultural and food exports, 59 percent of all nongrain and oilseed products exports, and over 75 percent of total shipments of such major export categories as beef and pork, live cattle and hogs, and sugar and maple products. In recent years, the United States has supplied about 60 percent of Canada's agricultural imports. Canada has ranked fifth (behind Japan, the USSR, the Netherlands, and Mexico) as an outlet for U.S. agrifood exports but has been the largest single recipient of U.S. exports of fruits and vegetables and the third largest outlet for exports of livestock and livestock products and soybean cake and meal.

The current and growing dependence of the Canadian agrifood system on trade makes the attainment of assured and improved access to foreign markets the principal objective of Canada's agricultural commercial diplomacy.

Table 1. *Destination of Canada's Agricultural Exports and Origin of Its Agricultural Imports, Various Years, 1977–84*
Percent

Country	1977–79[a]	1982	1983	1984
Export destination				
Developed countries	57.9	47.3	46.6	47.9
United States	16.4	17.3	18.3	21.7
Japan	17.5	13.4	13.6	13.6
European Community[b]	20.9	13.3	12.0	10.2
Others	3.1	3.2	2.7	2.4
Centrally planned economies	21.9	35.3	33.3	30.7
USSR	7.1	20.6	17.3	19.6
China	7.1	8.0	9.9	6.3
Others	7.7	6.7	6.0	4.8
Less developed countries	20.2	17.4	20.1	21.4
Import origins				
Developed countries	77.2	79.7	79.8	78.3
United States	57.3	60.5	60.1	59.0
Japan	0.5	0.5	0.6	0.6
Australia	5.2	4.6	3.5	3.0
New Zealand	2.3	2.4	2.7	1.7
European Community[b]	7.6	7.5	8.2	9.2
Others	2.0	4.2	3.7	4.8
Centrally planned economies	2.0	2.4	1.8	1.7
Less developed countries	20.8	17.9	19.4	20.0

Sources: Agriculture Canada, *Canada's Trade in Agricultural Products 1982, 1983 and 1984* (Ottawa: Ministry of Supply and Services, 1985), and *1979, 1980, 1981*, no. 82/3.
a. Average of three years.
b. Nine countries in 1977–79; ten thereafter.

Table 2. *Canada's Trade with the United States in All Commodities and Agricultural Products, 1985*
Millions of Canadian dollars

Goods	Exports	Imports	Balance
All commodities	90,377	74,377	16,000
Agricultural products	2,427	3,431	−1,004
Grains and grain products	257	264	−7
Animal feeds	37	82	−45
Oilseeds and oilseed products	113	388	−274
Live animals	394	71	323
Beef and pork	630	155	475
Other animal products	119	233	114
Dairy products	15	16	−1
Poultry and eggs	31	104	−73
Fruits and nuts	77	811	−734
Vegetables, excluding potatoes	86	531	−445
Potatoes and potato products	58	45	13
Seeds	19	55	−36
Maple products	26	. . .	26
Sugar	30	39	−9
Tobacco	31	5	−26
Other	440	632	−192

Source: Agriculture Canada, *Canada's Trade in Agricultural Products 1983, 1984, and 1985*, tables 7, 8.

Table 3. *Canada's Agricultural Exports to the United States as a Share of Total Exports, by Commodity Group, 1978–85*
Percent

Goods	1978–80[a]	1981	1982	1983	1984	1985
All agricultural exports	15.6	14.3	17.3	18.3	21.7	27.2
Grains	0.9	0.8	1.4	1.2	1.3	2.4
Grain products	34.4	31.7	55.4	57.2	51.7	62.5
Animal feeds	38.1	38.7	37.7	39.6	47.8	19.9
Oilseeds	3.5	9.5	6.7	8.4	6.3	8.5
Oilseed products	4.9	9.3	9.3	21.0	13.9	14.6
Live animals	86.8	82.8	88.6	87.6	90.4	90.6
Meats	47.7	52.2	59.0	61.5	71.9	76.4
Other animal products	22.3	23.3	20.7	23.7	22.8	27.0
Dairy products	7.2	4.2	3.8	5.0	5.8	6.9
Poultry and eggs	29.0	22.9	27.8	45.0	51.6	67.3
Fruits and nuts	61.5	44.8	53.7	62.2	65.3	73.3
Vegetables, excluding potatoes	28.0	22.4	30.8	38.8	40.0	37.7
Potatoes and potato products	32.7	58.3	47.7	45.2	50.3	60.4
Seeds for sowing	49.4	58.3	56.8	78.8	63.2	54.3
Maple products	84.2	85.2	89.9	87.3	83.2	81.3
Sugar	72.8	2.5	54.2	89.3	95.8	93.8
Tobacco, raw	13.9	16.0	28.0	25.0	24.1	33.3
Other agricultural products	67.1	59.6	64.5	74.2	79.1	83.7

Source: Agriculture Canada, *Canada's Trade in Agricultural Products*, various years.
a. Average of three years.

The larger context

Canada is integrated into the world economy to an unusual degree. In 1985, its exports of $116 billion of goods accounted for 24 percent of gross domestic product. And $90 billion or 78 percent of these exports went to the United States. Furthermore, the dependence of the Canadian economy on exports to the United States has grown over time. The Third Option of the Trudeau administration under which Canada sought to loosen its trade dependence on the U.S. market by diversifying its export outlets has failed.

In 1985, Canada imported $103 billion of goods, $74 billion, or 72 percent, of which were from the United States. The two-way trade of $164 billion was the global economy's largest bilateral merchandise trade flow.

The major consideration that has led Canadian authorities to seek to conclude a comprehensive bilateral trade agreement with the United States is the perception that Canada's access to the U.S. market—and hence present and future levels of national income and employment—is at risk. The threat to Canadian access is seen as arising in two forms. First, there is a perception that the U.S. Congress, U.S. industry, and organized labor are drifting toward a protectionist trade stance in response to such factors as the massive deficit in merchandise trade, persistent surplus capacity and unemployment, fears about the "deindustrialization of America," and mounting discontent with the trade barriers and practices of other countries. The protectionist mood is manifest in the drift of authority over trade matters from the executive branch to Congress, in draft trade legislation before Congress, in the pronouncements of many private interest groups, in the emphasis on "fair" trade rather than "free" trade, and in the proliferation of restrictive trade actions.

Second, the more vigorous application of the contingent protection provisions of existing U.S. trade law—that is, the trade remedies against unfair competiton due to subsidies and dumping and the safeguard measures against fair but intolerably disruptive competition—threatens future access for a wide range of agricultural, resource, and industrial products. Furthermore, Canada's exposure to U.S. contingent protection measures will continue to grow as U.S. authorities press the "fair trade for free trade" bargain offered by the administration to the Congress, and as new trade legislation widens the definition of what constitutes unfair competition and mandates retaliation against a host of measures that figure prominently in the instrumentation of Canadian economic and social policies. The latter include important elements of the sector-specific industrial policies and programs that are operated for agriculture in Canada under the rubric of national agricultural policy.

Canada therefore has three principal objectives in seeking a trade accord with the United States. It wishes to secure access to the U.S. market by limiting the effects of U.S. trade remedy laws on Canada and by developing clear and workable distinctions between acceptable assistance programs and unacceptable (and therefore countervailable) subsidies. It proposes to improve access to the U.S. market by lowering tariff and nontariff barriers to trade and obtaining national treatment for Canadian goods and services in markets affected by U.S. state and federal government procurement policies. Finally, Canadian negotiators hope to enshrine this access by establishing effective mechanisms for the adjudication and settlement of disputes.

Many Canadians favor free trade with the United States for less defensive and more positive reasons. These include the stimulus that would be given to the restructuring and diversification of the Canadian economy, the opportunities that would be created for the establishment of world-scale plants and for adding value in Canada's resource industries, and the improvements in productivity that would flow from the deregulation that would be forced on the Canadian economy by the need to compete in the continental market. To those who hold to this agenda, the creation of a free trade area is the centerpiece of a market-oriented industrial strategy for Canada.

For those who formulate trade policy for the Canadian agrifood sector, improving the security of access to the U.S. market for Canadian farm and food products is the only objective of any consequence. Restrictions on access are not now a major problem, and few see bilateral trade liberalization as an important element of a sector-specific industrial strategy. And even improved access to the U.S. market is viewed as a second-order objective, sub-ordinate to the larger imperatives of obtaining improved access to extracontinental markets for grains and oilseeds and creating better functioning world markets for these products.

The objectives of the United States in the negotiations are less clear, for U.S. authorities are responding to a Canadian initiative. Certainly, in a narrow bilateral context, the United States wants the improved access to the Canadian market that would result from a reduction in high Canadian tariffs and changes in a host of federal and provincial regulations that constitute nontariff barriers to trade. Beyond that, however, it appears that U.S. leaders view a bilateral accord as providing a signal to the rest of the world of the continuing commitment of the United States to a liberal international economic order. A bilateral agreement also can provide a model for the coming GATT round of multilateral trade negotiations insofar as it liberalizes exchanges between the world's largest trade partners and offers an opportunity to devise, test, and demonstrate codes of conduct and adjudication mecha-nisms—which would serve as prototypes for the GATT—in such new areas as trade in services and intellectual investment, as well as in old and intractable areas such as government procurement, technical barriers, subsidies, and agriculture. A bilateral accord would also serve as an alternative to the GATT if it proves that the multilateral commercial diplomacy followed in the postwar era has run its course.

For the United States, as for Canada, the specific trade and farm income benefits that might flow from better bilateral trade arrangements for farm and food products are not inconsequential, but again they are not decisive. For both countries, the primary focus of their commercial diplomacy in the agricultural sector is on trade in grains and oilseeds (which are not, and will not be, traded continentally in large quantities) with other countries

(Europe and Japan), and in another forum (the GATT). In this sense agricultural trade is caught up in the bilateral negotiations perhaps mainly because of its potential significance for the multilateral negotiations to follow.

Coincident Canadian agricultural and national interests

Canada has less reason than the United States for including agricultural and food trade on the negotiating agenda since it is apparent that the economic interests of some influential commodity groups and regions will be impaired and some farm programs and institutional arrangements will be jeopardized in an arrangement providing for free north-south (and, at home, freer east-west) trade. Nonetheless, the Canadian agricultural and national interests do coincide in three areas.

First, those competitive sections of Canadian agriculture that successfully export to the United States need relief from the uncertainty, harassment, and expense resulting from the sometimes quixotic application of U.S. federal trade remedy laws and the protectionist application by states of technical standards. This is most obvious for those commodity groups that have been or may become the subject of U.S. countervailing, antidumping, and safeguard actions and of states' regulations. These include hogs, pork, cattle, beef, potatoes, onions, carrots, tobacco, raspberries, cut flowers, and sugar.

Canadian producers of these products share the view that the provisions and implementation of U.S. contingent protection or trade remedy laws are a veil for protectionism and a vehicle for the harassment of Canadian traders by groups in the United States who prefer not to meet fair competition. They believe that these laws constitute an effective nontariff trade barrier insofar as the judgments made by U.S. agencies are inconsistent, subject to political influence, unpredictable, and expensive to contest. Definitions of what constitutes a countervailable subsidy are ever widening and increasingly unreasonable. Tests are not onerous for determining injury from imports to domestic U.S. producers and no causal link must be established between assistance programs and trade distortions and injury. Beyond that, U.S. contingent protection ignores the effect of U.S. subsidies.

For these reasons, affected or threatened commodity and product groups in the Canadian agricultural and food industry would welcome revised contingent protection arrangements that classified subsidies into three categories—prohibited, permissible, and countervailable—on proof of injury; had a higher de minimus definition; provided for common measures of distortion and injury; required higher standards of proof of causation and injury; had more rigorous standards for standing and specificity; placed limits on cumulation; confined countervailing duties to the net of the two nations' subsidies; and provided for binational administration of trade remedy laws, starting perhaps with joint fact-finding and impartial advisory mechanisms and moving eventually through binding arbitration to supranational operation of common legislation. Arrangements such as these would provide Canadian farmers and food processors with the assured access to the United States market that they need.

Second, Canadian producers of many farm and food products could expect to find expanded market opportunities in the United States if the United States would lower its tariff and nontariff barriers, presumably in a manner that would provide preferential access to the U.S. market for Canadian suppliers. Noncommodity groups hurt by the trade remedy laws would also feel the benefits of improved access; so too would producers of cole crops, asparagus, mushrooms, some flowers, fruits and nursery stock, oilseed products, maple products, animal feeds, seeds, and a very large number of processed foods in which Canadian suppliers are competitive.

Third, conceptually at least, since what constitutes "a level playing field of competitive conditions" would be defined by Ottawa as well as by Washington, Canadian authorities would have a vehicle for influencing those U.S. agricultural subsidies and industry aids that are perceived by Canada as providing unfair advantages to U.S. producers, processors, and merchandisers in competing with Canadians in continental and third-country markets. Such subsidies are legion, ranging from the deficiency payments made to U.S. producers of the basic crops, through the operation of U.S. marketing orders and agreements, to the subsidized supply of transport services, irrigation water, and rangeland.

Divergent agricultural and national interests   Notwithstanding the arguments for change, the major Canadian farmer organizations and many commodity groups are unequivocally opposed to the inclusion of agriculture in arrangements for free trade between Canada and the United States. And the numerous parliamentary groups, provincial governments, commissions, and research agencies that have addressed the matter have differed only in the degree of their reluctance to have Canadian agricultural policies and associated agricultural trade agreements disturbed. Even those who concede that agricultural trade might have to be included, and those few who actively advocate its inclusion, have emphasized that this will present exceptional difficulties and require special arrangements with respect to the extent, form, management, and timing of the integration of the food systems of the two countries.

The difficulties stem in part from fundamental differences in the instrumentation and parameters of agricultural policy in Canada and the United States. The two countries' policy objectives are similar insofar as they emphasize farm income support, preserving a family farm structure, assuring adequate food supplies, promoting development of industry, and the like. But Canadian agricultural policy differs from U.S. policy in many ways, including a higher overall level of intervention and regulation in agriculture and a less marked resolve to move to more market-oriented systems (even at the rhetorical level); the provision of distinctly higher levels of support for the dairy, poultry, horticultural, and red meats subsectors; a broader commitment to stabilize producers' returns for a wider range of products and generally to share with farmers the downside risks of markets; the more extensive use of explicit supply-management techniques that involve formula pricing and farm-level quotas and that require border controls for their operation; a deeper commitment to "orderly marketing" through producer-controlled national marketing agencies and provincial commodity boards; the active involvement of provincial governments in agriculture in ways that make them equal managing partners with the federal government, or that result in their effectively operating their own food sector assistance and development policies and programs; and the conviction that agricultural policy in Canada is an important means of attaining the national imperative of balanced regional economic development and of fostering cohesion in an intrinsically fragile economic and political union.

In addition, and perhaps more tangibly, the opposition of many farm and food industry groups to continental free trade in agrifood products stems from their perception that their economic interests would be adversely affected if the Canada-U.S. border were opened, if Canadian agro-industry assistance programs were outlawed or constrained, and if present institutional arrangements were jeopardized. Adverse economic effects are seen to include, first and foremost, lower prices, profits, and asset values from a reduction in the income transferred by border protection (tariffs, quotas, health and sanitary standards, technical regulations, and state trading); domestic market control programs (formula pricing, supply reduction, discriminatory marketing, and restrictions on food analogs); and direct subsidies to products (stabilization payments, industrial milk subsidy) and to inputs (transport, insurance, capital, and credit). Industry groups would also count as adverse developments the emergence of a more unstable and risky economic environment, a reduction in the degree of control exercised by producers over markets and over their economic destinies, and the circumscribing or foreclosure of future policy options.

Commodity implications

From a commodity-centered point of view, the economic and institutional effects of a fully open border and the equalization of competitive conditions do not look promising. To be sure, substantial benefits could accrue to participants in the Canadian agrifood system if Canada could persuade the United States to change its agricultural price and income support arrangements but there is pessimism about the feasibility of this. By contrast, the inventory of potential negative effects is large and easily calculated. Hence the antipathy of major Canadian commodity groups and some input suppliers, food processors, and provincial governments to free trade with the United States in farm and food products.

Grains

Bilateral free trade in grains would erode the ability of the Canadian Wheat Board to continue its control over the marketing of western grains; to provide equitable access to the Canadian elevator system and to markets; to exclude imports of wheat, wheat flour, and grain products; to extract a price premium for wheat consumed for food domestically; and to obtain a quality premium for grains sold off shore by maintaining the integrity of the control system for types, varieties, and quality standards. Open borders would create pressure to remove the transport subsidies provided by the Western Grains Transportation Act on grains shipped to U.S. markets via Vancouver or Thunder Bay, and by the Feed Grains Assistance Program on western-grown feed grains shipped into eastern Canada. And growers in central Canada would lose the price premium on soft wheats now secured under the Two Price Wheat Plan.

Oilseeds

Removal of the tariff on soybean oil would create difficulties for crushers. And termination of the import embargo on margarine would cause losses for oilseeds crushers, margarine manufacturers, and milk producers and dairy processors.

Dairy, Poultry Meats, and Eggs

Bilateral free trade would bring an end to cost-of-production pricing, supply management, regional market sharing, and marketing board monopoly powers. Prices would go down 20–30 percent as Canadian prices fell to U.S. border-state market levels (on fluid milk, poultry, and eggs) or support levels (on industrial milk). There would be a consequential reduction in profitability and asset values—including the loss of $6 billion in quota values. A significant reduction would have to be made in the numbers of producers and processors, and there would be some adjustments in the location of production in Canada.

Livestock and Meat

Most of the effects of freer and more secure trade in livestock would be positive, but there would be some risk to herd health if health and sanitary regulations were changed and a consequential threat to off-shore exports of breeding stock and semen. The permissibility or level of benefits provided under federal and provincial or "tripartite" price and margin stabilization programs would be challenged.

Horticulture

Various groups in this multiproduct subsector would be affected differently. Some producers would lose the protection afforded by seasonal tariffs in the 10–20 percent nominal range, the prohibition on consignment selling, and regulations on the use of containers. Capital grant programs for storage and processing facilities would end. The price setting and negotiating powers of some producers' marketing boards would be eroded.

Wine and Grapes

Open borders would end the protection provided against U.S. wines by the discriminatory procurement, listing, and margin policies of provincial liquor monopolies and by provincial "domestic content" regulations.

Tobacco

Free trade across the border would foreclose the proposed formation of a national marketing agency with price setting, market sharing, and supply management powers.

Food Processing

While the results for the heterogeneous and multiproduct food processing industry would be diverse, some processing sectors would face loss of protection now afforded by escalating tariffs, import quotas on supply-managed products, and regulated pricing systems for raw-product inputs. Canadian firms would face intensified competition from U.S. firms that enjoy longer production runs, higher labor productivity, lower wage rates, lower fringe benefit and social program costs, and lower costs of raw products, packaging materials, transport, and machinery. Processors would be victims of double jeopardy if prices and supplies of raw products continued to be regulated but trade in intermediate and final products were to be liberalized. And U.S. parents would be likely to move their branch plants out of Canada.

These potentially negative effects of freer agricultural trade on national and regional farmers' incomes, agricultural asset values, and farm numbers, and on established policies and institutions, are readily predictable. By contrast, the possible gains from improved and assured access for Canadian products in the U.S. market are distinctly less tangible and more speculative. Will the United States be willing to change its trade remedy laws and procedures in ways that provide more assured access for Canadian exports? What forms and levels of assistance will be deemed not to constitute unfair competition? Is it realistic to think that the United States will change the nature and parameters of its agricultural programs in response to Canadian demands for a "level playing field" on which to compete? Will a strengthening of the Canadian dollar eliminate the expanded market opportunities that changes in the present conditions of access to the U.S. market would otherwise provide? However one looks at it, it appears to most participants in the Canadian food system that there is a fundamental asymmetry within bilateral negotiations between the benefits that realistically can be secured for the Canadian agrifood sector and the agricultural concessions that the United States will most assuredly seek.

With this perception it is not surprising that the weight of organized agricultural opinion in Canada has favored the selective exclusion of entire commodity subsystems from the negotiating agenda. Farm organizations advocate dealing with the specific problem of threatened access for farm and food products in a general accord on contingent protection law and practice. They would then treat the multilateral negotiations in the GATT as the primary vehicle for seeking improved access to markets since this is the arena in which expanded market opportunities might be obtained for Canada's largest and most competitive export sub-sectors, grains, oilseeds, and red meats.

Such a strategy does not appear to be acceptable to the United States. American authorities are animated by concerns about the United States' $170 billion (in U.S. dollars) merchandise trade deficit (including a $16 billion deficit in 1985 with Canada), with its shrinking agricultural trade surpluses with the world and with Canada (table 4), and with the badly needed trade balance and farm income benefits that could result from increased sales of agrifood products to Canada. In addition, agriculture is one of the few major industry groups in the United States that continue to support a liberal international economic order, and it must be kept "on side" if the administration's attempt to make world trade freer and fairer in a new round of multilateral trade negotiations is to succeed.

It would also be a bad precedent for the GATT round if agriculture was excluded from a bilateral accord. For if the United States and Canada cannot agree to open their borders to each other's farm products and to change their national agricultural policies in ways that remove their distorting effects on trade, what hope is there of engaging Europe and Japan in meaningful negotiations on improving the multilateral trading system for agricultural products? And the United States, of course, is hoping that the bilateral negotiations will generate constructive approaches to global agricultural trade policy issues that can subsequently be adopted in the GATT.

There are, nevertheless, features of a bilateral accord on agriculture that would be highly unwelcome to U.S. authorities, the Congress, and some U.S. commodity groups. First, more open

Table 4. *Canada's Agricultural Trade Balance with the United States, 1979–85*
Millions of Canadian dollars

Year	Exports to the United States	Imports from the United States	Trade balance
1979	1,007	2,678	−1,671
1980	1,113	2,916	−1,803
1981	1,260	3,264	−2,004
1982	1,606	3,060	−1,454
1983	1,736	3,118	−1,382
1984	2,236	3,609	−1,373
1985	2,427	3,431	−1,004[a]

Source: Agriculture Canada, *Canada's Trade in Agricultural Products*, various years.
a. In 1985, Canada had a surplus of $447 million in its trade with the United States in alcoholic beverages.

access for Canadian farm and food products would complicate the operation of U.S. commodity programs for grains, dairy products, and sugar. Second, U.S. producers of oilseeds, tobacco, potatoes, other root vegetables, soft fruits, and a range of processed foods would resist further penetration of the market by Canadian products. Third, neither U.S. authorities nor U.S. farm groups would welcome challenges from Canada to U.S. commodity price and income support policies, import quotas, and agricultural resource pricing policies.

Possible
outcomes

Once negotiations are fully joined, a range of outcomes is conceivable both on issues that cut across commodity lines and on those that are commodity-specific.

On the crosscutting issues, the principal task is to get a grip on the trade-distorting nontariff measures that are linked to domestic agricultural price and marketing policies. And of these, subsidy policies are the most important. Possibilities include a ban on the use of export subsidies in bilateral agricultural trade (not a significant problem at present) and codification of the relationship between the use of subsidies to production and the application of countervailing duties in response to them. For Canadian agriculture the key elements of a bilateral production subsidies code are definition of the types of subsidies, industry aids, and expenditures on public goods that are and are not countervailable; agreement that countervailing duties should not exceed the net difference in subsidies between the two countries; more onerous burdens of proof of injury and higher injury thresholds than those now in effect; and the creation of an impartial dispute settlement mechanism. In practical terms, Canada's highest priority must be to secure agreement by the United States that the stop-loss, market-oriented, low-slung economic safety nets available to producers under the Agricultural Stabilization Acts of 1975 and 1985 and the Western Grains Stabilization Act of 1976 have a neutral effect on production and trade and, therefore, are not countervailable.

On commodity-specific negotiations three broad possibilities can be envisioned. First, it is conceivable that a decision could be reached that, for selected commodities, trade should not be liberalized and that existing farm programs, institutional arrangements, and border measures should be left substantially intact. This might be the preferred outcome where the two countries operate parallel systems of economic regulation but with different program instruments and parameters; where very little additional trade would result from opening the border and changing national commodity programs; where severe dislocations in terms of incomes, asset values, farm numbers, and institutional arrangements would nonetheless occur in one country if support and trade arrangements were changed; and where the regulatory systems are a burden on the citizens of the country that employs them rather than on the trading partner. These four conditions might all be met, for instance, by Canadian pricing, marketing, and trade arrangements for fluid and industrial milk, poultry meats, and eggs, which are the subsectors most vehemently opposed to being included in a bilateral trade arrangement. The same conclusions might be reached with respect to U.S. support and trade regimes for sugar and, less certainly, for grains and dairy products. In short, a reciprocal agreement might exclude particularly difficult agricultural subsectors that offer little scope for substantial trade creation.

A second possibility is that the trade and farm income objectives of the country with the lower prices and costs might be satisfied with a negotiated marginal increase in its market share in the country with the higher prices (plus the rents that accompany market management). This would permit the country conceding improved access to retain its regulatory arrangements for the correspondingly reduced domestic output. Such a settlement might be negotiable concerning U.S. access to regulated Canadian markets for dairy and poultry products.

The third possibility is, of course, that borders might be fully opened and national agricultural assistance programs that distort competitive conditions be harmonized or eliminated. There is no doubt that this would require adjustments in parts of the Canadian agrifood system, especially among primary producers of milk, poultry meats, eggs, grapes, and some horticultural products and among several sections of the food processing industry. To ameliorate the pressures of adjustment, the exchange rate between the Canadian and U.S. dollars could be left as it is (where it seems likely to provide substantial protection to Canadian producers for some years to come) and the phase-in period for agreed arrangements might be as long as a decade, so that abrupt dislocations would not be required. Finally, a bilateral trade accord should certainly permit (and equity and political realities will require) the provision of generous adjustment assistance to firms, industries, and regions that suffer losses as a consequence of the creation of a comprehensive bilateral trade agreement.

Concluding observations

An intense debate is being conducted in Canada about the merits of entering into a closer trading relationship with the United States. Much of the debate is concerned with what is nonnegotiable if Canada is to obtain net economic benefits while preserving its national sovereignty and cultural identity. At present there is a consensus only on the imperatives of Canada retaining its social programs, cultural subsidies, and regional development grants; obtaining the right to provide adjustment assistance over lengthy phase-in periods; and preserving the freedom to control its exchange rate. The negotiations may finally founder because it proves impossible to conclude an agreement that satisfies such vital Canadian interests as these.

Apart from those who have mercantilist notions about the purposes of trade policy, and they are numerous, the opposition in Canada to the inclusion of agriculture in a trade arrangement with the United States boils down to a preference by some for a continuation of the subsidization of high-cost agricultural production in Canada and for preserving familiar regulatory systems and cherished producers' marketing institutions. Only time will reveal whether these matters are in fact "below the bottom line."

Meantime, an urgent task for policy analysts is to elicit the information needed by policymakers and industry participants. They must identify the interventions and regulations that may have to be changed in response to the opening of borders and the equalization of competitive conditions. And they must measure empirically the impact of this development on such variables as prices, output, consumption, trade flows, incomes, asset values, and producer numbers. Other dimensions that need to be explored are cross-commodity effects, effects on pricing and marketing systems and institutions, vertical effects within the food system, and impact on regions and communities and on third countries. Little work on these matters has been done on either side of the border; hence the negotiations are not yet being illuminated by research-based knowledge about the size and distribution of economic benefits and of dislocation and adjustment costs.

There is a real possibility that the experience of grappling on a bilateral basis with the nontariff measures that impede and distort agricultural trade will lead to lessons and models that can guide and catalyze the subsequent multilateral encounters in the GATT. Thus, it is realistic to anticipate that bilateral progress in containing the use of subsidies to agriculture and the response to them, in devising new modes of dispute resolution, and in banning the use of technical standards as trade barriers and limiting their incidental trade effects by harmonizing them will lead to approaches that subsequently can be carried over to the multilateral talks in Geneva. However, it is easy to have unrealistic expectations in this regard, particularly in the all-important matter of subsidies. For the bilateral negotiations on subsidies will focus largely on the response by one partner to the subsidies to production that the other gives for commodities that are exported. They will have little to say about the subsidized import substitution and subsidized export competition in third markets that will be the centerpiece of the negotiations to revise and strengthen the articles of the GATT and the subsidies code negotiated in the Tokyo Round.

Neither country's agricultural industries are in the van of those seeking to construct a Canadian–United States free trade agreement. For farm groups in Canada, the losers and losses are more numerous and surer than the gainers and gains, there are few benefits for the key grains and oilseeds sectors, and wrenching adjustments might be required of some other commodity groups. For the United States, the prospects are for minor trade and income gains for minor products, little trade creation for the major U.S. agricultural export products, and the prospect that the support arrangements for grains, dairy products, and sugar will be compromised and challenged. Nevertheless, both countries' broad agricultural interests mandate that the negotiations encompass agriculture, for both need tangible agricultural benefits to present to particular commodity interests and to national legislators if the draft agreement is to attract the support needed for ratification, and both governments fear the disastrous precedent that would be set for the Uruguay Round if the two major advocates of global agricultural trade reform were seen to be unable to open their borders and curb their use of subsidies. In short, Canada and the United States are fated to negotiate about continental agriculture, where the outcome does not much matter, if they wish to negotiate about agriculture globally, where it matters a great deal.

Possibilities in the United States

JOHN A. SCHNITTKER

A CANADIAN newspaper reporter called me in November 1985 to inquire about the attitude and response of U.S. agricultural interests to Prime Minister Brian Mulroney's initiative toward building a Canadian-American free trade area. I pleaded urgent business and offered to call him soon. In fact, I had not heard of the Canadian proposal. When I telephoned U.S. farm organization leaders to ask for their ideas on the matter, I found that they did not know what I was talking about, or had not considered the question.

That is still largely true, seventeen months after the Canadian initiative and less than a year before the Canada-U.S. free trade negotiations are scheduled to be completed and sent to Congress for approval. In the U.S. government, the Canada talks are overshadowed by preparations and expectations for the multilateral trade negotiations. In the countryside, the Canada negotiations are overwhelmed by the frustration and fears arising out of the continuing loss of the export markets that were gained in the 1970s, the decline of over 30 percent in the value of farm assets since 1981 with more losses still ahead, and the near-disappearance of the once huge positive balance of trade in agricultural products.

The Canada-U.S. talks on agricultural issues are also dwarfed in importance by the American preoccupation with domestic farm policy, the bruising political struggle of 1985 to adopt a farm bill designed to get back "our fair share" of export markets, and the disappointing aftermath during which corn, wheat, and oilseed exports have not been increasing at all in tonnage and have declined sharply in value. The apparent importance of the talks to U.S. agriculture is also minimized by the nature of the product mix in trade between Canada and the United States. That list is dominated by fruits and nuts, vegetables, and animals and animal products—all of which the United States exports to many countries, but none of which are looked upon as the export products that will save our economic skin even if we can recapture what farm interests believe to be our fair share of world markets.

184

Finally, a "good guy–bad guy" preoccupation with the European Community (EC) and its common agricultural policy has diverted U.S. agricultural interests from the truth, or truism, that increases in farm exports must be gained cargo by cargo, and box by box, in commerce with nearly every country in the world. Similarly, but to a lesser extent, our love affair with the Soviets as grain buyers, and China's brief dalliance with us in grain markets, has long distracted U.S. interests from the business of selling wherever we can, and from emphasizing such rudimentary considerations as credit, quality, contacts, and a business–government partnership to insure that larger and larger sales are made from year to year.

Dr. Warley notes that "Canada has less reason than the United States for including agricultural and food trade on the negotiating agenda since it is apparent that the economic interests of some influential commodity groups and regions will be impaired and some farm programs and institutional arrangements will be jeopardized in an arrangement providing for free north-south" trade. This statement is supported by the fact, evident from the start, that most agricultural commodity groups in Canada want to be left out of the free trade talks.

What about U.S. institutional arrangements and U.S. commodity groups? Would they necessarily be disturbed by movement toward a Canada-U.S. free trade area? Do U.S. farm interests also want out?

The classic trade-restricting institution for U.S. agriculture is section 22 of the Agricultural Act of 1949, as amended. This provision authorizes the president to place quotas and fees on imports that materially interfere with any price support or stabilization program for agricultural products. Section 22 quotas now apply to cotton, sugar, peanuts, sugar blends and mixtures, sugar-containing products, and dairy products. Section 22 has been in effect on wheat and rice and is available to restrict corn, tobacco, and oilseed imports as well.

The International Trade Commission (ITC) has been rather conservative in applying section 22 to new commodities in recent years, recommending no restrictive action in the absence of a finding of material interference in two tobacco cases where evidence showed large increases in U.S. imports concurrent with increased U.S. tobacco stocks. That kind of evidence would have brought an automatic import quota recommendation from the ITC in the 1950s and 1960s, and an immediate presidential proclamation virtually stopping all imports. Farm interests no longer look to section 22 as confidently as they once did. Any move to modify or terminate actual and potential protection under section 22 on dairy or sugar products, however, would be met by strong opposition. Other commodity groups would join that opposition. In any case, reports on the U.S.-Canada talks state that modification or termination of section 22 is not likely to be offered to Canada, since it is expected to be a major U.S. offer in the multilateral negotiations and should be held for the main event, not used as a warm-up.

American programs to support wheat and corn prices and the incomes of grain producers are sure to be issues in the bilateral talks, even though grains are not major elements in U.S.-Canada trade. The United States has increased its levels of protection (margin of total support above world trading values) by close to 50 percent, by dropping price support levels while maintaining income support levels. The United States now spends $10 billion a year or more encouraging farmers to produce more grain, and urging them not to do so at the same time, and coping with the inevitable aftermath of such contradictory policies. This is extremely harmful to Canada, Australia, Argentina, and some other grain-exporting countries and contributed last year to the organization of the Group of Fourteen countries in opposition to U.S. and EC agricultural policies.

While it appears superficially true that the United States has the machinery in motion to reduce its levels of protection for grains over the next few years, the letter of the present law would suggest that they will either be increased slightly or stay the same. Target price levels will fall slightly beginning in 1988, but market support (loan or intervention) levels will also decline, keeping payments at today's high levels. In the meantime the 1988 congressional and presidential elections virtually guarantee against any substantial reduction in grain, dairy, cotton, and rice subsidies before about 1990, unless such reductions are driven by overall budget policy. It is true that the president's proposed budget for 1988 would reduce the overall level of protection for wheat, coarse grains, cotton, and rice very substantially by 1991—the last year of operation of the Food Security Act of 1985. This portion of the White House budget is not expected to be considered seriously, however.

Levels of protection for grains are also scheduled to be major items offered by the United States in the multilateral trade negotiations. Talks with Canada may prove to be useful rehearsals for grain negotiations in the multilateral talks, where the United

States and Canada will be allied against the European Community
on grain issues and, at the same time, will be at odds with each
other over the sharply higher levels of subsidy for grains in the
United States relative to Canada and over the effects on trade of
the divergent grain marketing systems of the two countries.

There seems to be little prospect for any progress toward free
trade in grains and oilseed between the two countries in the
current negotiations. In fact, there has been a set-back to free
trade in corn, which further complicates agricultural trade relations. Canada has found that the United States subsidizes corn
production substantially—more than $1.00 per bushel—and has
imposed substantial countervailing duties on corn imports. This
has raised tensions among commodity groups in the United States
who fear that other countries may have similar ideas.

The U.S. action last year countervailing against live hogs, but
not against pork imports, has surely worsened the climate in
Canada for freer agricultural trade, just as Canada's corn action
has in the United States. Rising impatience among U.S. soybean
growers and associations over imports of canola (oil) from Canada,
concurrent with legal and rhetorical skirmishes over Procter and
Gamble's advertising of its canola-containing product in an effort
to limit or stop canola use in the United States, is another example
of the difficulty U.S. negotiators face in producing tangible gains
in products with substantial trade flows.

Big-ticket items, however, do not exhaust the list of possibilities
for progress beneficial to both sides in the U.S.-Canada talks.
The U.S. Department of Agriculture has produced a thirty-three-
page, single-spaced paper entitled "Canadian Federal Assistance/
Subsidy Programs." This is accompanied by sixteen pages on
Saskatchewan, British Columbia, and Ontario agricultural aids,
which means that the paper for all provincial subsidies must run
close to fifty pages. Canadian subsidies cited range from subsidized
interest on advance payments to potato growers, to rather massive
aids for transporting grains to market, to counseling for farmers,
and to the Oil Royalty fund to reduce farm fuel costs in Saskatchewan.

Canada doubtless has an even longer paper, with substantially
more programs and much larger numbers citing and describing
the hundreds of subsidies the federal and state governments provide
farmers in the United States. The negotiations give the two
governments the opportunity and obligation to review these
programs and the spending associated with them. They can provide
the U.S. government with the leverage for change in minor

federal programs, even as program reviews are delayed. The U.S. government, however, has virtually no leverage to modify state programs that may subsidize or otherwise benefit farmers and may influence U.S. trade in agricultural products with Canada.

Attention to the multitude of minor programs and issues that impede or otherwise affect trade between Canada and the United States is surely a worthwhile endeavor for 1987. The results will be positive; the accord will be acceptable to the U.S. Congress and will be valuable preparation for the multilateral negotiation.

Clearly, the United States has a basis for only the most limited concessions to Canada on trade in agricultural products. Canadian intervention in agriculture is more pervasive than American intervention and is substantially controlled by provincial law which is not immediately responsive to national decisions. Two big-ticket items on the agenda for changes in the U.S. system— grains subsidies and section 22—will surely be reserved for the multilateral talks, as will U.S. marketing orders which occupy a special place in U.S. agriculture.

Dr. Warley's suggestion that Canada wishes the United States to limit the effects on Canada of U.S. trade remedy laws is an interesting idea but surely a nonstarter in the present climate. Commodity groups and Congress are becoming increasingly militant in the use of unilateral remedies against what are deemed to be unfair trade practices. It seems rather far-fetched for Canadians to think that they might be inoculated against retaliation by the United States in response to real or imaginary threats to U.S. farm interests.

There is a lesson for the bilateral negotiations in the outcome of the recent U.S.-EC confrontation over the trade effects of the accession of Spain and Portugal into the Community. American negotiators hailed the settlement as a substantial victory, since Europe gave somewhat more than it had originally offered. But the U.S. farm interests most directly affected, represented by the National Corn Growers Association, called the same settlement "a sellout by the U.S."

That is the fate of trade negotiators, to achieve more than was expected in very difficult circumstances, but less than might have been achieved if the other side had been forthcoming, and far less than the commodity constituencies thought would have been fair.

General Discussion

Doug Bereuter opened the discussion by saying that neither country's farm organizations had given much consideration to the impact of a Canada-U.S. free trade agreement on their respective agricultural sectors.

In his view, an agreement would do little to create agricultural trade but would be a source of great disruption. The two countries have gone a long way toward achieving the complementarity that is available in their agricultural trade. As far as the United States is concerned, such complementarity applies principally to semi-tropical crops, and even in that area the United States might have cause for concern. In examining how the Caribbean Basin Initiative is working, he had found that the United States is losing out as a source of supply for vegetables and fruits in the domestic market. It is less likely to be supplying those products to Canada in the future.

His concern about including agricultural products in a free trade arrangement with Canada centers on the changes that would take place. It would be extremely difficult to reduce or eliminate a variety of subsidy programs relating to farm commodities. That difficulty would be as great in Canada as in the United States in view of the fact emerging from this conference that government intervention in agriculture is greater in Canada than in the United States.

In short, Bereuter thought there would be only small gains in some relatively minor products. Fundamentally, Canada and the United States are competitors in agriculture, which is why, as Warley had noted, the Canadian preference is for the status quo, for the familiar, and for the continuation of the subsidization of high-cost agricultural programs. Much the same attitude exists in the United States.

Bereuter is also troubled because he believes that the Canadian agricultural sector has more political clout in legislative bodies at the provincial and national levels than the American agricultural sector has in U.S. politics. That worries him from a parochial point of view, since he comes from an agricultural state and the western grain belt. In geopolitical terms, furthermore, the United States, as a superpower, occasionally has felt obligated to take positions on trade that are not in the best interest of its agricultural and industrial sectors.

For these reasons, Bereuter does not want dramatic movement toward free trade in agricultural commodities and believes such a move would generate strong opposition in the U.S. agricultural industry. Because U.S. agriculture is diverse, some significant sectors are likely to support such a move. Most of those in opposition have not yet expressed their position. Even so, he noted that when the administration first expressed its intention of negotiating an agreement with Canada, it ran into a hailstorm of opposition in the Senate Finance Committee, which is composed of members who might be expected to show support. When Americans begin to focus on the possibility of a free trade area with Canada, opposition will emerge in full force from all sectors, and most vehemently from agriculture.

Warley said he found his own and Bereuter's pessimism disappointing. If Canada and Canadian agriculture are to achieve their potential, deregulation is imperative. It is essential to shed the cocoon of regulations built up over fifty years and to become more market oriented. If this is not done on a continental basis, it will be difficult if not impossible to persuade Europe and Japan to move in the same direction. Failure to make progress in agriculture bilaterally sets a bad precedent for the multilateral negotiations.

MacLaury asked Bereuter whether the Congress will in any event have to find some way to reduce the cost of agricultural supports. If so, is there not a case to begin dealing with that necessity by making some progress bilaterally?

Bereuter said that is the common wisdom. Many of his congressional colleagues take that position back home and it also gains visibility from op-ed pieces in the newspapers. He does not, however, see any urgency in the Congress to reduce agricultural subsidy programs, despite the continual decline in the political clout of agriculture. Therefore, he did not see the budgetary argument as a driving force on this question.

Schnittker agreed with Bereuter's position as it applied to the next two to three years—the time frame of the Canada-U.S. negotiations and the early stages of the multilateral trade negotiations. In the longer run of ten years, however, there might be a transition period bringing into effect the deals negotiated bilaterally and multilaterally. Assuming that the budget deficit continues to be an issue in the United States, agricultural spending levels will be brought down.

Dawson, commenting on the need to include agriculture in the agreement, struck a more optimistic note. As with financial services, a great deal has already been accomplished by Canada and the United States in agriculture. Arrangements for cattle, for instance, already come very close to free trade. Tariffs are coming down to one cent a pound and differences over health regulations, as they affect trade, have been resolved within the two cattlemen's associations. With study, a number of groups and associations have changed from being against to being for some agreement on agricultural trade. Some specific sectors will require more time to adjust, but there is no need for agriculture to stay off the table. To the contrary, agreements on agriculture in the Canada-U.S. context are vital to the future of the GATT negotiations insofar as they affect agricultural trade.

A participant noted that Warley had raised the possibility of using the net subsidy concept in dealing with contingent protection. He said that the fish industry had gone through two years of countervailing duties and never could understand why some concept of balancing subsidies had not been applied when the American industry argued that the playing field was not level. Instead of retaliatory countervailing action and two sets of subsidies and duties, why not define a level playing field in terms of net subsidies? Is there any chance of that concept growing out of this negotiation? Is that something Congress might buy?

Warley said he would go further than net subsidies and also take into account the costs a domestic industry suffers as a consequence of other policies. That is a difficult procedure to apply and it opens a Pandora's box, but the OECD is now engaged in a study that seeks to measure the level of effective protection, commodity by commodity and country by country. He claimed it would not be too difficult to add as an offset certain increases in costs that producers face. Furthermore, he said, what is really being discussed in the OECD—and he hopes in the GATT—are ways of measuring the level of protection and binding it. That revives a concept advanced by the Europeans more than twenty years ago. It was then called *montant de soutien*, or level of support.

Schnittker pointed out that on that score the United States is in a particularly fortunate position now, a position similar to that of the European Community in 1966 or so. At that time the

Community had just adopted the common agricultural policy, which raised their levels of protection very sharply. Consequently they were in a position to offer to bind and, over a long period, reduce them. As a result of the 1985 agricultural legislation, the United States increased the level of its agricultural protection; it could now take the high ground in the GATT negotiations and offer to bind and, over time, reduce it.

Bereuter emphasized that it is extremely difficult to measure accurately the level of agricultural subsidization and protection. That is now being tried in the GATT negotiations and is going to be a nightmare. The OECD is doing much the same thing in trying to measure the amount of export subsidy involved in mixed credits and tied aid. It has been politically difficult to start this exercise and technically difficult to carry it out.

Hudec also threw in a word of caution. Net subsidies sound attractive as a way out of ameliorating the countervailing duty problem. But pursuing that course, or even worse taking into account Warley's additional costs that an industry might claim, would put a level playing field even further out of reach.

To clean out all subsidies on one side and take account of all artificial disadvantages on the other might be a way of working back to the ideal of a state of nature as a basis for international trade—that is, a price that exists nowhere but in people's minds. The main result may be additional employment for lawyers but not necessarily a solution to this problem.

Weiss disagreed. He argued that applying a countervailing duty requires officials in the importing country to determine what constitutes a subsidy and how large it is for the exporting country; they can make the same determination for the competing industry in their own country. If it can be done for fifty-five fish programs on the Canadian side, what does it take but another three or four weeks to determine it for the thirty-three fish programs on the U.S. side, and then balance the two sides to determine what has to be done to level the playing field.

Hudec replied that once you try to examine offsetting subsidies, the logic of the situation pushes you into all the other factors that distort the state-of-nature costs of each of two competing enterprises. He agreed it could be done; the law is capable of answering any question. But it would take a long time, and he is uncertain that the end result would be less protective than what existed to begin with.

Jack Crean expanded on a geopolitical comment initially introduced by Bereuter. He pointed to the Soviet military buildup in the Pacific, which in his view increased requirements for defense expenditures in Canada. Heretofore Canadian defense activity has been directed to the support of NATO. He emphasized that holding an alliance together was less difficult if its members were not in the middle of trade wars. The changing strategic situation, therefore, is an added reason to work for a free trade arrangement in North America.

Weiss commented that, in the past, the United States had said it would be willing to renounce section 22 of the U.S. agricultural legislation if in return the Common Market made appropriate changes in its agricultural policy. He asked three questions. Does this U.S. position still obtain today? If it does, would a settlement with the Community along these lines also be a means of negotiating a liberalization of Canadian restrictive practices in agriculture? And could such an agreement with Canada be deferred until after September 1987, subject to working out the deal with the Common Market?

Schnittker replied that he would guess the United States will advance the modification and ultimate termination of section 22 during the Uruguay Round on the condition that appropriate amendments are made in the European Community's common agricultural policy (CAP) and in the policies of other countries as well. American negotiators recognize that the CAP is not going to be very negotiable, but they also know that Europe is being forced by costs of the CAP to avoid increasing its levels of protection or to slowly reduce them. Some small accommodation could very well be made in this round. Since the termination of section 22 will not be advanced in the Canadian negotiations, any relationship it has to trade with Canada would have to be deferred for five, six, or seven years—that is, until after the multilateral negotiations are settled. In any event, he did not believe this would be an important factor in Canada-U.S. agricultural trade, since sugar and sugar mixtures are probably the main products affected by section 22.

A United States Official View

A Vote of Confidence

CLAYTON YEUTTER

I WOULD LIKE to set at rest any reservations that anybody has about the importance to the United States of the free trade negotiations with Canada and any doubts that our friends in Canada have about the U.S. attitude toward them. There have been comments to the effect that the United States has not taken the negotiations seriously or, at the least, has not put a high enough priority on them. I do not agree with these propositions.

In my view, the Canada–U.S. trade negotiation is the most important bilateral negotiation this country has ever had. I have said this repeatedly in speeches over the past nineteen months. This negotiation represents an opportunity to open the border between the United States and Canada so as to provide large economies of scale to the business firms of both countries and improve their competitive position internationally. That is the basic value of these negotiations, which ought to be recognized by anyone who has any experience in business. Canadian firms will benefit in a variety of ways because of the extension of their markets in the United States and the resulting economies of scale. American firms will enjoy similar benefits.

I do not believe American firms will benefit nearly as much as Canadian firms, but that is not important. This is not a zero–sum game where somebody wins and somebody loses. Both countries will be significant beneficiaries.

Not every firm in both countries will benefit and not every industry in both countries will benefit. Structural adjustment will be required as a result of this kind of arrangement, but that is to be expected. Such adjustment is a part of growth and evolution in a capitalistic society, whether or not there is a free trade arrangement. Canada goes through it all the time, as does the United States. A free trade arrangement may accelerate the adjustment process to some degree, in some areas. But that is a reflection of strength and vitality, not of weakness. It should not be a deterrent to the negotiations. Completion of the free trade arrangement is very clearly in the economic self-interest of both Canada and the United States.

This negotiation can also have multilateral benefits. If we do this job well and achieve an open border between Canada and the United States—and I am convinced we can—it will set an excellent example for the rest of the world. I see that as constructive bilateralism, the kind that fosters and facilitates multilateralism. It will serve as an example for the rest of the world and a stimulus for opening markets everywhere. It would come at a propitious time, setting an example for the Uruguay Round of the multilateral negotiations. There will be a lot of skirmishing in those negoti-ations in 1987, just at the time that the United States and Canada hope to bring their bilateral negotiations to a conclusion. If the Geneva negotiations enter a serious stage in 1988—as I believe they will—what is achieved in the Canada-U.S. free trade ar-rangement can clearly provide not only an example but in some respects even a model.

Comments are in order about the negotiation process itself. The fast-track authority expires at the end of 1987, which means, as a practical matter, we would need to reach final agreement around October 1 so as to present it to the United States Congress in a timely way. That constitutes a significant negotiating chal-lenge; there is not much time and there are a lot of issues to cover. That time schedule does not intimidate me and I hope our friends in the government of Canada are not intimidated by it either.

The United States has a number of interagency working groups that have been functioning for some time. I am sure similar groups exist in Canada. We have had to wait for the advice of the U.S. International Trade Commission in regard to tariffs and that advice is now at hand. The United States is in a position to move forward aggressively on the tariff negotiation now and very soon will be able to move on all other aspects of the agreement.

If the United States can do what Peter Murphy and his colleagues have set out to do and what I believe Simon Reisman and his colleagues in Canada have set out to do, a comprehensive agree-ment can be put together by October 1 or thereabouts.

I understand that concern has been expressed in your discussions that the U.S. administration has not consulted adequately with the Congress and with the private sector. I do not agree with that allegation for several reasons. First, consultation is a time-con-suming process. There is no reason for our negotiators to consult with members of Congress or to call members of the private sector to Washington unless there is something worth talking about. Both they and our negotiators are pressed for time.

In fact, the negotiations have gone through a skirmishing phase over the past several months, without either side having much to say. Now that we are getting down to business in an intense way, there will be a lot to consult about and ample opportunity to do so before October. The administration is appreciative of any input coming from the members of the U.S. Congress and the private sector. We will listen and try to finish with a product acceptable and marketable on Capitol Hill.

Apparently someone made the point here that there is a difference in rank between Peter Murphy on the U.S. side and Simon Reisman on the Canadian side, or at least argued that the United States is at a disadvantage because Ambassador Murphy reports to me, and Mr. Reisman, allegedly, reports directly to the prime minister.

How Canada organizes itself for the negotiations is the business of the Canadian government. Ambassador Murphy is a skillful negotiator. He may not be as skillful as Simon Reisman and, therefore, the United States may end up on the short end of this negotiation. I am willing to take that chance. I will accept responsibility for the ultimate product, and if it turns out badly for the United States, then everybody in the United States can castigate Ambassador Yeutter for the results. That judgment should be made, however, when the exercise is finished, not now.

It is not desirable to second-guess the skills of the negotiator when active negotiations have just begun. If second-guessing is appropriate, it belongs at the end of the process.

The United States would like to go farther with this agreement than it did with the U.S.-Israel agreement. That may be ambitious, but it is not unrealistic.

In particular, the United States would like to achieve progress bilaterally in some areas that are of interest to us multilaterally as well. These include topics that we emphasized at Punta del Este and will emphasize in the new GATT round. We hope we will be joined by Canada in that effort. I refer to establishing rules for intellectual property, services, and investment. There are major difficulties in these three areas around the world and good opportunities to resolve problems internationally. The Canada-U.S. agreement should set an example and provide models for what may be achievable in the GATT round.

Agriculture also is a high priority to both of us in the new

GATT round in Geneva. I know there has been considerable discussion on that issue here and questions raised as to just how much can be achieved in agriculture bilaterally. I agree that agriculture is a global problem, not a Canada-U.S. problem. There are certain facets of the agricultural situation, however, that can be dealt with effectively by the two countries and should be built into the negotiating exercise.

Canada and the United States can do a lot to reduce barriers to agricultural trade between us. Agricultural tariffs can be reduced and problems in regard to standards affecting agricultural trade can be cleared up. Furthermore, problems inhibiting trade in agricultural products that are not likely to be on the multilateral agenda—such as specialty crops—can be addressed. We should try to resolve such problems and open the border between Canada and the United States in these products as well.

The big-ticket items, such as grains, clearly are multilateral in scope and will have to await the results of the Uruguay Round. The results achieved there could be folded into the free trade arrangement at a later date.

With respect to other issues—nontariff measures, automobile issues, all tariff questions—the United States seeks to achieve major results. I assume that is true for Canada as well.

Clearly, agreements on this scale will come into force only over a period of years. Neither Canada nor the United States is going to make major changes overnight in most of these areas. In the Israel-U.S. arrangement we used a program phased in over ten years. I suspect something of that order will emerge in the Canada-U.S. negotiation.

How unfair trade practices will be handled is another important question. It seems to be a priority of the government of Canada to discuss the issue of subsidies and countervailing duty and antidumping laws. The United States believes those are proper subjects for discussion in this negotiation. In my judgment, everything should be on the table in the Canada-U.S. negotiation. The United States is prepared to have everything on the table, if Canada is.

What can be done that makes sense in that area is another matter. We ought to try to design measures that will discourage unfair trade practices on both sides of the border, not generate new ones. That is going to take some creative thinking and negotiating. The United States is prepared to listen to any suggestions or recommendations that are brought forth, either on this side or on the Canadian side of the border. We should try to develop some models and see where they take us.

One analogy in that regard is the U.S. semiconductor agreement with Japan. Though the agreement at the moment is having its problems, the concepts encompassed in it are sound. One objective of the semiconductor arrangement is to provide for what I would call "preventive dumping." The system seeks to deal with the practices of firms in such a way that they are discouraged from dumping, rather than being punished for it. It amounts to preventive medicine, rather than curative medicine. If it is possible to effectively discourage the dumping of semiconductors by the Japanese, perhaps there are ways to use that model in this exercise. In trade as in medicine, it is better to prevent problems from arising than to have to come along afterward and attempt to cure them.

My final comment relates to the general outlook for the negotiation. I am told that there is a considerable amount of pessimism in this conference about the likelihood of bringing this exercise to a successful conclusion. There is a consensus that a free trade arrangement is a good idea but a lot of doubt as to whether it will ever come to pass.

I see no reason to be pessimistic about bringing a good idea to fruition. We ought to be able to find the skills, the commitment, and the determination within the governments on both sides of the border, and within our respective private sectors, to bring this about.

I am convinced it is a sound idea—and that it can be brought to fruition. Those in this room can join with those in government to bring a positive outcome into effect by October 1. Worthwhile objectives are usually difficult to achieve, but with a sufficiently strong commitment, the difficulties can be overcome.

Questions and Answers

Question. Has there been a new high-level directive or political push recently to move more aggressively toward a trade agreement?

Yeutter. A strong U.S. commitment to the negotiations existed from the start. The recent visit of Vice President Bush and Secretary Baker to Ottawa, at the invitation of your government, was a positive step. It confirmed the commitment and determination of the government of the United States to move forward but did not represent a new push.

Question. The *New York Times* the other day reported that you or the U.S. Trade Representative's Office was more or less told not to take action against Canadian steel because a repetition of the action against lumber, if applied to steel, would set off land mines for Prime Minister Mulroney and torpedo the free trade talks. Has there been such a directive?

Yeutter. There has not, but I would like to comment further. I have said repeatedly that both Canada and the United States should separate consideration of short-run issues from long-run issues. That is difficult to do. There is inevitably some link between them, but the attempt should be made to separate them. The free trade arrangement will benefit both nations in immeasurable and indispensable ways over the next half century or century. To suggest that this necessary and invaluable negotiating exercise should be held hostage to individual bilateral trade problems, no matter how important, is not a sensible proposition. Current, but essentially transitory, trade problems should be disposed of by our two countries in a relatively short period of time—independent of the free trade negotiations.

After all, if this agreement is negotiated in 1987, approved by both governments, say, in 1988, and then phased in over a period of ten to twelve years, it will not be fully in effect until the year 2000. To suggest that what is happening in 1987 on timber or steel should dissuade the two countries from moving forward with an agreement that will be beneficial to them both in the year

2000 is not comprehensible to me. I hope people on both sides of the border will come to the same conclusion.

The two countries should be able to deal with difficult bilateral trade problems of a temporary nature, whether softwood lumber, or shakes and shingles, steel, or any one of a dozen issues. We should deal with them one by one and resolve them amicably. These problems may be difficult and contentious, and they may have political implications on both sides of the border. Nevertheless, we ought to be able to handle them in such a way as to emerge better friends than we were before.

The United States went through a comparable discussion with the European Community recently in its GATT article 24-6 negotiation on the trade damage it would suffer from the accession of Spain and Portugal to the Community. The Community argued that if the United States did not rock the boat on this issue, it might be able to support an agricultural negotiation in the new GATT round. Here again the same analogy applies. The agricultural negotiation in the new GATT round is too important to be linked to a dispute over corn exports to Spain. The GATT agricultural negotiation is of great importance to the world and will set the environment in which agricultural trade will be conducted over the next ten, twenty, or thirty years. To suggest that it should be put on hold because of a relatively minor trade issue strikes me as wrong. It was possible in the end to settle that dispute with the European Community without jeopardizing the larger agricultural negotiation. It should be possible to settle disputes with the government of Canada on steel or anything else while still proceeding with the free trade negotiations.

Question. How will automobiles be treated in the negotiations?

Yeutter. Automobiles represent a major item of trade between the two countries and raise some complicated issues. The two governments have not yet reached agreement on how these issues will be managed. The United States has raised with the government of Canada a number of problems relating to the automobile trade. Some of these, notably the Canadian duty remission scheme, have received considerable attention, both within the administration and in Congress. They will require further discussion and debate. Conclusions about how they will be resolved are premature.

Question. Current pessimism about the negotiations seems to apply not so much to the desirability of the ultimate outcome but to the feasibility of negotiating a free trade arrangement by October 1. New, important, complicated areas such as services are covered; it may be difficult to achieve substantive agreements before the

deadline. What happens if the job is not completed by October 1?
Yeutter. Both governments will have to appraise the situation at that point and decide what to do. My judgment is that we should not try to extend the time available. In effect that would mean that the U.S. administration would have to get an extension of the fast-track authority. I would rather not go that route and prefer that we meet the deadline. But all aspects of the situation would have to be evaluated on October 1, if that becomes a necessity.

Whether the Congress would grant an extension of the additional fast-track authority at that time is an open question. It would probably depend on what the potential outcome looked like then. If major progress had been made and only a few loose ends remained to be wrapped up, I would assume that the U.S. Congress would extend the deadline for the fast-track authority. Based on my experience as a negotiator, I believe a warning is in order. Negotiations usually go as fast as they need to go. Extending deadlines is usually an excuse for postponing decisions.

Question. Would it be possible to have staged agreements rather than to seek an extension of the fast-track authority?

Yeutter. That would be possible. It is not a very realistic approach, however. Trade-offs would be necessary within and among the different agreements. Either each agreement would be self-balanced and could stand on its own, or some way would have to be found to calculate net advantages and disadvantages for each country that would have to be offset in succeeding agreements. That would add a complexity to the negotiations that would not be helpful. It is far preferable to complete the entire exercise as one package. That would help in terms of legislative approval here in the United States and, I suspect, in Canada as well.

Question. During your remarks you used the phrase, "everything is on the table." That has come up a couple of times during the discussion today. Don Macdonald is the one who said that although that sounded like a very reasonable proposition in the abstract, to some Canadian ears it means that such things as cultural autonomy are likewise on the table. Are you not offending some people in Canada who might be strong supporters of an agreement by the sweeping statement that "everything is on the table"?

Yeutter. Perhaps the question is whether Canadians or Americans are more concerned about preservation of their cultural autonomy. In a sense both have their cultures at stake. I am prepared to take the risk of having American culture subject to greater Canadian influence under a free trade arrangement. I hope Canada is prepared to run the same type of risk.

I do not mean to be facetious about this. I recognize this is a serious issue in Canada. I also recognize that Canada, as a sovereign nation, can decide to take things off the table, whether cultural or anything else. There is a price for doing that since its negotiating partner can do the same thing. This will happen in the bilateral negotiations between the United States and Canada or in the multilateral negotiations in Geneva. It is not realistic to expect one negotiating partner to take a sector off the table while its negotiating partner leaves everything on the table. To go that route will shrink the terms and parameters of the negotiation.

I believe it is in the best interest of both countries to move as far as possible toward an open border. I am not enthusiastic therefore about proposals designed to shrink the negotiations, even though there may be very good reasons to do so.

Question. There may be some confusion of terms on this subject. Most trade negotiators would agree with your point that for one country to take something off the table would have consequences for the other party and would lead to a smaller area for negotiation.

But a large disparity exists in cultural exchange between the larger and smaller North American partners, and the uniqueness of Canada, whatever that is, is very precious to Canadians. It would be a matter of concern to Canadians, therefore, to conclude that their worry about being able to evolve as an independent North American partner was equated in your mind with withdrawing some commercial matters from the negotiating table. That certainly would not be the way most Canadians would feel about their desire and capacity to live with the United States as two separate entities in North America.

Yeutter. That is one of the difficulties of dealing with abstract concepts. I am not sure what the government means when it says that cultural sovereignty cannot be a subject for negotiation. More specificity is needed to assess what complications that has for the negotiations. That might best be left for the negotiating table where people can be specific in setting forth positions in terms of trade.

Question. You said that both Canadian culture and American culture could be at risk. Specifically, how might a free trade agreement put American culture at risk?

Yeutter. In the same way that it would put Canadian culture at risk. I do not see this as being a major concern, but it is a concern in Canada. I hope that our Canadian friends can articulate just what is encompassed in this term and what constraints that may have on the negotiating process.

I realize that this is an issue of great sensitivity in Canada, and the United States, therefore, will try to be accommodative. But it will have to be done in terms that are more specific about what is meant and what trade implications are involved.

Question. What progress is likely on the U.S. trade deficit in the coming year, and what effect will that have on congressional attitudes toward trade?

Yeutter. It is dangerous to estimate changes in the trade account because they are dependent on many factors, including what happens in Western Europe and Japan, among other countries. I subscribe to Fred Bergsten's thesis that the U.S. trade deficit will shrink in 1987 by some $30 billion to $40 billion. That is not an unreasonable expectation in the economic conditions prevailing today. I believe improvements are ahead, but we are starting from a very large base, that is, a U.S. global deficit now running at an annual rate of $170 billion.

What effect will that have on the Congress? Certainly, an improvement in the deficit will be psychologically beneficial in the Congress and everywhere. But those who seek legislative action to counter the trade deficit will continue to use the argument that even though it is improving, it is still too large. Both opinions will be articulated on Capitol Hill at great length in 1987.

As to the relationship of the deficit to this exercise, again I would make the basic distinction between short and long run. I do not believe we should pay much attention in this exercise to what the global or bilateral trade deficits happen to be this year in Canada or in the United States. The same point applies to the exchange rate. I have a hard time understanding why these matters should be of major concern to a trading regime that will not be fully in effect until the year 2000. I see the present situation getting better, but that issue has little to do, one way or the other, with the discussion of the merits of the free trade arrangement.

Question. You mentioned that you would like to see such issues as services and intellectual property discussed. Yet Canada is just starting to analyze proposals for regulatory reform. This will take time. Several observers have suggested that trade in services be dropped from the fast-track negotiations. But you have suggested that you do not like partial agreements. Do you think then that it would be possible to deal with such topics in broad strokes?

Yeutter. I believe we should try to achieve positive, significant results in all these areas because they are important to both countries and to the world. The services trade between the United States and Canada today is enormous. Establishing a sound system for the conduct of services trade between the two countries would ensure that it will expand in the future. Trade in services is likely to be a growth area internationally for both Canada and the United States.

As for intellectual property, a similar situation exists. International piracy in the intellectual property area is not defensible anywhere. It is in the interest of both countries to support strong, effective regimes for the protection of intellectual property rights both in Canada and the United States and in the rest of the world.

A third area is investment. Trade and investment go hand in hand. It would be incongruous to negotiate a trade regime intended to open the border and not do the same for investment. Businessmen do not separate trade from investment. They make trade and investment decisions together. How do you say to a businessman that the border will be open to your products, but not to your investment in the other country? In many respects they are two sides of the same coin.

Therefore, we ought to try to make progress in all three areas. Can the job be completed by October 1? I do not know; time will tell.

Question. What about the political sensitivities of this entire exercise? Have they had some impact on the scheduling timetable and the process of the negotiations?

Yeutter. The general question of a free trade area is much more sensitive politically in Canada than it is in the United States. As an economist, I would argue that this negotiation ought to have widespread support in Canada, because Canada will be by far the greater beneficiary.

If that is the perception in Canada—and I have seen no persuasive evidence to suggest otherwise—the negotiations ought to be a source of broad support for the Mulroney government, which started the exercise. There should also be support for the negotiating result when it is finally presented to the Canadian Parliament. I see the agreement as a big winner for the government of Canada over the next half century.

In that connection, it is interesting to note our free trade arrangement with Israel. There is no question about who has become the major beneficiary of the U.S.-Israel free trade arrangement. Much more of Israel's exports move to the United States than vice versa. Analogies between Israel and Canada cannot be pushed very far because Canada obviously is a much larger trading partner and one that is nearby. Nonetheless, I believe that the same result will apply to the Canada-U.S. agreement.

That is acceptable to me. Canada may gain more, but the United States will also gain a great deal from free trade. As long as both nations benefit, the agreement is both attractive and supportable.

To go a bit further, there has always been concern that there is little public support, or even attention, to these negotiations in the United States. I hope Canadians are not bothered by that phenomenon. If a sound agreement emerges, I believe it will gain public as well as congressional support in the United States. The administration will have to consult effectively, which will require a substantive product that justifies support. I believe such a product will emerge from this negotiation and that it will generate the necessary support in the United States.

Attitudes in the United States toward the new GATT round provide a useful analogy. When I returned to government some eighteen months ago and visited Capitol Hill, members of Congress said that they did not hear anything about the desirability of a new round of trade negotiations, either from the business world or from their constituents generally. Why then is the administration pushing for it? Now that the new round is under way, support for that negotiation has come out of the woodwork. I happen to think that it was there all the time.

Latent support also exists for Canada-U.S. free trade. It will surface when the outlines of an agreement become clear.

Question. It is evident from the discussion at this conference that Canada's first priority is to achieve changes in the U.S. antidumping and countervailing duty laws. I take you at your word that those, like everything else, are on the table. My question to you is: What would it take in the way of a packaged concession and structuring of this problem to get these issues from the table into a bill that the administration would be willing to submit to the U.S. Congress?

Yeutter. My judgment is that those issues will have to be handled carefully by both countries. There is just as much interest in them on the Canadian as on the U.S. side of the border. There is just as much of a challenge in getting a bill that will be approved by the Canadian Parliament as there is in getting a bill that will be approved by the U.S. Congress. This is not an easy issue on either side because it deals with trade practices that are traditionally construed to be unfair. Nobody in Canada is going to be enthusiastic about a negotiated result that will permit American firms to engage in unfair trade practices to penetrate the Canadian market, any more than Americans will be enthusiastic about proposals that will permit Canadian firms to penetrate the U.S. market through unfair trade practices.

So, the problem cuts both ways. Canada is not the only country with export subsidies. The United States has some too. I believe there are fewer here than elsewhere in the world, but they exist. Dumping cases have been filed against American companies in Canada and elsewhere, just as there have been dumping cases filed against Canadian companies in the United States.

So the issue will have to be addressed; no one is going to support engaging in unfair trade practices with impunity. How will it be possible to keep trade fair between our two nations so that the issue does not arise, or how do we deal with it if that fails and it does arise?

Furthermore, there is no point in producing a result in that area that will not fly in the U.S. Congress or in the Canadian Parliament. Nobody wants to be attacked for approving unfair trade practices. That is not a salable proposition for the public or business community in either country.

That is an abstract answer. But there is no way to be specific now about the creative sorts of things that might be done. That is something that we will have to work on between now and October 1.

Conference Participants

Matthew J. Abrams
President, Canamco

Raymond Ahearn
Specialist in International Trade, Congressional Research Service

Richard Anderson
Government Research Center

Stacy Augustine
Office of U.S. Representative Jim Kolbe, Republican of Arizona

Ian Austen
MacLean's

Ellen Reisman Babby
Executive Director, Association for Canadian Studies in the United States

Harvey Bale
Assistant U.S. Trade Representative

Francine Bastien
Canadian Broadcasting Corporation

Shelly Battram
Osler, Hoskin and Harcourt

Jacques Beauchesne
Program Representative, Canadian Broadcasting Corporation

Steve Beckman
International Economist, United Auto Workers

Carl E. Beigie
Chief Economist, Dominion Securities

Murray J. Belman
Thompson and Mitchell

Tom Bernes
Director, International Economic Relations, Canadian Department of Finance

Ivan Bernier
Centre Québécois de Relations Internationales

Doug Bereuter
U.S. Representative, Republican of Nebraska

Thomas Brewer
Director, Office of Canada, U.S. Department of Commerce

211

Alastair Bruce
Program Manager, Public Affairs, IBM

Ron W. Bulmer
President, Fisheries Council of Canada

Tom Burns
Senior Consultant, Public Affairs International

John Coleman
Assistant Deputy Minister for International Trade and Finance, Canadian Department of Finance

Stephen J. Collins
Director, International Affairs Division, Motor Vehicle Manufacturers Association of the United States

David Conklin
Institute for Research on Public Policy

Peter Cook
Toronto Globe and Mail

David Cooke
Chairman, Ontario Select Committee on Economic Affairs, Ontario Legislature

Robert A. Cornell
Deputy Assistant Secretary, U.S. Department of the Treasury

Edward Cowan
Washington Manager, Ried, Thunberg and Company, Inc.

David Crane
Editorial Department, Toronto Star

Jack Crean
Toronto

Peter Dawes
Senior Vice-President, Canadian Importers Association

Richard Dawson
Senior Vice-President, Cargill, Ltd.

Germain Denis
Assistant Chief Negotiator, Canadian Trade Negotiations Office

Charles G. Derecskey
Program Director, IBM

Rod Dobell
President, Institute for Research on Public Policy

Charles F. Doran
International Economist, Committee on Banking, Finance and Urban Affairs, U.S. House of Representatives

Cameron Duncan
International Economist, Committee on Banking, Finance and Urban Affairs, U.S. House of Representatives

Robert M. Dunn, Jr.
Professor of Economics, George Washington University

Helen Ericson
Reporter, Journal of Commerce

Lawrence A. Fox
Vice-President, International Economic Affairs,
National Association of Manufacturers

John Frahm
Manager, International Affairs, Minnesota Mining and Manufacturing

Isaiah Frank
Professor of International Economics, Johns Hopkins University

Walter Freedenberg
Correspondent, Scripps Howard Newspapers

Harry L. Freeman
Executive Vice-President, American Express Company

Edward R. Fried
Senior Fellow, Brookings Institution

Richard Gardner
Professor of Law, Columbia University Law School

Norman I. Gelman
Executive Vice-President, Newmyer Associates Inc.

Giles Gherson
Washington Editor, Financial Post

Pierre J. Gosselin
Minister-Counsellor, Embassy of Canada

Norma Greenaway
Correspondent, The Canadian Press

Joseph A. Greenwald
Attorney and Trade Consultant

Sally Hall
President, Consumers Association of Canada

Richard G. Harris
Professor of Economics, Queen's University

Michael Hart
Canadian Trade Negotiations Office

Eric Hartman
Legislative Assistant to U.S. Representative Sander Levin,
Democrat of Michigan

Jean Hennessey
Research Fellow in Environmental Studies, Dartmouth College

Bob Hepburn
Washington Correspondent, Toronto Star

Michael W. Hodin
Vice-President, Public Affairs, Pfizer International

James Holbein
Economic Officer, U.S. Department of State

Harry J. Horrocks II
Director of Government Affairs, National Lumber and Building Material Dealers Association

Robert E. Hudec
Professor of Law, University of Minnesota Law School

Tom Jennings
U.S. International Trade Commission

William Johnson
Washington Bureau Chief, Toronto Globe and Mail

Bill Jvetski
Business Week

Julius L. Katz
Vice-President, Consultants International Group, Inc.

Samuel I. Katz
Professorial Lecturer, Georgetown University

Bogdan Kipling
Columnist, Kipling News Service

Andrew Kniewasser
President, Investment Dealers Association

Mordechai Kreinin
Professor of Economics, Michigan State University

Peter Karl Kresl
Associate Professor of Economics, Bucknell University

Bob Kyle
Legislative Counsel to U.S. Senator Max Baucus, Democrat of Montana

John J. LaFalce
U.S. Representative, Democrat of New York

Leonard H. Legault
Economic Minister, Embassy of Canada

Jennifer Lewington
Reporter, Toronto Globe and Mail

Norman T. London
Academic Relations Officer, Embassy of Canada

Patrick Luciani
Office of Special Trade Advisor, Government of Ontario

Anne McCaskill
Arnold and Porter

John H. McDermid
Parliamentary Secretary to the Minister of International Trade, Canada

James McDermott
Senior Economist, U.S. General Accounting Office

David MacDonald
Editorial Columnist, Winnipeg Free Press

Donald S. Macdonald
Partner, McCarthy and McCarthy; Chairman, Royal Commission on the Economic Union and Development Prospects for Canada

John McKay
Washington Correspondent, Broadcast News, Ltd.

Bruce K. MacLaury
President, Brookings Institution

René Marleau
Counselor, Quebec Government House

Robert Martin
Canadian Trade Negotiations Office

Rosemary A. Mazon
Director, International Affairs, Allied-Signal Inc.

Allan I. Mendelowitz
Senior Associate Director, U.S. General Accounting Office

Peter G. Morici
Vice-President, National Planning Association

Andrew Moroz
Assistant Director, International Economics Program, Institute for Research on Public Policy

Ronald C. Morrison
President, Kodak Canada Inc.

Cornelius J. Murphy
Senior Vice-President, Eastman Kodak Company

Peter Nicholson
Senior Vice-President, Bank of Nova Scotia

William Niskanen
Chairman, Cato Institute

Jim Oberstar
U.S. Representative, Democrat from Minnesota

Jo Oberstar
Executive Director, JO Associates

Richard O'Hagan
Senior Vice-President, Bank of Montreal

Jacques Parizeau
Professor of Economics, Ecole des Hautes Etudes Commerçiales

Sidney Picker, Jr.
Professor, Canada-United States Law Institute, Case Western Reserve University Law School

Joe Pietroski
Vice-President and Secretary, Manufacturers' Life Insurance Company

Alfred Reifman
Senior Fellow in International Economics, Congressional Research Service

Burke G. Reilly
International Trade Associate, Ford Motor Company

Daniel Roseman
Research Associate, International Economics Program, Institute for Research on Public Policy

David Ruth
Director, International Government Affairs, American Express Company

Arthur Sackler
Time Inc.

J. Robert Schaetzel
Former U.S. Ambassador to the European Community

Frank W. Schiff
Consultant, Committee for Economic Development

John A. Schnittker
President, Schnittker and Associates; Former Under Secretary of Agriculture, United States

Terence F. Shea
Washington Correspondent, Detroit News

Susan Skucas
International Trade Analyst, U.S. General Accounting Office

Guy Stanley
Managing Partner, John Doherty and Company

Hugh Stephens
U.S. Trade and Economic Relations, Canadian Department of External Affairs

Paula Stern
Carnegie Institute; Former Commissioner, U.S. International Trade Commission

Frederick W. Stokeld
Director, International Business Relations, Chamber of Commerce of the United States

Frank Stone
Director, International Economic Program, Institute for Research on Public Policy

Elaine L. Swanson
Research Associate, Mitsui and Company (USA) Inc.

Mary Thomas
Reporter, International Trade Reporter

Bill Thorsell
Editorial Writer, Toronto Globe and Mail

Philip H. Trezise
Senior Fellow, Brookings Institution

Max Turnipseed
Manager, International Affairs, Ethyl Corporation

Janet Vangrasstek
Reporter, Washington Trade Report

T. K. Warley
Professor of Agricultural Economics, University of Guelph

Jake Warren
Special Advisor for Trade Negotiations, Government of Quebec

Leonard Weiss
Atlantic Council Trade Committee

Paul Wonnacott
Professor of Economics, University of Maryland

Clayton Yeutter
U.S. Trade Representative